Bending with

ຮ່ວງການສຶກສາ ເສິມທ່ງກ່ານ
ຂ້າວ໌ດຕ່ງ່ງຶເລ໌ງ໌ ດຮະ

Thank you for
purchase this book

[signature]

Bending with the Wind

Memoir of a Cambodian Couple's Escape to America

Bounchoeurn Sao *and*
Diyana D. Sao

As told to Karline F. Bird

McFarland & Company, Inc., Publishers
Jefferson, North Carolina, and London

LIBRARY OF CONGRESS CATALOGUING-IN-PUBLICATION DATA

Sao, Bounchoeurn.
　　Bending with the wind : memoir of a Cambodian couple's
escape to America / Bounchoeurn Sao and Diyana D. Sao ;
as told to Karline F. Bird.
　　　p.　　cm.
　　Includes bibliographical references and index.

　　ISBN 978-0-7864-6377-0
　　softcover : acid free paper ∞

　　1. Sao, Bounchoeurn.　2. Sao, Diyana D.　3. Political refugees—
Cambodia — Biography.　4. Political refugees— United States—
Biography.　5. Political atrocities— Cambodia.　6. Cambodia —
Politics and government —1975–1979.　7. Cambodia. Kanyodhabal
Khemarabhumind.　8. Cambodian Americans— Biography.
I. Sao, Diyana D.　II. Bird, Karline F.　III. Title.
DS554.83.S36 [A3 2012]
305.895' 9320730922 — dc23
[B]　　　　　　　　　　　　　　　　　　　　　　　　　　2012003912

BRITISH LIBRARY CATALOGUING DATA ARE AVAILABLE

On the cover: Diyana and Bounchoeurn Sao in Olympia,
Washington (photograph from the personal collection of
Bounchoeurn and Diyana Sao); background © 2011 Shutterstock

Manufactured in the United States of America

*McFarland & Company, Inc., Publishers
　Box 611, Jefferson, North Carolina 28640
　www.mcfarlandpub.com*

To all the Cambodian people who lost their lives
during their escape to Thailand. — **B.S.**

To all my students whose own journeys
have inspired me to write. — **K.B.**

Contents

PART III — SAO BOUNCHOEURN AND SAN BOUNRIEM

Acknowledgments

I am grateful to Bounchoeurn Sao, Bounriem Sao, and her older brother Phath San for sharing their experiences with me, even when the memories were painful. I appreciate all the hours Bounchoeurn and Bounriem spent in interviews, graciously answering every question. Your memoir is much richer for your ready willingness to provide more detail.

Thank you, again, to Bounchoeurn, for translating the interviews with Phath, meeting Rick and me at the airport in Phnom Penh, and taking us to Takeo to visit your birthplace in Tang Russey and to meet extended family. We will never forget the wild ride through western Cambodia to Svay Chek, close to Bounriem's birthplace, to meet your family's dear friends Plong Chin and Liem Nee.

I wish to express my gratitude to my husband and fellow traveler Rick Bird for willingly accepting the task of first reader, providing invaluable insight, critiques and suggestions, and for unfailingly giving love, support and encouragement throughout.

To my daughter Stephanie Bird, second reader, a special thanks for being almost more critical and observant than even your father. I value your input. Thank you to my other readers, sister Tedi Sacco and Vicki Lynn Braun, for encouraging me and finding errors even after many revisions. To son Ryan Bird, sister Stephanie Claire, and mother Teddy Topp, thanks for your encouragement and support.

Thank you to photographers Craig Faustus Buck, Charles C. King, and Bruce Sharp for generously allowing me to use your photographs of Cambodia. A special thank you to Vonda Witley of VisionSeed Publishing for your professional help in developing the map of Cambodia.

I am indebted as well to Todd Keithley for early advice on finding a publisher.

— **Karline Bird**

CAMBODIA

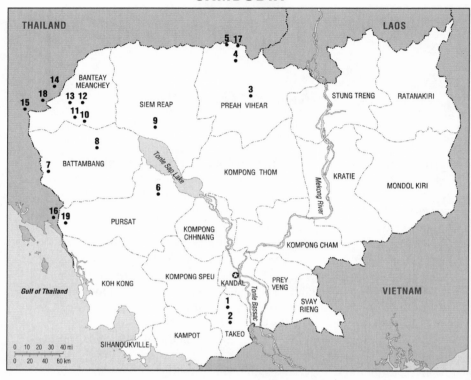

✪	Phnom Penh	
1	Tang Russey	
2	Takeo City	
3	Tbeng Meanchey	
4	Choam Khsant	
5	Prasat Preah Vihear	
6	Pursat City	
7	Pailin	
8	Battambang City	
9	Siem Reap	
10	Mongkol Borei	
11	Sisophon	
12	Svay Chek	
13	Sam Rong	
14	Ta Phraya	
15	Aranya Prathet (Khao-I-Dang)	
16	Trat	
17	Chheuteal Kong	
18	Lum Pak Refugee Camp	
19	Sok San Resistance Camp	

Glossary

A-5: one group of five Cambodian Special Forces men

Angka: The "organization" of the Khmer Rouge; the leadership of the Khmer Rouge

apsara: heavenly nymph or angelic dancer frequently found in Khmer sculpture

baht: Thai currency; one baht = five cents in 1968

Chaul Chnam: New Year

Chaul Chnam Khmer: Khmer New Year, a three-day celebration in mid–April

chhlop: spy

Deum-ko: "Be mute, like the kapok tree." Don't speak.

Free Khmer: *Khmer Srei*; Cambodian resistance fighters against the French, then the Khmer Rouge, then the Vietnamese

hectare: a metric unit of land equal to about two and a half acres

Hmong: hill tribe people from Laos and Thailand

INS: Immigration and Naturalization Services in the United States

Khmer Rouge: Cambodian Communists, "Red Khmer," who seized control in 1975, causing the deaths of approximately two million Cambodians during the following four years

Khmer Srei: Free Khmer; Cambodian resistance fighters against the French, then the Khmer Rouge, then the Vietnamese

khru Khmer: Cambodian traditional healer

kilometer: a metric unit of measurement of about ⅝ mile

kosang: Khmer Rouge disciplinary meeting

krama: traditional checked Cambodian scarf worn around the head, neck, or waist

Lao: Laotian; people from Laos

lok: mister

Min aiy te: "Never mind." Similar to the Thai expression "Mai pen rai."

MSG: monosodium glutamate, frequently used to enhance flavor in Cambodian cooking

new people: people who lived in the cities, especially Phnom Penh, during the civil war in Cambodia, who, the Khmer Rouge believed, were associated with Lon Nol and western influences old people: people who lived in liberated areas during the civil war in Cambodia; the rural people, who, the Khmer Rouge believed, were free from western influences

P'Chum Ben: Cambodian Festival of the Dead, a kind of All Soul's Day in September

phnom: mountain

quinine: medicine used to treat malaria

Radio Beijing: Communist radio programs broadcast out of China all over Southeast Asia

riel: Cambodian currency; 4 riel = $1.00 in 1980 after Vietnamese liberation; 4100 riel = $1.00 in 2011

stupa: dome-shaped Buddhist shrine where ashes or bones of deceased family members are interred

Thai *Dang*: Thai Communist, "Red Thai"

Vespa: low-powered, motorized, two-wheeled vehicle

Viet Cong: Vietnamese Communist guerrillas who fought against the South Vietnamese government and the United States during the Vietnam War

wat: Buddhist temple

Year Zero: the year the Khmer Rouge seized power; 1975

Names and Relationship Terms

Part I: People

This list presents names of people in this book, with their identifications, as they would appear in Cambodian — the family, or "last name," first, and the given, or first name, second (and no comma between). To enable readers to quickly find anyone and yet to ascertain easily which name part is the "last name," all Cambodian names are given both ways below; those with an equal sign = indicate, immediately after the =, what the "last name" is (first entry: "Sao" is the last name and "Sao Amarin" is the proper Cambodian listing). Single names represent the given name only, as "last name" is unavailable.

Western names are presented in the usual fashion: last name, comma, first name.

Names in italics provide names that may also be referred to in this book or to nicknames, or explain relationships; see Part IB: Relationship Terms.

Amarin Sao = Sao Amarin
Annmarie Sao = Sao Annmarie
Asuan: Bounriem's childhood classmate
Bird, Rick: former director of Olympia School District's ESL program; author Karline Bird's husband
Bonker, Don: U.S. representative from Washington State's third Congressional district, 1975–1989
Bounchoeurn Sao = Sao Bounchoeurn
Bounriem San = San Bounriem
Bounrien San = San Bounrien
Bounroeurn San = San Bounroeurn
Bun Kim: Bounchoeurn's mother; *Mae* Kim
Bun Kith: Bounchoeurn's aunt; his mother's younger sister; *Ming* Kith
Bun Ngin: Bounchoeurn's uncle; his mother's older brother; *Thom* Ngin
Bun Sok: Bounchoeurn's cousin; Bun Yoeun's son

Bun Yoeun: Bounchoeurn's uncle; his mother's younger brother; *Poo* Yoeun
Champea: tribal girl in Ratanakiri, who becomes Bounchoeurn's girlfriend
Cheally Sao = Sao Cheally
Chek: Bounchoeurn's step-mother; Pich Cham's second wife; *Ming* Chek
Chham Pich = Pich Chham
Chheang: former monk from Takeo; part of Bounchoeurn's escape group
Chhouy Theuk = Theuk Chhouy
Chin Plong = Plong Chin
Chum: villager's wife in Choam Khsant; *Ming* Chum
Doch Sak = Sak Doch
Dorn Pich = Pich Dorn
Evans, Dan: governor of Washington State, 1965–1977; U.S. senator from Washington State, 1983–1989
Gardener, Booth: governor of Washington State, 1986–1993
Gorton, Slade: U.S. senator from Washington State, 1981–1987 and 1989–2001
Ham: Bounriem's Lao sister-in-law; San Phan's wife
Hannah, Grace: ESL teacher; wife of Lacey Baptist Church pastor
Heng Long = Long Heng
Here San = San Here
Hoeung Pich = Pich Hoeung
Hor: one of Bounriem's suitors in Lum Pok Refugee Camp; Bounriem called him *Bong*
Jae: Bounriem's sister-in-law; San Phong's wife
Kantuoch: Bounriem's friend in Lum Pok Refugee Camp
Karien: Bounriem's friend in Lum Pok Refugee Camp
Kath Sum = Sum Kath
Kel: monk at Wat Chambak Bethmeas; later Khmer Rouge; *Lok Bong* Kel
Ken Saret: business partner with Bounriem in Sao and Ken Janitorial Services
Kennedy, Ted: U.S. senator from Massachusetts, 1962–2009
Ketesak Sao = Sao Ketesak
Khim Yon: Bounriem's sister-in-law; San Phath's wife; Yon
Kim Bun = Bun Kim
Kim Hai Sak = Sak Kim Hai
Kim Heng Sak = Sak Kim Heng
Kin Vann: Bounchoeurn's army friend, now living in Olympia, WA
Kit Bun = Bun Kit
Koes Eav = Eav Koes
Kon: male student at Tonle Bati High School; Bounchoeurn's friend; later Khmer Rouge
Lan Los = Los Lan
Leiy: Bounriem's uncle; her mother's younger brother; *Mia* Leiy

Lek: little girl in Tang Russey

Liem Nee: Plong Chin's wife; Sao family friend in Svay Chek; called *Bong Srei* by Bounchoeurn and Bounriem, meaning *older sister not related*

Long Heng: Pich Satom's husband; Bounchoeurn's brother-in-law

Los Lan: Bounchoeurn's mother-in-law; Kim Heng's mother; *Mae* Lan

Lowery, Mike: governor of Washington State, 1993–1997

Mii La: Bounriem's best friend when she lived with the monks and nuns

Mukh: San family friend in Sam Rong; *Ta* Mukh

Munro, Ralph: secretary of state for Washington State, 1980–2001

Muth Nem = Nem Muth

Naren Sao = Sao Naren

Nee Liem = Liem Nee

Nem: Bounchoeurn's younger cousin

Nem Muth: Bounriem's aunt; her mother's younger sister; *Ming* Muth

Nem Yan: Bounriem's mother; *Mae* Yan

Ngin Bun = Bun Ngin

Oung Sareth: Cambodian refugee student at Jefferson Middle School; Sareth

Oung Un: Sareth's uncle; a minister of the Alliance Church

Peo: elderly lady at Din Daeng Transition Center; *Yeay* Peo

Pha San = San Pha

Pha: one of Bounriem's suitors in Lum Pok Refugee Camp; Bounriem called him *Poo*

Phan San = San Phan

Phath San = San Phath

Pheav San = San Pheav

Phin San = San Phin

Phol: village headman of Bounchoeurn's last Khmer Rouge work camp; *Kanak Phum* Phol

Phong San = San Phong

Pich Chham: Bounchoeurn's birth father; *Ow* Chham

Pich Dorn: Bounchoeurn's half-brother; Pich Chham's son; Dorn

Pich Hoeung: Bounchoeurn's half-sister; Pich Chham's daughter; Hoeung

Pich Satom: Bounchoeurn's half-sister; Pich Chham's daughter; Satom

Piset Sao = Sao Piset

Plong Chin: San Phong's friend in Svay Chek; now a Sao family friend; called *Bong* by Bounchoeurn and Bounriem because he is the same age as an older brother and sister

Powers, Fern: sponsor of the Sao family and many other refugees to Olympia

Prom Soeung: Bounriem's sister-in-law; San Bounroeurn's wife

Puy: San family friend in Lum Pok Refugee Camp; *Poo* Puy

Rean: captain of Thai border police; *Phu Kong* Rean

Rieng San = San Rieng

Rin: Bounchoeurn's cousin, son of Bun Kith; later Khmer Rouge

Rivera, Zenaida: Garfield Elementary School teacher

Sa Luan San = San Sa Luan

Sadee: family friend to Bounchoeurn's family in Tang Russey; part of Bounchoeurn's escape group; *Poo* Sadee

Sak: Bounchoeurn's "aunt-in-law," who was married to a family friend in Tang Russey; *Ming* Sak

Sak Doch: Bounchoeurn's brother-in-law; Kim Heng's younger brother

Sak Kim Hai: Bounchoeurn's sister-in-law; Kim Heng's younger sister

Sak Kim Heng: Bounchoeurn's first wife; Kim Heng; Kim

Sak San: Bounchoeurn's father-in-law; Kim Heng's father; *Pa* San

Sam El Sao = Sao Sam El

Samphao San = San Samphao

San Bounriem: the eleventh San child; Bounchoeurn's second wife; Diyana D. Sao; nicknamed *Gnep*, meaning *tiny person*, and *Mii Own*, a term of endearment used by her family

San Bounrien: Bounriem's second elder brother; *Bong* Bounrien

San Bounroeurn: Bounriem's eldest brother; *Bong* Bounroeurn

San Here: Bounriem's father; *Ow* Here

San Pha: Bounriem's fourth elder brother; *Bong* Pha

San Phan: Bounriem's sixth elder brother; *Bong* Phan

San Phath: Bounriem's fifth elder brother; *Bong* Phath or *Lok Bong* Phath

San Pheav: Bounriem's eighth elder brother; *Bong* Pheav

San Phin: Bounriem's seventh elder brother; *Bong* Phin

San Phong: Bounriem's third elder brother; *Bong* Phong or *Lok Bong* Phong

San Rieng: Bounriem's older sister; *Bong* Rieng

San Sa Luan: San Phong's daughter; Bounriem's niece

San Sak = Sak San

San Samphao: first San daughter, who died as a baby before Bounriem was born

Sang: captain of Thai soldiers on border with Preah Vihear; *Phu Kong* Sang as a captain; later *Phu Phan* Sang as a colonel

Santephear Vachana Sao = Sao Santephear Vachana

Sao Amarin: daughter of Bounchoeurn and Kim Heng; their third child

Sao Annmarie: daughter of Bounchoeurn and Bounriem; their second child; Annmarie

Sao Bounchoeurn: Bounriem's husband; nicknamed *Choeurn*, no special meaning; *Pa* Piset; Bounchoeurn

Sao Naren: Bounchoeurn's half-sister; Sao Sam El's daughter

Sao Cheally: son of Bounchoeurn and Kim Heng; their second child; nicknamed *Bdei*, meaning *husband*

Sao Piset: son of Bounchoeurn and Bounriem; their first child; Piset

Sao Ketesak: son of Bounchoeurn and Kim Heng; their fourth child

Sao Sam El: Bounchoeurn's step-father; *Papa*

Sao Som Il: Bounchoeurn's uncle, abbot of Wat Chambak Bethmeas; Papa's youngest brother; called *Lok* because he is a monk and *Poo* because he is an uncle, *Lok Poo* Som Il

Sao Santephear Vachana: daughter of Bounchoeurn and Kim Heng; their first child; nicknamed *Phosda*

Saret Ken = Ken Saret

Sareth Oung = Oung Sareth

Saron: Phnom Penh girl in Bounchoeurn's last Khmer Rouge work camp

Satom Pich = Pich Satom

Savoeurn: Sak family's twelve-year-old neighbor boy

Soeung Prom = Prom Soeung

Sok Bun = Bun Sok

Sok: Bounriem's aunt; Leiy's wife; *Ming* Sok

Sokang: Chinese female student at Tonle Bati High School; Sokiang's twin sister

Sokiang: Chinese female student at Tonle Bati High School; Bounchoeurn's girlfriend

Sokim: Bounchoeurn's paternal cousin; Khmer Rouge

Som Il Sao = Sao Som Il

Sophal: Sao family friend in Lum Pok Refugee Camp; *Ming* Sophal

Sophi: Bounchoeurn's paternal cousin; Khmer Rouge

Sophon Chan = Chan Sophon

Sum Kath: master sergeant over Bounchoeurn in Chheuteal Kong; Sergeant Kath

Suong: young Khmer Rouge boy in Tep Prasa

Sy: Bounchoeurn's cousin-in-law in Tang Russey; Rin's wife; *Neang* Sy

Ta: elderly monk with whom the child Bounriem lived and traveled; *Lok* Ta

Ta Mukh: Grandpa Mukh; San family friend in Sam Rong

Ta Nem: Grandpa Nem; Bounriem's maternal grandfather

Ta Noy: Grandpa Noy; Bounchoeurn's maternal grandfather

Tep: Bounchoeurn's boss in Lum Pok Refugee Camp; *Lok* Tep (here, *Lok* means *Mister*)

Theuk Chhouy: wife of San Bounrien; Bounriem's sister-in-law

Ti: Bounchoeurn's uncle; his mother's youngest half-brother; *Poo* Ti

Tun: San family friend in Lum Pok Refugee Camp; *Ming* Tun

Un Oung = Oung Un

Vanara: Bounchoeurn's old school friend; later Khmer Rouge

Vann Kin= Kin Vann

Yan Nem = Nem Yan

Yeay Lay: Grandma Lay; Bounriem's maternal grandmother

Yeay Noy: Grandma Noy; Bounchoeurn's maternal grandmother

Yeay Peo: Grandma Peo; elderly lady at Din Daeng Transition Center

Yim: Bounchoeurn's uncle in Tang Russey; *Thom* Yim

Yoeun Bun = Bun Yeoun
Yon Khim = Khim Yon
Youn: Bounchoeurn's Vietnamese Cambodian aunt; Bun Yeoun's wife; *Ming* Youn

Part II: Relationship Terms

A nga: little brother; male younger than you; son
Bong: brother or sister, friend older than you
Jae: sister-in-law
Kon: son
Lok Bong: term showing respect for a man who is or was a Buddhist monk
Mae: mother
Mia, *Poo* or *Thom*: uncle
Ming: aunt; woman your parents' age
Mit: comrade or friend; term of address by Khmer Rouge
Neang: little sister; female younger than you; daughter
Ow or *Pa*: father
Phu Kong: Thai army captain
Phu Phan: Thai army colonel
Poo: uncle; man your parents' age
Smat mit: best friend, best comrade; term of address by Khmer Rouge
Ta: grandfather; man older than your parents
Yeay: grandmother; woman older than your parents

Preface by Karline Bird

The story of Bounchoeurn and Bounriem (Diyana D.) Sao began more than 60 years ago in a small village in Cambodia. Since that time they have become known as strong, intelligent, courageous, and compassionate people, whom many consider themselves fortunate to know. I am one of those lucky ones.

My personal journey and connection to Southeast Asia began many years ago when John F. Kennedy challenged Americans: "Ask not what your country can do for you — ask what you can do for your country." After the Peace Corps was formed, recruiters visited college and university campuses around the nation, including the University of Oregon, where I was a student, and the University of Utah, where my future husband, Rick Bird, studied. After taking the language aptitude test and filling out the applications, we were invited to join the Advanced Training Program at Northern Illinois University for TEFL (Teaching English as a Foreign Language) in Thailand. During the summer after our junior years, one hundred college students traveled to NIU to study Thai language, culture, and TEFL methods. Rick and I met and fell in love, went back to our separate universities to complete our senior years, and married a year later before completing the second phase of our Peace Corps training in Honomu, Hawaii. Forty new Peace Corps volunteers arrived in Bangkok, Thailand, in August 1968, and then headed out to our assignments. Rick and I spent the next two years in the provincial capital of Chiang Rai, in Chiang Rai, Thailand, the northernmost province bordering Laos and Burma, teaching English to Thai high school students, immersing ourselves in Thai culture, and making lifelong friends with students and colleagues.

After our Peace Corps service was over, we returned to the United States to attend graduate school and start our family, finally settling in Olympia, Washington, to work in the Olympia School District in 1973. Several years later, after the fall of Saigon and Phnom Penh, Washington governor Dan Evans opened the doors to welcome the Southeast Asian refugees to our state. As the start of the new school year approached in the fall of 1979, the OSD expected to have 18 refugee students enrolled in the school district. On the

1

first day of class, however, the district discovered it had 135 refugee students on its doorsteps. Because of our Peace Corps experiences in Thailand, with TEFL and speaking the Thai language, Rick became the ESL (English as a Second Language) teacher at Garfield Elementary School, where the vast majority of the students were enrolling. I was hired to teach ESL at Jefferson Middle School, where a small number of Cambodian, Lao, and Vietnamese students had enrolled. Rick was also made director of the district's ESL program. The OSD had already hired a Vietnamese educational assistant and translator to work with the Vietnamese students, but it soon became apparent that we needed people who could work with the Lao and Cambodian students.

With that in mind, Rick drove to St. John's Episcopal Church to visit the adult English language classes. Arriving just as the men were outside having a break, he stood on the bumper of his car and shouted, "Is there anyone here who can speak Cambodian, Lao, Thai, and English?" One man slowly and hesitantly raised his hand. "You're hired," Rick announced with a sigh of relief. Thus began our friendship with Bounchoeurn Sao. Since that time, Bounchoeurn not only worked with the refugee students in elementary, middle and high school, as well as translating for the district, but he also helped with translations for the local hospitals, doctors, and law enforcement, wherever needed. He has been such an asset to the community that he has been honored and invited to the governor's mansion for community service awards on two different occasions.

One day when Bounchoeurn was working with my Cambodian students at Jefferson, during a break the students began talking about unusual Cambodian names. A new student happened to mention the nickname of Bounchoeurn's son, prompting him to show the student his son's photograph. Our student was able to assure Bounchoeurn that at least two members of his family were still alive in Cambodia. When I heard of this serendipitous occurrence, I became more and more intrigued with Bounchoeurn's story of how he and his wife Bounriem came to be in Olympia, Washington.

After watching the movie *The Killing Fields*, I thought more about my students and Bounchoeurn, wondering how each one of them had survived the horrors of that time to end up in my classroom. The more I read, the more I wanted to know and write Bounchoeurn's and Bounriem's stories. After reading *Children of Cambodia's Killing Fields: Memoirs by Survivors*, compiled by Dith Pran, whose story was told in the movie, I heard Pran's charge that Cambodian Americans learn the stories of the survivors of the Khmer Rouge reign of terror in Cambodia. All Americans need to know these stories.

When I approached Bounchoeurn with the idea of telling his story, he was interested and agreeable. After I retired from teaching English and correcting essays, Bounchoeurn and I were ready to begin. Initially, I had planned to write only Bounchoeurn's story, but as our work progressed, I learned that Bounchoeurn was very proud of his wife and her accomplishments; he told me several times I needed to write her story, too. My plan was to write a second book about Bounriem later.

Our family and friends were first introduced to Bounchoeurn's wife as Bounroeurn, and that's what we called her for years. It wasn't until she started her janitorial service and I received her business card that I learned Bounroeurn had changed her name to Diyana. But we all still called her Bounroeurn, and when Bounchoeurn spoke about his wife to us, he also called her Bounroeurn. Imagine my surprise last year when I began interviewing Bounroeurn and learned that her name was really Bounriem. I had a choice of three names; I decided to use the name given to her by her parents for her story — Bounriem.

Cambodians do not use names the way westerners do. The last name, or family name, is presented first, with the given name second, as in Sao Bounchoeurn. In the book while the Saos and Sans are in Cambodia, I write their names in the Cambodian way, but after they immigrate to the United States, I present their names in the western way, as in Bounchoeurn Sao. More important to Cambodians, though, are relationships. The elderly are called *yeay* and *ta*, grandmother and grandfather. Men and women the same age as your parents are called *poo* and *ming*, uncle and auntie, even if they are not related to you. People the same age call each other *bong*, meaning friend, older brother, or older sister. If the woman is younger than you, she is called *neang*, younger sister, while a younger man would be called *a nga*, younger brother. I have tried to minimize confusion by referring to people by their relationships in italics and their given names. For example, I refer to Bounriem's older brother Phan as *Bong* Phan, while Bounchoeurn calls his father's friend Sadee as *Poo* Sadee. Cambodian words are written in italics with the definition often following. I've included Cambodian words and their definitions in the glossary.

Bounchoeurn and I began our project in the latter part of 2006, logging over thirty hours of interviews, generally two hours at a time. After each two-hour session, I spent more than two hours transcribing each interview into workable text and deciding what information needed further explanation and detail. The next session would first be spent asking Bounchoeurn to elaborate on a number of parts to his story before proceeding further. At the end of each session, I would ask Bounchoeurn to reflect upon a certain period of time for the next session's focus. Once I began the actual writing process, I printed the completed chapters so we each had a copy. Bounchoeurn would read his chapters at home, marking any corrections, then bring them back to my house for discussion. Sometimes I read chapters to Bounchoeurn, as he followed along, making sure each page was correct as written. Meanwhile, my readers were asking for further clarification and detail for certain events. Many revisions later Bounchoeurn's story was finished by the end of 2009, in time for my husband and me to meet Bounchoeurn in Cambodia to visit several of the places where he lived and worked. Rick and I have visited Cambodia three times before, but always to spend our time in the Angkor temples of Siem Reap or the Royal Palace museum and temples of Phnom Penh. This time we were able to meet Bounchoeurn's extended family in Takeo and friends in Banteay Meanchey, as well as follow parts of his journey from Phnom Penh to the Thai border.

Early in the spring of 2010, I received word that McFarland was interested in publishing Bounchoeurn's story and was asked if I would consider including another Cambodian's story as well. I was more than happy to include Bounriem's story along with Bounchoeurn's. Bounriem and I began the interview process in the summer of 2010, logging more than eighteen hours together. As with Bounchoeurn's story, I printed out copies of chapters, reading them to Bounriem as she followed along, making corrections and revisions as we went. Once again, my readers continued to question and probe, asking for more.

Because I interviewed Bounriem in her home, I was privileged to meet her brother Phath. After learning Bounriem's story, I realized that Phath's experiences shed light on and completed Bounriem's family history. He was willing to share his painful story with me, so we spent three hours in interview with Bounchoeurn as translator.

The book is set up in three parts: Part I tells Bounchoeurn's story up until he first sees Bounriem in the refugee camp; Part II tells Bounriem's story up until she first sees Bounchoeurn; Part III continues their story together, alternating chapters with Bounchoeurn or Bounriem as narrator.

And so I've written of the survival of Bounchoeurn and Bounriem Sao—that their children and grandchildren, my students and their children, the people of Olympia, and people everywhere may know their stories.

Part I

Sao Bounchoeurn:
He Was Just a Soldier

CHAPTER 1

Give Back Only Bone and Eyes

In the little village of Tang Russey, in the district of Bati in Takeo Province, south of Phnom Penh, I was born on October 21, 1946, and named Bounchoeurn. My parents had also been born in Tang Russey. My mother Bun Kim was a housewife, and my father Pich Chham was a farmer. I called my mother *Mae* and my father *Ow*, the Cambodian words for mother and father.

When I was young, I remember my parents and I lived in a small house on stilts—nine big, round posts—commonly seen in rural Cambodia. We had built the house above ground so we could tie cattle underneath at night. The house had only one large room, an open space. When we went to sleep, we hung up curtains and slept on mats.

As a child, I especially liked to play with clay. I would go to the rice fields and find a termite hill, cut it in half, take the dirt from the hill, add some water, and squeeze and squeeze until it was soft. I would mold the clay into animals that I saw, like a cow or a water buffalo. My village wasn't very far away from Highway 2 to Takeo City, and Takeo wasn't very far from Phnom Penh, so my friends, who called me Choeurn, and I saw cars going back and forth. Sometimes my friends and I, who were all about the same age, would make a car. We'd pick a palm fruit and carve it to make the car wheels. Then we'd get a bamboo stick, split it to make an axle, and fit it together with the wheels to make the car. We ran and made noises with our mouths, "Rmmmm, rmmmm, rmmmm," little kids running around with no shirts, some with no pants, just running in the field. Sometimes we used another kind of fruit that looked like a star fruit. We'd take a palm leaf, cut it and tie it to the fruit, then tie it to the wheel. We ran it so it would make noise. Young Cambodian children are free to play and rarely have to do any work, just small chores. I had the same freedoms. When my mother was cooking and ran out of something, she'd ask me to go buy it for her, or she'd ask me to bring in a few sticks of wood, stored outside the house. Mostly, I played.

When I was young, I especially liked to eat sour soup, *samla machou*. *Mae* Kim cooked sour soup, sometimes with fish in it, *samla machou banle*.

Apsara gate at the entrance to Bounchoeurn Sao's childhood village in Takeo Province, 2010 (photograph by Rick Bird and from the personal collection of Karline and Rick Bird).

In Cambodia when I was a child, we rarely had meat, eating mostly fish, but not every day. People would go to the rice fields and get fish or little crabs, and they liked to make *prahok*, preserved fish, that had a strong smell. Our family lived about three or four kilometers from the water, but at that time, I was too little, so my mother wouldn't let me go to fish by myself. Fish was cheap, so *Mae* Kim would buy it in the market. The fishermen took fish from the lake to our village, and she could buy it there. We never bought vegetables because we had our own garden. If we didn't have a certain vegetable we wanted, we would just ask a neighbor and trade something for it. In addition to having a garden, *Mae* Kim planted fruit trees on our lot — star fruit, mango, and banana. I planted a very small, sour fruit called *kantuat*. My mother also liked to plant taro in the back yard, but we didn't have coconut palms. *Mae* Kim bought coconuts from the market when she wanted to make coconut curry.

Our family also raised chickens, so in April when Cambodians celebrated *Chaul Chnam Khmer,* Khmer New Year, my favorite holiday, my mother could make delicious coconut chicken curry. My other favorite New Year's dishes were fried noodles and Cambodian sweets—rice cakes and a solid coconut pudding. After *Mae* Kim and her sister Bun Kith, my *ming* or aunt, cooked all the special foods for Chaul Chnam, we would take some of it to my grandparents' house, along with money to buy material to make clothes, to honor them. After honoring my grandparents, *Ta* and *Yeah* Noy, we would come back home to get more food to take to the temple to give to the monks. Of course, we also ate some of the holiday food ourselves.

My parents divorced when I was very young. This wasn't common in Cambodia at the time. My mother eventually remarried a man from the neighboring village of Khla Kon. My stepfather, Sao Sam El, whom I called Papa, loved me very much. He's the one who sent me to school and forced me to learn. Papa is the one who gave me the family name Sao. I didn't have any brothers or sisters. After my mother divorced, she had a baby boy with my stepfather, but he died when he was very young.

Because they had already passed away, I didn't know my paternal grand-

Cambodian boy in front of a shop similar to *Mae* Kim's shop in Tang Russey, 1991 (photograph by Bruce Sharp).

parents. My birth father *Ow* Chham had sisters, though. His big sister loved me very much. Since *Ow* Chham's family were farmers, they didn't have money to give as gifts, but they gave me special foods. I called my stepfather's parents *Ta* and *Yeay*, just as I did my maternal grandparents. Mostly I saw my maternal grandparents because we were in the same village, but sometimes I would walk to visit Papa's parents who lived only a kilometer and a half away.

My mother didn't want to depend on her husband's salary, so she kept a little store, at the front of the house, to sell everything the villagers needed, a common sight in Southeast Asia. When people came to buy special items for a holiday celebration like the New Year, she would be very happy to sell to them. Since our village was only about twenty kilometers from the market at Takhmau, close to Phnom Penh, *Mae* Kim would buy the needed items there for her little store. It was easy for her to tend the store as well as our family. When we lived in the house on stilts, her kitchen was outside, under the house, right next to her store.

Both of my fathers had an elementary education. They had studied in the temple in the village, where I would later study. When they were children, girls did not go to school, only the boys, so *Mae* Kim was not educated. Since there was no public school in the village, if boys wanted to go to high school, they went to the city of Takeo to study. Otherwise, if they wanted to learn in the village, they became monks.

When I was old enough, my parents sent me to the same elementary school where my fathers had studied, in the temple Wat Chambak Bethmeas near Tang Russey. It didn't cost money to go to school, but the teachers were very strict. When *Mae* Kim took me to school on the first day, she said to the teacher, "Now I give my son to you. I want you to give back only bone and eyes." The teacher could discipline the children with a stick, but not break their bones or blacken their eyes. The parents always said, "I need only eye and bone."

Mae Kim's brother, my favorite uncle *Thom* Ngin, had no children, so he paid attention to all the nephews and nieces. He was also strict: he would not let us stay home from school at all. Every morning before he went to the fields, he would go from house to house. "Who is not going to school?" he shouted. "All the children must go to school."

While most of my friends never left the village, *Ow* Chham gave me the experience of visiting and staying in Phnom Penh. At that time Cambodia was under French control. Most of the Cambodian people didn't like the French and wanted to remove them from Cambodia. A rebel group was formed called *Issarak*, meaning freedom. The Issarak movement wanted freedom from the French. When the Issarak rebels were fighting against the government, and I was about four years old, Papa decided we would not be safe in the village because he worked for the government. *Ow* Chham took me to Phnom Penh. At that time in the early 1950s, Phnom Penh was much different than it is now. It looked like a forest to me. I remember only the palace and the road that is now Monivong Boulevard with only one little light on it. Of course, there were restaurants, radio and *cyclos*, bicycle pedicabs, but Independence Monument had not yet been built. We stayed with *Ow* Chham's friend until it was safe to go back to the village. These people were kind to my family, especially to me.

After the divorce we didn't live in the house on stilts very long because the French government burned it down for political reasons. Even though Papa worked for the government as a soldier in the army, they accused him of working for the rebel Issarak. I was about eight years old at the time. I remember the French government soldiers coming to the house and asking if my stepfather had any children. My grandmother *Yeay* Noy took my hand and told the rebels, "This is my son," then took me to her house. *Yeay* Noy was my mother's stepmother. When *Mae* Kim's mother died, her father married a young woman just a few years older than my mother. *Yeay* Noy did not have any children of her own, and because of her young age, it was believable that I could be her son. Although the soldiers burned my house, my parents were able to escape by running into the woods. Even though these soldiers worked for the French government, they were Cambodians, so their sympathies were with the villagers. As they neared the village, the soldiers talked and laughed loudly, making noise so the villagers would hear them. Since most of the villagers were spies for Issarak, they quickly ran to warn our family that the government soldiers were on their way. Following the fire, my family built a single-story house out of wood with walls made of palm leaves. Shortly after this the people who worked for the government had to move, so my parents and I left, while *Yeay* Noy remained in Takeo.

Because my stepfather was a soldier and part of the intelligence unit, our family had to move several times when the army reassigned him to a unit in another province. That meant I had to withdraw from school to go with my parents. I was eight years old at the time. My parents knew it was hard on me when they moved during the school year. First, Papa was sent to Kompong Cham on the Vietnamese border, so I stayed in the village with my grandmother. Just after they moved, my mother saw that there was an elementary school there, so she came back to Tang Russey to take me to live with them. When I was about ten years old, we moved to Kompong Thom Province. I lived there until I completed the eighth grade. Here I was able to go to public school, not in the temple. Unlike when my mother was a girl, when I was a student, girls were able to go to school, too, but most parents didn't want their daughters to go to school. They were afraid that if their daughters learned to read and write, they could write letters to their boyfriends. This was the common belief.

As a young student, I loved to study Cambodian language and math, and I rarely got in trouble at school. Since I lived three kilometers from school, I brought my lunch from home — rice, sometimes dried fish, whatever leftovers my mother had. Cambodian schools had physical education classes, but PE was held after school before the students went home for dinner. Everybody came out to exercise, and then they went home. The schools didn't have fancy PE equipment. No one had balls for sports at home, only in school. Each school had a volleyball and a soccer ball. These balls were not provided by the government; the parents had to pay one *riel* each, the price of a school lunch, every month to buy the two balls for the school so their children could play after-school sports. The school also didn't have uniforms. Because I loved to play volleyball, my parents bought the uniform for me themselves.

About this time, the administrator of the government office where Papa worked was accused of and arrested for supporting the rebels. The pro–French supporters also wanted to arrest all the people who worked in Papa's office. Papa didn't know what to do, so he ran off to the forest to join Issarak. He joined the rebels to fight against the French until 1953, when the French lost power and left Cambodia. The new government called all the Free Khmer rebels back, giving them positions to join with Prince Norodom Sihanouk, including Papa.

CHAPTER 2

Speak for Yourself

When village boys complete the eighth grade, most of them quit school so they can become monks. That way they can pay respect to their parents. At this time *Thom* Ngin, my mother's older brother, told Papa, "I want Bounchoeurn to become a monk." I didn't want to become a monk, so Papa wouldn't allow it. He wanted me to go to school and do the best that I could. In the village of Tang Russey, I am the only one who went on to receive a higher education.

For my eighth grade year, I went back to Tang Russey because Papa was transferred to the post in southern Takeo down on the Vietnamese border. There was no elementary school near the post, so Papa didn't want me to stay there and not go to school. My grandparents were still in the village of Tang Russey, but I lived at first with my favorite aunt, *Ming* Kith. She had one child, Rin, who was younger, lazy, and spoiled. I had to help my cousin with his homework, and *Ming* Kith complained that her son wouldn't do anything. She complained so much, it was disruptive, and I didn't want to live like that, so I went to live in the temple.

The abbot of Wat Chambak Bethmeas, the temple in Tang Russey's Bati District, was Papa's youngest brother, Sao Som Il, so I lived with him in the monk's dormitory. Since Sao Som Il was my uncle, even though he was the head of the temple, I called him *Lok Poo*. While living in the temple, I did not become a monk. Papa gave me the choice, and I chose not to be one. Instead, I lived there, served the monks, and went to school on the temple grounds. Every day, I boiled water, made tea, and when the monks went out early in the morning to ask for rice, I would carry the alms bowl for one of them. When I lived at the temple with *Lok Poo*, I felt like I had a great deal of freedom. All I had to worry about was going to school. I just studied and played with my friends, as long as I respected the monks and the workers hired to help the monks.

Some temples had schools for the monks, as well as the government schools for the children. Wat Chambak Bethmeas, the Bati District temple in

Contemporary Cambodian house on stilts, similar to Bounchoeurn Sao's childhood home in Tang Russey, 2010 (photograph by Rick Bird and from the personal collection of Karline and Rick Bird).

Takeo Province, had a government school for the children and a school for the monks. There weren't many children there, only about thirty, but there were one hundred monks because they came from other temples around Takeo Province. I studied and lived here until I completed the eighth grade.

Lok Poo Som Il was a kind but strict abbot. He never made the children who lived in the temple work in the morning because he knew they must go to school. He fed them with the rice cooked for the monks. The old nuns living in the temple cooked breakfast and lunch for the monks every day. *Lok Poo* told them, "Feed the children first; they have to go to school." When the monks went to ask for rice from the villagers, *Lok Poo* divided it — some for the monks and some for the children to eat.

Although I was homesick for my parents when I first went to live in the temple, soon I was fine. Papa sent me money every month, which my mother brought to me. This was an act of love on *Mae* Kim's part; it was difficult to travel between the post on the Vietnamese border and Tang Russey. The distance wasn't far, but at that time the roads were terrible; during the rainy season, they were completely unusable. Then *Mae* Kim would have to travel by boat, but the boat didn't go every day. My mother would bring one hundred riels, though she wouldn't give it to me. She gave it to my uncle to keep for me; when I needed to buy something, I would just ask *Lok Poo.*

In Tang Russey my neighbors didn't approve of my ideas about religion and proper behavior. The older people at that time were old-fashioned, and they wanted the children to follow their beliefs and ideas and agree with everything they said. If the young people said, "Yes, yes, yes," to everything the old people said, it made them happy. I was the one who was against their ideas. I was considered naughty when I was thirteen because I didn't listen to them, mainly because they weren't my parents. The villagers were Buddhist, and so was I, but sometimes their beliefs were not logical and didn't make sense to me. They wouldn't listen to me, but all the kids in the village liked me and my ideas.

I helped when the elders asked me, though. When the village was going to hold a fair or festival, the older people needed the help of the younger people to build booths or put up tents because of their greater strength. The elders flattered the young people when they helped by saying, "Oh, you're going to go to Heaven. You're so good to help."

But I said, "How are we going to go to Heaven? You're seventy or eighty years old. You better come and help or you won't go to Heaven. I'll be there by myself. You'll go to Hell if you don't come and help." The elders of the village didn't like my comments and thought that I was disrespectful.

One time the radio announced, "King Sihanouk is going to come to Takeo by car along Highway 2 at noon." All the people were out there waiting for him alongside the road. As a student, I belonged to a youth group. We were required to dress in our uniforms and all go out to wait for the king to drive by. The king was supposed to come at noon, so the youth group had to be there at eight in the morning. Then Sihanouk wouldn't arrive until two or three in the afternoon. Everyone had to wait and wait in the hot sun. I think Sihanouk did this to show his power. He would wait to come until an auspicious time, so the people would think he had special power. If the king waited until the rain started to fall and it clouded over, the people wouldn't be so uncomfortable. They believed that he brought the good weather. He was their God King. I told them, "I think the king was born the same as I was born."

A neighbor replied, "No, it's not the same because he's the king."

"No, it's the same," I argued. "I know he's the king, but when he was born, he had no clothes, just as I had no clothes when I was born."

Another day a big water buffalo bull walked through the village, so I said, "Wow! That bull is so big, if I killed it, the whole village could eat for a month."

"See there," one of the old people said. "You are a sinful boy."

"Why?" I asked.

"Because you want to take that water buffalo's life," answered the old man.

"No, I didn't do it; I just said it," I explained.

"If you say it, that's sinful, too," the old man told me.

Later on, I said to the neighbors around me, "Oh, if I had a lot of money, I would build a big temple and invite the monks and feed them. Probably I would go to Heaven."

"You can't go to Heaven unless you do it," an old man said. "You haven't done it, so you can't go to Heaven. You shouldn't say that. It's just like if you say, 'Oh, I'd like a bowl of noodles,' but you don't have it and you don't eat. How can you be full?"

"I don't understand," I said. "The other day you said I'd go to Hell for saying if I killed a water buffalo, we'd all have food for a month. Now I said I want to build a temple; why can't I go to Heaven?"

"You are a bad boy," the old man said, and he walked away. He was the man most respected in the village, the village elder. He influenced the way the other adults thought, and he thought I went against their beliefs. He probably wished that my parents would come home so I wouldn't talk like that. Even though the elders disapproved of me and my ideas, they didn't do anything to me out of respect for my father. They also didn't tell my parents or my relatives; it wasn't that bad.

Later my parents moved back to Bati District and took me with them. I went to the public school when I went to high school. First I went to Tonle Bati High School, and then I transferred to Preah Utei High School when we moved to Takeo City. I lived with my family in the fort, about thirty kilometers from Kompong Chay, the city where I lived while my father was in transit. When we first arrived there, Papa helped to build a new fort for the 18th Battalion. Then we lived in the new fort.

Most of the public schools were really not provided for by the government. The people in the community and the monks in the temple gave the money to build the elementary schools and some of the high schools and provided for them. Frequently, the monks would hold fund-raisers to collect money to be distributed in different ways—to take care of the monks, to take care of poor students, and to help improve the schools.

Tonle Bati and Preah Utei High Schools were government schools, so they had many more resources, materials and equipment than the temple schools. The city high schools had all certified teachers, while the village temple schools used both certified teachers and monks as teachers. The teachers were required to be certified, but if a school didn't have enough money to hire them, the monks could teach the beginning classes to help.

At the time I went to school, the schools were mixed for boys and girls. But although they were together in the same class, they were separated by space. The girls sat in the front and the boys sat in the back. In between them was a large space, so they couldn't reach each other. My high schools in Takeo also had boys and girls attending together. Generally, when the Cambodian people built a high school, they built it next to the temple because there was no available land. The school was not ruled by the monks; it was a government school on the temple grounds. The monks merely maintained the buildings. The teachers were educated and certified people hired by the government.

Cambodian communities had many Chinese living in them. The Cambodian people thought the Chinese were smarter because they liked to live and work in town, buying, selling and trading. The Cambodians, on the other hand, had land and rice fields, so most of them were farmers and preferred working on the land. Both groups of people were prejudiced against each other. The Chinese children went to the same schools as the Cambodian children, and both groups were allowed to be friends with each other. The parental expectations of their daughters were the same. However, neither group would allow Chinese and Khmer to marry each other. Both sets of parents chose the ones their children would marry.

A beautiful Chinese girl named Sokiang went to Tonle Bati High School, as did I, for a year; she was two years younger. One day my friend Kon asked me to talk to Sokiang for him. "Speak for yourself, Kon," I teased.

"I can't, Choeurn; I'm afraid to talk to her," responded Kon. I didn't think Kon was serious, but two days later, Kon asked me why I didn't go to talk to Sokiang for him. So I agreed to talk to her.

The next day Sokiang went to the pond to get water, as she always did, so I went to take a bath there. I wore a *krama* tied around my waist, as all Cambodian men do when bathing. "Sokiang," I said, "Can I ask you something?"

"Yes," she replied.

I then asked, "Do you know my friend Kon? He loves you. What do you think?"

She started to say something negative about Kon, so I told her, "*Min aiy te,* never mind. I just asked for him. Don't be mad at me, OK? Whether you like him or not, don't be mad at me. He wanted me to ask you."

"He should speak for himself," Sokiang stated. "Do you know who I like and who I love?"

"No," I answered.

"You will know," Sokiang promised and went back to her house with the water.

A few days later, my younger cousin Nem, who lived in the same temple, came to me, saying, "Here's a letter for you."

"Who's it from?" I asked.

"I don't know," Nem answered, giving me the letter.

After I opened and read it, I responded, "Ohhh, yeah." The letter said that Sokiang loved me, but if I didn't love her, to please not tell anybody or think that she was a bad girl. At first I didn't do anything; I just ignored it. But Sokiang kept sending me letters, so I finally answered, "OK." The parental concern about girls learning to read and write was apparently true.

Several days later Sokiang wrote, "Tonight, if you have time, I want to meet you in the market close to Phnom Penh." After I told her I would have time, she wrote, "Meet me at the small public market half way from our temple to Phnom Penh." Her mother asked her to take a message to a friend in Phnom Penh, and her father, who was a nurse, needed medicine from the Chinese hospital in Phnom Penh, so she was going to run errands for both of her parents.

Sokiang took a bus, and I rode my bicycle; it was only two hours from the temple by bicycle to meet her there. When we finally met, we rode on my bicycle together, talked, and had pictures taken together. Sokiang confessed that she had loved me for a long time, but I had ignored her. In Cambodia girls liked boys who were smart and not afraid. If the boy's parents were of high rank, that was also what girls liked.

Eventually, Sokiang became my girlfriend, but we were not open. We didn't let anyone know. We couldn't date. Cambodian teenagers were not allowed to date at all. If there was a temple fair, or something like that, then all the girls and boys could go together. The parents would know their children were with a group. I had a bicycle, and others had bicycles, so we could all go together that way.

One day when Sokiang's parents were in Phnom Penh, she told Nem and gave him some money, so he gave me the message. She lived across the street from the temple, so I went to her house to see her. Sokiang had a twin sister, Sokang, who sat out in front studying and watching for someone to come. Sokiang and I were in her room talking. Sokiang showed me some things she had made, including an embroidered handkerchief. She was good with art and did Chinese embroidery. "I made this for you," she said. She had embroidered the letters "B" and "K" in French for our names. Suddenly, Sokang came running and knocked on the door. Since there were only the three of us in the house, I shouted, "What's the matter with you?!"

"Oh, *Yeay* is coming! My grandmother is coming!" cried Sokang.

I panicked; Sokiang panicked. Where was I going to go? I wanted to hide under the bed, but Sokiang whispered, "No! Don't go there!" I tried to run out the back door, but I couldn't because *Yeay* was coming and would see me. The family had a space where they kept all the rice sacks by the wall, so I slipped behind the rice sacks. But that made one of the rice sacks fall. "Who put this sack like that?" Sokiang asked. Then she took the rice sack and put it on top of me. She was scared, but made herself calm. The rice still had husks on it, not yet ready to cook, so it was dusty. The dust made me want to sneeze, but I couldn't.

Yeay talked and talked, and because it was nighttime, she walked around to check all the doors and windows, as elderly Cambodians always do before they go to bed. They make sure everything is where it belongs in the kitchen, and nothing is out where the mice could get it. Then I heard Sokiang's grandmother say, "Okay, time to go to bed. Make sure all the lights are out." She didn't know I was there, and Sokiang didn't know I was there either. She thought I had run out the back door. Nobody knew. She was behaving normally because she thought I was gone. She had heard her uncle's dog barking, so she thought it barked at me when I ran away.

My body was sweaty and I was scared. Sokiang's grandmother did not go to bed right away. She decided to chew some betel nut, so she was pounding the betel leaves and nuts in the mortar, mixing it with powdered slake lime, rolling it, and then chewing it. Yet she didn't go to bed. Because she was Buddhist, she next said her prayers. I was still hiding behind the rice sacks, and I didn't know what to do. Finally, after about two hours, hoping *Yeay* was finally asleep, I moved carefully and quietly; then I knocked softly on Sokiang's door.

When Sokiang opened the door, she was startled. "What are you doing?!" I told her I'd tell her the next day. I just needed her to help me leave. "Come in here," she whispered. The window with its metal bars and latch was very difficult to lift up. Finally, Sokiang, Sokang, and I were able to do it together. As I crawled out the window, Sokiang called to her grandmother, hoping that her voice would cover up any sounds I made. She also didn't want *Yeay* to hear me outside her own window. My shirt caught as Sokiang was putting the window down, and it tore as I ran away. Fortunately, *Yeay* did not see me when she came into the girls' room.

I told only one person about Sokiang and me — one of the teachers, who also lived at the temple school. When I told my teacher about Sokiang, he said, "OK; that's fine," and never told anyone.

One other person knew about Sokiang and me, though, and that was Kon, the boy who was afraid to speak for himself. From the time Nem brought me the first message from Sokiang, Kon knew that she loved me and not him. He was angry and accused me, "You just spoke for yourself, not for me."

"No, I talked for you. I told her about you. I don't know what happened," I reassured him. But Kon was unhappy, and after two months he quit school. I went to his house and told him not to do that because this was his future.

I told Kon, "A lot of girls you can have, but even if Sokiang loved you, you couldn't marry her. I can't marry her either. She's Chinese. We're just friends." But Kon was too angry. He never returned to school and later joined the Khmer Rouge. He wasn't living in the village of Tang Russey; he came from a district far away. I am lucky I never saw him again.

CHAPTER 3

I Fell in Love with a Tribal Girl

Until I was sixteen, I lived in the temple in Takeo. When my parents left the village, *Mae* Kim rented our house to one of the rural development teachers. Cambodia had two kinds of teachers; one taught children in school, and one taught the villagers improvement skills, such as making their houses stronger, implementing clean water systems, and eliminating mosquitoes. At that time rural development was paid for by money from the United States. When my parents moved back to Takeo, the rural development teacher continued to rent the house, while our family moved into the fort, where Papa was serving in the army. Families could stay with their soldiers in the fort, so I moved in with my parents.

In 1965, I graduated from high school, and because I didn't have a job, I remained at home with my parents. Then I heard I might apply for *Enfants Troupes*, but I was too old because I was nineteen. Enfants Troupes takes only children whose parents are in the military. Even though my father was in the military, I couldn't join because this military academy was for boys ages ten to sixteen. I didn't know what to do.

At that time my uncle, a retired commander from the military, was made a mayor in the province of Stung Treng, next to the Lao border. He asked, "Would you like to join the police force now that you're graduated from high school? As a mayor, I can help and hire you. My district needs policemen."

"No," I replied, "I don't want to be a policeman. I want to join the army." But in Cambodia, it wasn't like in the United States where they recruit for the military every day. Here young men might wait four or five years before the army recruits again. Luckily, I heard that students who had graduated from high school were needed and could apply to join the army. Only seven hundred people would be accepted. First we had to apply, then take a test, and finally have the physical examination. During this time, a lot of people had no jobs, so many men came to apply, even those who had master's degrees. Those who had completed four years of college did not have to take the test.

21

Volleyball teams of Cambodian soldiers and Thai university students on the Thai-Cambodian border, Preah Vihear, 1972. Bounchoeurn Sao is standing at the far left of the second row (photograph from the personal collection of Bounchoeurn Sao).

They were accepted right away and could become commissioned officers. I had to take the test. I passed, so next came the physical.

On the day of the physical exam, I went to the Ministry of Defense and stood in line with three thousand candidates, all waiting to take the physical for seven hundred positions. While I was standing in line, I became hungry and wanted something to eat, but I didn't want to lose my place in line. One of the captains who worked there called to me, "Hey, boy; come here."

"No," I answered, "I don't want to lose my place in line."

"*Min aiy te*; go buy coffee for me," he said. "Give me your application. I'll put it in for you." He gave me money to buy coffee for him, took my application, and submitted it for me. Then he wrote a note for me, saying, "Give this note to the examiner when you go to have your physical." I gave the note to the doctor when it was my turn and passed the physical examination.

Two weeks later the list was posted at the Ministry of Defense, giving the names of the men who were chosen. I went to look for my name, but I didn't see it. I was so upset, wondering what I was going to do. After two more weeks, a message came that there were two parts to the recruitment. The first names that were called went to boot camp, and after they finished, the military cleaned up the camp. Now they were ready for the second group. This time when I went to look at the list, I saw my name. I was so happy. The list said these men needed to come to the Ministry of Defense to receive permission papers to ride the train. I immediately went to pick up my papers, including a free train ticket.

"Don't lose it," growled the man behind the desk.

"No, Sir!"

While we were waiting in Phnom Penh to go to the military camp, I stayed in the temple where one of the monks lived who had studied at my temple. When he left the temple in Takeo, he went to the monks' college in Phnom Penh. I stayed with him for one night. "My train leaves at 7:00 in the morning, so please wake me up early, OK?" I asked him. He woke me up in plenty of time, and I took a pedicab to the train station, along with all the other new recruits. When our names were called, we boarded the train for the military camp. I trained there for almost a year.

While I was in boot camp, I sent Sokiang a letter. She wrote back: "Well, now, do you have a girlfriend there or not?"

"No, I don't have one," I answered.

Sokiang would come to see me sometimes. "How about if I go to live with you?" she asked. That means she wanted to marry me. I said no, although at first I wanted to marry her. Her parents had found out. The teacher that loved her was jealous, so he told them about us. Sokiang told me her mother hit her because she heard I had been to see Sokiang. She also asked Sokiang if I had come into the house, but Sokiang said no, and her sister supported her.

"From now on, you don't come to meet me anymore, OK?" I told her. "I still love you, but I don't want you to get in trouble." Sokiang's parents knew we loved each other, but they didn't want that; right away they found a match for her. They made her get married.

I was sad, but I knew from the beginning, it wouldn't work. Not many Chinese girls married Khmer men, unless the men were of high rank, like a teacher. Then the parents would allow their Chinese Khmer daughter to marry a Khmer man, but this might happen only in a village, not in the city. Many Chinese Khmer men married Khmer women, but very few parents allowed Chinese Khmer women to marry Khmer men. If the family had recently emigrated from China, the parents would never have allowed their daughter to marry a Khmer man. Chinese parents preferred that their daughters marry Chinese men.

In 1966 I finished military training. When we graduated from boot camp, the soldiers were sent to our different posts. Three hundred fifty of the new soldiers went to the Thai border, to Odor Meanchey Province, where the

Khmer Serei, a different group of antigovernment rebels, was fighting the Cambodian army. The other half of the recent graduates, my group, went to Ratanakiri Province. Some were sent to fight another group of Khmer Serei, and the rest of us were sent to build houses. We went to help the retired military people in the northeast part of the country. At that time the province of Ratanakiri was underdeveloped, with a lot of malaria and few roads. The existing roads were very bad. Because of no running water and no electricity, no one wanted to go to Ratanakiri. Only tribal people lived there. But the Cambodian government offered land to retired military men, as well as rubber trees to enable them to set up rubber plantations. In exchange the government promised to build roads, develop water systems, and provide electricity. I was sent there for five months to help build houses for these retirees. After we built the houses, then we would go to our posts.

While I was working in Ratanakiri, I met a beautiful tribal girl named Champea. She had a good education. The tribal people in Cambodia were able to go to college. At that time the minorities were given scholarships to go to school, and Champea's parents wanted her to be educated. Many people in her village were educated. But when these educated people were in the village, they had to follow the tribal customs. The unmarried women go topless, wearing only a sarong. Then they go to the fields where they do dry rice farming. The women clear the land, then take a stick, poke a hole in the ground, and drop rice seeds in it. At harvest time they gather the rice in baskets they have woven. When the college students come home, they do the same. They must maintain their customs.

Another tribal custom is the girls of the village build a bamboo house in the middle of the village. At night the young men come together and sleep in that house. The girls then build a house a bit farther from the parents' houses. The girls stay there by themselves. The parents have to protect their sons because the girls walk around at night looking for boys, so the old men chase the girls away.

I wasn't a part of the village, so when I talked to Champea, she said, "OK, you can come in." At night it was difficult to enter the village because they had it protected from wild animals, like tigers. The villagers used a crossbow to set up a trap. When someone stepped on it, the arrow would fly. Champea told me, "I'll wait for you outside the village and take you inside." I asked her to show me the place where there was no trap. Not only was Champea beautiful, she was also smart. She was educated and still going to school. At that time she was getting a master's degree. She went to school in Stung Treng, the province next to Ratanakiri. She lived only about three kilometers from where I lived.

At the end of 1966, we finished building the houses in Ratanakiri. The military trucks were full of soldiers, taking them to all the different posts. Some came to Ratanakiri, some were sent to Takeo, some were sent to Stung Treng, and twenty of us were sent to Kompong Cham, northeast of Phnom Penh. We were there for only three days when a military alert was called, so we all went to Kompong Thom, to the northwest and closer to Preah Vihear, where the fighting had broken out on the border with Thailand. Thai soldiers had invaded Cambodia in the area of an ancient temple, also called Preah Vihear, built on the crest of the Dangkrek Mountains. The temple was famous historically, but more importantly, it was a strategic military location. The soldiers were given orders to gather their weapons and go to Preah Vihear that night.

"All those soldiers who just came from Ratanakiri must be checked first before they can go," stated the military doctor. Since I had just come from there, I had to be checked; the blood test showed that I had malaria.

"I think I'll be OK," I told the doctor.

"No, you have malaria," he replied. I did not feel sick, but he wouldn't let me go. He found a total of four soldiers with malaria, so we were sent by ambulance to the military hospital in Phnom Penh.

I didn't feel sick and complained, "Why do I have to go? I don't feel sick." But by the time we got to the hospital, I was really sick. I stayed in the hospital for two weeks.

While I was in the hospital, my parents were able to visit me in Phnom Penh. They told me they had made a match for me with the parents of a girl named Sak Kim Heng. Although she didn't come from my village, I had known her since we were young. Her parents were friends of my father, and we used to live next door to each other in the fort in Takeo. At the time she was sixteen and I was twenty-one. "No," I told my parents. "I fell in love with a tribal girl."

"No," my mother said. "You cannot marry that tribal girl." So I told them all about Champea, how beautiful and educated she was. But my parents didn't accept her. *Mae* Kim explained, "I already have a girl ready for you."

"Why didn't you ask me first?" I questioned.

"No," she replied. "You have to marry Sak Kim Heng."

I didn't know what to do. I had just been transferred to Kompong Thom away from Champea in Ratanakiri. According to Cambodian culture, I had to do what my parents said. I didn't even write a letter to Champea, telling her that I couldn't marry her. It was difficult to send letters at that time; it would take about a month for a letter to get to Ratanakiri because of the road situation, and I didn't even know which fort I'd be stationed at in Kompong Thom. I felt terrible. There was nothing I could do. I never saw Champea again.

CHAPTER 4

Encounters with a Wild Boar and a Tiger

After I recovered from malaria, I returned to the fort at Kompong Thom, but all the soldiers of the 15th Battalion had gone to take part in the frequent skirmishes with the Thais up on the Thai border in Preah Vihear Province. Only the office people stayed. I told them I wanted to go with the rest of the soldiers, but they said no, they needed me to stay there. In Cambodia, the wives and children of the soldiers were allowed to stay in the fort, but when all the soldiers were up on the border, there weren't enough soldiers left to guard the fort. That meant the military wives had to guard the camp. They had to know how to fight and carry weapons and were issued guns so they could be guards. The remaining officers wanted me to supervise the wives guarding the fort, so I stayed behind rather than join my battalion. Since I was only engaged, not yet married, Kim Heng was not living with me at the fort.

Kim and I were married in a traditional Cambodian wedding in 1966 in Kompong Speu Province where she was raised. After the border war with Thailand was over, I took Kim with me to my next assignment with the 2nd Company at Fort Kompong Thmar in Kompong Thom Province. After she became pregnant and was close to giving birth, Kim returned to Kompong Speu to be with her parents. There our first child was born, a girl we named Sao Santephear Vachana. Her nickname was Phosda. When Phosda was about two months old, she and Kim rode the bus back to Kompong Thmar to be with me. I grew to love our little Phosda.

Eventually, I was transferred to the 35th Battalion stationed in Choam Khsant District in Preah Vihear Province. Five military trucks loaded twenty soldiers and their families from the forts in Kompong Thom and Kompong Thmar and headed out to Preah Vihear Province, about 150 kilometers north of Kompong Thom. There was no pavement, just dirt roads. We moved during the rainy season, and because the roads were so muddy, it took us two days to arrive at Tbeng Meanchey, the capital of Preah Vihear Province. We stayed in Tbeng Meanchey for a week, waiting for the rains to stop and for transportation from the 35th Battalion to pick us up.

While we were waiting for the monsoon rains to subside, the villagers warned us to make a raft for sleeping. Since Kim and Phosda were with me, I needed to be especially careful. During the monsoons, sometimes the rains would begin up in the mountains of Thailand and the river would come raging down, destroying everything in its path. If this happened at night and you were sleeping on the ground, you would be drowned. One of the villagers told me to build a raft, with my tent on top, and tie the raft loosely with vines to a tree, making sure that the tree was smooth and slippery, without rough bark. That way when the floods came while we were sleeping in our tent, the raft would rise with the water, and the vines would slide up the tree. Fortunately, this never happened to us while we were stranded in Tbeng Meanchey, but it did happen to a friend, who survived because of the villagers' advice.

Since there were no roads to Choam Khsant, we had to use elephant paths. It was only about sixty kilometers to the fort from Tbeng Meanchey, but it took us two weeks. The stream and creek were flooded; we were stranded. My commander sent ten ox carts to pick up the women and children. The men had to stay with the trucks to push them when they were stuck. I did not like being separated from Kim and Phosda. Everything made me sad — the singing of a cicada, looking at the sunset, and hearing the sound of a gibbon. I missed my wife and daughter, but was happy they were able to ride in the ox cart and arrive safely in Choam Khsant.

I was sent to the isolated village of Chheuteal Kong close to the Thai border, next to the Thai provinces of Ubon Ratchathani and Si Saket. Having the lowest rank of sergeant, I was in charge of a section of thirty soldiers there, with one officer, Master Sergeant Sum Kath, above me. I couldn't return home much: sometimes for only two or three days to report to my commander. I walked between Chheuteal Kong village and Fort Choam Khsant.

Phosda became sick with fever, causing seizures. The hospital was far away in Tbeng Meanchey, but there was a military field hospital in the area. I asked the army nurse to come look at Phosda, which he did, but he said it was too late. The nurse didn't know what was wrong with her. Phosda was sick for only three days before she died. The nurse wasn't an expert and had no lab to find out why she died. His experience was with treating malaria, taking X-rays, and dealing with war wounds.

I was not with Kim when Phosda died; I was at work at the fort. I felt terrible because I was not home with her when it happened. Kim and I were so sad, we cried and cried. But all the villagers helped us and comforted us.

At that time I had to spend most of my time at the fort, and there wasn't room for the families to live with the soldiers, so I rented a big house in town where many of us lived together when we could come home. After Phosda's death, though, we didn't want to live there anymore. It made us sad to see where our adorable daughter had lived, crawled, and played. Kim could go to the border with me, but I was afraid something would happen. Cambodia was so poor, with no radio for communication and only dirt roads through the forest.

It was then that Kim and I rented a room close to the fort from a villager in Choam Khsant. The villager and his wife Chum let Kim stay with them and took care of her. They considered us part of their family and told us to call them aunt and uncle. Both Ming Chum and her mother-in-law loved Kim and treated her like their daughter. At first Ming Chum said, "Yes, I'll rent a room to you for 150 riels," but after several months, she said, "No, I don't want the money."

We lived and cooked together like a family, and when they went to the fields to cut rice, Kim would go and work with them. She didn't know how to cut rice, but she learned. When they needed to go out to their garden in the field away from the village houses to pick some eggplant or squash, Kim would say, "I'll go with you." Kim was so young; it looked just like a family going out to the garden together — grandmother, mother and daughter.

One day I walked down to Choam Khsant to visit Kim. After three days it was time for me to go back to Chheuteal Kong. She packed my backpack with things I needed—cigarettes, salt, MSG, dried and smoked fish. As I started back up the mountain alone, I wasn't afraid because I had my rifle. Suddenly, about a hundred meters from a fork in the trail, I saw a big, wild boar running toward me. I yelled as loudly as I could to scare it away, but it still kept coming. I tried to grab my rifle, but my backpack came off my shoulder. I ran to a big tree, but couldn't climb it, so I climbed a small one instead. The boar paced around and around the tree. Again, I yelled and shook the branches, hoping to scare it away. Then the branch I was sitting on broke, and I fell down on top of the boar. It was so surprised it ran away. Breathing a huge sigh of relief, I stood up, wiped the dirt from my uniform, shouldered my backpack and rifle, and walked as fast as I could toward camp.

Still shaken by the incident with the boar and my fall, I arrived at Ayoung Stream. I was thirsty, so I walked into the stream to take a drink of water. Suddenly, I saw a tiger in the bushes. I was so frightened; I started walking slowly backward, aiming my rifle at the tiger. While I was walking slowly backward, the village boys who herd the water buffaloes came along and saw me.

"What are you doing, *Sep*?" one asked, calling me sergeant because I was in my uniform.

Contemporary Cambodian soldiers at the ruins of Prasat Preah Vihear, the 9th century Angkorian monument built on top of a south-facing cliff of the Dangkrek Mountains on the border between Cambodia and Thailand. This location continues to be the site of frequent skirmishes between Cambodian and Thai soldiers, as recently as 2010 (photograph by Charles King).

"There's a tiger in the bushes!" I whispered.

They all laughed and ran to get the tiger. I didn't know the tiger was already dead because it had stepped on the villagers' trap. I couldn't believe I had encountered a wild boar and a tiger on the same day.

The villagers of Chheuteal Kong had a local militia with guns to protect the village, which was only six kilometers from the border. The village needed protection, not necessarily from Thai soldiers, but from robbers who might come at night to steal cattle. There was no longer fighting between Thailand and Cambodia over Preah Vihear. That was over.

The people who lived on the border could speak Thai as well as Cambodian. After I was in Chheuteal Kong for a while, I noticed that no one could read and write. The same was true in the neighboring village about five kilometers away. This bothered me, so I talked to Sergeant Kath about the problem. "I think we should build a school so these children will be able to read and write," I said.

"I agree; that's a good idea," he replied.

Next I talked to the villagers and asked how many would agree to come together to build a school. They all wanted to help. The men cut down trees and sawed them in their mill, while the women cut thatch and tied bundles together to make a roof. My soldiers made tables, benches and a chalk board. In just one week, we built a classroom for those children.

Then I went down to Choam Khsant and talked to the principal of the local elementary school and also to the mayor. I explained to them what I had done and told them that now I needed a teacher. Unfortunately, no one wanted to go to Chheuteal Kong because it was so isolated. Just like the temple of Preah Vihear, it's very difficult to reach from the Cambodian side, requiring a steep climb up the mountain. From the Thai side, however, the road is easy.

Another reason people didn't want to move to Chheuteal Kong was it had no hospital. Some people could read and write Cambodian, but no one could read and write French; the medicine labels were written in French. I was trained by the army to give injections and taught which medicines were given for the different illnesses. I was given a bag of medicine so I could treat the soldiers and villagers who had basic illnesses. I was known as the medicine man. If a person was really sick, he was taken to Choam Khsant where there was an army nurse. There was no doctor, only one nurse for an entire battalion. The nurse had a helper, if someone wanted to be trained, so when the nurse had to go to Phnom Penh to pick up medical supplies, the trained helper would be the one to take care of any sick people in the battalion.

When I returned to Chheuteal Kong without a teacher, I talked to my soldiers and found one who could read and write because he had been a monk. I asked him to be the teacher, and I became the principal. Next we needed school supplies; I told the principal in Choam Khsant I needed paper, pencils, books, and whatever he could spare, so he gave me the necessary materials. There were no organizations to help the children in Cambodia then. That's why I was so strict. I told the children, "You must come to school. No one must be sick. If you are sick, you need to go to see the military medicine man." I knew the children didn't want to do that because they hated the taste of the medicine — especially aspirin and quinine.

It wasn't long before the children were beginning to read and write in Cambodian. Anytime I went to Choam Khsant or Phnom Penh, I asked my friends to give me their used, easy children's books to take back to the village school. My house became a lending library; if the students wanted to read, they could borrow books from me. When I was called back to the fort, a year and a half later, all the villagers got together to write a letter and sign it, asking me to stay. But I had to go back to Fort Choam Khsant and the 35th Battalion.

I was removed for making friends with the Thais. One day Sergeant Kath and I took a group of soldiers and villagers to patrol the area of the border covered by the Thai Border Police. We climbed the mountain and walked through the stream in Cambodian territory. Soon, we heard people laughing and singing in the stream. Sergeant Kath and I ordered our men to surround them, but not to shoot unless the intruders shot first. We had happened upon Thai Border Police who had come to patrol the frontier between Thailand and Cambodia. It was during the dry season, and it was hot, so they were bathing in the stream. All of the police had put their weapons down on the rocks, and no one was standing guard. When they saw me standing on a rock aiming an AK 47 at them, they were really frightened. The Thai team leader got out of the water to talk to us. Sergeant Kath knew how to speak Thai well because he went to school in Battambang when Thailand occupied that province.

"We are just ordinary people," the Thai leader said. "We shouldn't fight each other."

"I don't want to fight either," Sergeant Kath answered. "I want to be friends."

Then we started to exchange cigarettes, and the Thai men got out of the water and put their clothes back on. We sat and chatted with them, and Sergeant Kath and I ate lunch with the Thai border patrol. Thai men like to drink alcohol; they had brought some Mekong whiskey with them, so they offered some to us. We drank just a little bit because we didn't trust them. We talked together for about an hour. Then the Thai leader told us they wanted to meet us again next week and have a party.

"What do you think, Choeurn?" Sergeant Kath asked me.

"OK," I replied, but I didn't trust those men; I planned to send more troops and village militia to the area one day before the party. I knew if something happened, my team would have a better place than the Thais did because we would be on top of the hill.

The day of the event, I asked the villagers who were good hunters to get some venison. They killed three deer, which we took to the party. The Thai border patrol lived at a high elevation, and they could drive their truck close to the stream where we would meet. They brought their commander and all their wives. The Thais brought whole roasted chickens, the spicy northeastern pork called *lap,* sticky rice, ice, Mekong whiskey, and a lot of other food. They also brought a portable radio, so we ate and drank with them while listening to music. They didn't even bring their weapons. I had taken five soldiers and five village militia men with me and told them not to drink too much. But the Thai people seemed to trust us, and we didn't want to hurt or kill them. Because the Thais brought so much food, we didn't cook the venison. We gave it to them as a gift, and they thanked us. Before we parted, we exchanged cigarettes and wine and agreed to meet every two weeks.

The next time, the Thai governor of Si Saket Province, the police commander, and the mayor came, as well as all their wives. The place looked like a picnic. We had good relations, but it was not like that before between Thais and Cambodians. The Thais asked us what we needed and what they could do for us.

"Seeds," I answered. "Could you give us some seeds?"

The next time the Thais came to visit, they brought seeds—cabbage, lettuce, daikon radish, pandanus—and helped us plant them. One soldier was assigned to tend the garden. The villagers didn't have these vegetables, only vegetables like squash and sweet potatoes that they could plant every year. They had never seen lettuce before, and they didn't know how to use it.

The Thais invited us to visit them in Si Saket. Sergeant Kath went, but I didn't go.

"When you go," I told him, "I will wait for you for three days. If you don't return, I will come to fight. I know where that police camp is."

But it was a safe trip. Sergeant Kath was gone for three days, and when he came back, he brought gifts from the Thais, including a shirt for me. We decided to give them something Cambodian in return. Thai people like pots made from copper, but they don't know how to make them. Cambodians have that skill, so we gave copper pots to the Thais. Because the Thai side of the border didn't have much wildlife, and the Cambodian side did, I asked the village hunters to kill two elk and two deer to give the Thais, also. They were very happy to receive the gifts. We continued to have a good relationship, something that did not exist between our two countries before. For this I was called back to the fort. Apparently the heads of the Thai and Cambodian governments didn't want to be friends.

CHAPTER 5

If You're Not Afraid, We're Not Afraid

In 1970 when the United States and South Vietnam jointly invaded eastern Cambodia, driving the North Vietnamese further west, I was in the north on the Cambodian-Lao border, guarding artillery. We were aware of bombings in the east, but we were given information only when we needed to know it. My wife and family were with me at this posting. Then when the 28th, 35th, and 39th Cambodian Army Battalions retreated back up the mountains in Preah Vihear, the wives and children were sent to Kantharalak Refugee Camp in Si Saket Province in Thailand, right across the border from Preah Vihear. The Thai military and the United Nations said it was too dangerous for the women and children because they believed there would be fighting. But the Viet Cong never came. The women and children stayed in the Kantharalak Refugee Camp until the fighting moved to Siem Reap, and the 28th and 39th Battalions were sent from Preah Vihear to Siem Reap. Only the small 35th Battalion was left behind in Preah Vihear.

One day a small group of U.S. Army men came to our camp, asking for men to be in a Special Forces group. Many of us wanted to join because of the better equipment and pay we would receive. Out of all the men in our company, thirty-two passed the tests of physical ability, mental ability, and education in order to join the group. I was one of them.

We trained at Nam Yen Camp near Kantharalak in Si Saket Province, where my family was also able to go. They were able to move from the refugee camp in Kantharalak because the danger of fighting with the Viet Cong in Preah Vihear was over. The Special Forces soldiers were given U.S. Army uniforms and weapons. It was cold in the mountains of the north, and the new uniforms were warm and better than what the regular Cambodian army was wearing. We trained in parachuting, tracking, and reporting on the Viet Cong, working in small groups of five men; I was the leader of one group called A-5. After training, we returned to Preah Vihear, in northern Cambodia.

My group A-5 observed the Viet Cong in Preah Vihear Province, to report on their movements, numbers, and weapons. The Viet Cong came from Ratanakiri and Stung Treng Provinces, as well as from Laos, along the Ho Chi Minh Trail into Preah Vihear. The terrain where we observed was forest, and we never used the same trail twice, but would come and go on different routes. I carried four weapons, including an M-16, a pistol, and two M-72 rocket launchers. We carried water and instant rice to eat so we wouldn't have to light a fire to cook. We also carried hammocks and a mosquito net, which we put up in the trees at night for sleeping. One of the men carried a radio on his back so we could report back. We would go for a few days and then come back to our base camp.

It was difficult to tell who the Viet Cong were; there were many Vietnamese civilians living in Cambodia, and many of them were spies for the Viet Cong. They could all speak both Cambodian and Vietnamese. They looked just like any other person. There was danger, but we had studied the procedures and trained to do this job, and if we followed the rules, we had a good chance of being safe. Some other teams didn't take the job seriously, saying this was Cambodia, and the Viet Cong wouldn't come into the forest. They made mistakes and they died. That's why I was so strict. Some of my men didn't like me because I was so strict, but I told them, "I know you don't like me, but I don't want your wives to lose their husbands and your children to lose their fathers."

When we were tired and needed to rest, I told them, "OK, one of you can rest over there behind that tree, another one over there behind another tree," making sure none of us was close together and not in the deep forest. We didn't sleep on the ground, and we chose an area where the trees were far apart to put up our hammocks. First we would make a little camp and set up tents; then an hour later, we would leave that area, walking backward to another place two or three hundred meters away where we would sleep for the night. We left the tents as decoys, so the Viet Cong would think that we were there. We were aware of them, and they were aware of us. Even though we carried weapons, we were not allowed to shoot. If something happened, we were to run for our lives. The only time we were allowed to shoot was if our lives were in extreme danger, and we knew we would die if we didn't shoot.

When we were in danger and would run, we each had a map and knew where to meet up with each other again. We had a password and our maps, so we could always regroup. Every day we had to change our password, but it would be something simple, like the number "five." My A-5 group was always careful, and no one was ever killed, but other teams found themselves in deadly situations.

Sometimes the Viet Cong would find an observer and force him to tell them the password. The Viet Cong might give the correct password, so the observers had to be very careful and try to go around and look at the man to see if we recognized him and his voice. Since there were only five in each group, we knew each other very well. We were also never supposed to travel together, so if two men came up together and gave the same password, we would know that something was wrong.

It was frightening to be in front of the enemy line, but it wasn't frightening to be behind it. At night when we crossed over enemy line, we took out our clothing that made us look like everyone else, hiding our uniforms, weapons and equipment. No one knew us, but we had to know where we came from. When we talked to people, we wouldn't ask about the Viet Cong, we would just talk about every day happenings, like how many sacks of rice were taken in that year.

I might say, "Yes, I didn't have that many rice sacks this season, and the Viet Cong keep going back and forth and they want rice to eat, so I don't know what to do."

The villager might say, "Yes, me, too. And we have Viet Cong staying in our houses. It's hard to provide for everybody."

In another village a person might say, "Oh, the Viet Cong are kind; they give us lots of medicine." And then we would know the Viet Cong were in this area and later radio the information back to our headquarters. We had to tell detailed information, including the map coordinates of where we were, but also facts like what the two villagers we met were wearing, if the husband was with his wife, were they going out to their garden, and were they carrying garden supplies. We didn't talk too much to people, and we didn't ask questions, otherwise the villagers would suspect us. We were always walking and just passing the time of day, saying that we had to keep going so we would be back home before dark.

The American Special Forces camp was in the Kantharalak District in Si Saket. When we patrolled far away from the base, we needed a radio that could reach the Special Forces camp. A walkie-talkie didn't have enough power to reach them. My team belonged to the Americans, so we couldn't report to anyone else. The Special Forces built their camp on Thai soil, but it was close enough so we could contact them on the border. They also built an airport for small planes to land. We could contact this small camp or the big American base in Ubon, Thailand.

It soon became evident that the international Morse code could not be used because everyone could understand it. In 1971, the Americans decided to make a special Cambodian Morse code. I was selected, along with five other men, to train how to operate a radio and translate Morse code into

Cambodian. The training took place at the Thai army base in Hua Hin, Thailand, south of Bangkok on the Gulf of Thailand, for two months. Our instructors were Thai soldiers. While I was training in Hua Hin, my family remained in Si Saket. When I came back, I was stationed where I was before.

Toward the end of 1972, the Cambodian army created a Special Forces unit. We were told we could not be in two Special Forces. The Cambodian government told the U.S. Army to give us back to the Cambodian army because they needed us, too. The U.S. Army agreed. When I became part of the Special Forces for Cambodia, the Americans still provided materials for us. The Cambodian Special Forces were trained in Thailand by the Americans. At that time, despite what the Cambodian army said, I was still a double agent, part of the American Special Forces and part of the Cambodian Special Forces. I received two salaries, one my regular Cambodian army salary, but also the salary paid by the Americans in Thai baht.

The Cambodian Special Forces went to fight in Prey Veng Province near Phnom Penh. I took my wife, children, and mother, who lived with us at the time, to stay in Phnom Penh with my parents-in-law, Kim's family. I was sent to Phnom Penh because I knew how to do the Cambodian Morse code. Sometimes the messages were secret; Cambodian Special Forces couldn't send them in English because everyone would know. Even the Viet Cong and Khmer Rouge knew the English Morse code, but they didn't know the Cambodian Morse code. I was stationed in Phnom Penh, radioing back and forth to the Cambodian Special Forces.

In 1973, my team was sent to Prey Veng for two months because of increased fighting there. By now the Viet Cong were gone, so the fighting was against the Khmer Rouge. I wasn't fighting, though; I was observing the Khmer Rouge and sending messages. I had to see how many Khmer Rouge there were, what kind of artillery, and how much of it they had. I also reported on their movements. At that time we had a big American 155-millimeter gun that could shoot almost thirty kilometers. It was installed east of Phnom Penh on Highway 1. The Khmer Rouge had installed artillery on Kong Mountain. My job was to go there and observe where they installed their artillery. They fired every morning and evening into Prey Veng City. When my team found their artillery, I called the base and told them. They were firing from about ten to fifteen kilometers west of Prey Veng City; that was as close as they could fire. Every time they fired the artillery, they retreated. They would fire and run, fire and run. They fired it only in the morning and evening, so they could retreat afterward. They were afraid the Cambodian forces would shell them with the big 155-millimeter gun. I'm not sure if the 155-millimeter gun ever destroyed the smaller Khmer Rouge artillery in Prey Veng. It probably did. I had seen explosions from where the big gun hit. The Khmer Rouge were everywhere, but I usually wasn't afraid; my team wasn't afraid. We knew we would win.

One time I was really afraid, though. The Khmer Rouge were fighting in the south of Prey Veng in the morning, as they usually did. When the fighting stopped and the Khmer Rouge retreated, we went out to look for casualties. I found a Khmer Rouge lying on the ground, so I went to turn him over with the barrel of my rifle to see where he had been shot. When I nudged him with my rifle, he jumped up, put his palms together, and began to *sampeah* to me, saying, "Don't shoot me! Don't shoot me!"

I was so surprised and gasped aloud. "Whoa!"

He had an American-made M-72 rocket launcher and six rockets with him. He immediately sat down and pleaded, "Look, I didn't fire my gun and shoot a rocket. I don't want to fight, and I don't want to go back."

"Why did you pretend to be dead? Why didn't you just sit down so I would know you didn't want to fight?" I asked him.

"I was afraid if I sat down, you were going to kill me," the young Khmer Rouge explained.

"Probably I would have," I said, "but why did you have to scare me half to death?"

I was so unsettled from my shock; I stopped checking for casualties and let the rest of the team finish the job. I don't know what happened to that young man. He wasn't my responsibility. After my team did the job we were asked to do, we left the area and went on to the next assignment. The officer in charge of the fighting in Prey Veng probably took the Khmer Rouge soldier as prisoner.

Another time all of our team was frightened. We were still in Prey Veng and now it was the rainy season, so the Mekong River was flooded. We wanted to know how many Khmer Rouge were living in a certain village on the river, but in order to reach the village, we had to go by row boat. We were dressed in our farmer clothing and rowed in our boat with our weapons and equipment stored in the bottom of the boat. We had to wait until the light was right so we wouldn't be seen by anyone on the bank. We quietly rowed under a big tree to wait until nine or ten o'clock when we would be safe.

Prey Veng has a lot of snakes, and during the floods, the snakes climb up in the trees and can't be seen. Just when we were ready to row the boat to land, a huge python dropped down into the boat. We were so scared, we jumped out of the boat into the water, yelling and screaming. The Khmer Rouge heard us and started shooting at us. We had to swim and push the boat away, all the time trying to get the snake out of the boat. Finally we were able to shake the snake into the water, making sure our equipment remained in the boat. By then the Khmer Rouge had stopped firing at us, but we were still so shaken, we turned our boat around and headed back to the opposite shore. We had had enough excitement for one night.

In 1974, the fighting moved close to Phnom Penh, so my team was sent from Prey Veng back to Phnom Penh. Shortly after, I was sent back to Preah Vihear, and I took my family with me. In 1975, the Khmer Rouge were fighting around Phnom Penh; again I was transferred to Phnom Penh. I went back and forth from Preah Vihear to Phnom Penh. Finally, I was transferred to Battambang in western Cambodia to help train Cambodian Special Forces. I was going to be there for two months, so I took my family with me. One day I needed to leave Battambang briefly to go to Phnom Penh to report, but the Khmer Rouge had blocked the roads, so I couldn't go that way. While I was waiting, the American Consulate, which was close to our base, had a small plane that had room on it. They asked, "Who wants to go to Phnom Penh?"

They let only the military go, not the families. I didn't want my family to go to Phnom Penh because I had heard that the Khmer Rouge launched rockets into Phnom Penh every day. Kim's family home was behind the palace in Phnom Penh, and the Khmer Rouge were launching the rockets across the Mekong River, not that far away.

Cambodian soldiers at rest during Special Forces training in Hua Hin, Thailand, circa 1971. From left to right, Sam Ol, Pich Koeun, Sao Bounchoeurn, and Keo Hok Ly (photograph from the personal collection of Bounchoeurn Sao).

"You don't need to go to Phnom Penh," I told Kim. "Just stay here in Battambang."

"If something happens," I told my Cambodian friends, "please take my family back to Preah Vihear."

I also went to the American Consulate and asked them, "If something happens, would you please take care of my family?"

"Don't worry," they assured me.

Off I went to Phnom Penh, where I was sent to the area of heavy fighting west of the city. After three days in the battlefield, my commander asked me if I would take care of the para commando unit because their leader was sick. I had the rank of lieutenant at the time.

"Wounded?" I asked.

"Yes, wounded," he replied.

"How about the assistant? Why don't you let the assistant be the leader?"

"No," he explained, "he doesn't want to be the leader."

My para commandos and I fought and never lost a skirmish. Back and forth we fought with the Khmer Rouge for about ten days. Then we were ordered to be part of a big attack. I told my men, "We have to be on the offensive early in the morning."

"OK," one soldier spoke for the group. "If you're not afraid, we're not afraid."

Early that morning the entire unit launched a surprise attack, gaining about three kilometers. At that point my commander told me to stop because we were in front of the rest of the unit.

"Dig a trench for yourselves," I ordered my men. "We're stopping to rest." This is what I had taught my men. When we stopped to rest, they must dig a trench to stay safe.

The next day the Khmer Rouge didn't come forward. Instead, they launched grenades and artillery, and some of the other teams' members got hit. I stayed, studying the map, trying to figure out what to tell my soldiers. Nobody died, but the other teams ran away. The ones who got hit cried and cried, but nobody helped. They were not my soldiers; my men had dug their trenches and were safe.

"Help me; help me!" I could hear the wounded soldiers crying.

I told my assistant to stay in the trench in case the Khmer Rouge launched rockets. The wounded soldiers crawled toward us. I went forward to carry one of them, about a hundred meters away, and when I heard the rocket, "B-b-b-btt," I stopped and dropped. Then I went again. When I heard it, I stopped again. Back and forth I went, carrying five wounded soldiers.

The ambulance was waiting for us behind the lines. Because I helped the wounded soldiers, I soon had blood all over myself. I was exhausted so I lay down by the side of the road. One of the ambulance drivers taking the men to the hospital saw me. "Lieutenant Bounchoeurn has been hurt!" the driver shouted.

My men saw and thought I had been hurt. Actually, I wasn't hurt; I was in shock and exhausted. They picked me up and put me in the ambulance with the wounded men. "Where are you wounded?" one of the soldiers asked me.

"I'm not wounded; I'm just so tired," I told him.

"I was worried about you!" he shouted angrily. "Why didn't you tell me?"

"I am so tired," I answered.

The ambulance took us to the hospital in Phnom Penh. One of the wounded soldiers lived next to my parents-in-law. When his family came to visit him, they saw me on the cot with an IV in my arm, a routine procedure, and blood all over my clothes, so they thought I was seriously wounded. They went home and told Kim's family what they had seen. Soon, her family came to the hospital, and everyone was crying.

"No, I'm not wounded," I explained. "I'm OK; I was just tired."

They were so happy to hear I was not wounded. I threw away my bloody clothes, put on the clean ones they had brought me, and left the hospital with them. Two days later, I was back with my commando unit.

Shortly after my return, the company lined up together. I thought the Khmer Rouge should surrender at that time. Our brigade had more weapons, tanks, and soldiers. We had much more than the Khmer Rouge did. But when I called up for more artillery to be sent to us, I was told no. All the artillery was sent back to the Olympic Stadium in Phnom Penh, and the tanks had no gas. I asked for more ammunition but was told there was no more.

"What happened?" I asked. My commander told me to come back to Phnom Penh. I asked again, "What happened? What do you want me to do now?"

He answered, "You have to take all of your belongings back to Phnom Penh."

"But what about all those soldiers, my para commandos?"

"Leave them there and let someone else take care of them," he replied.

I was so frustrated. I went back to my men and told them, "I'm sorry, but I have to go back to Phnom Penh; I can't stay with you. So stay safe."

They looked at me, and one soldier spoke, "If you're going to go back, then we're going to go with you."

"Don't do that," I told them. "You need to stay, and I've been ordered back to Phnom Penh."

When I went back to Phnom Penh, I was put to work in the office. "I don't want to work in the office; why don't you let me go fight?"

"There is no one left in the office, so you have to work here," my commander told me. "Besides, you need to go for special training."

"What kind of training is this? Why didn't you say something to me before?" I asked.

"We looked at everyone, but nobody else would do. You don't need to know everything. You need to do as you are told. I am not sending you back to the front lines!"

Kim and the children were still in Battambang. I knew I had to go back there. Instead, I was stuck in Phnom Penh. And then on April 17, 1975, Phnom Penh fell to the Khmer Rouge.

Looking back on it now, I don't think the Cambodian army was truly out of men, weapons, and gasoline. America had been talking to the North Vietnamese, and they wanted to get out of Southeast Asia. Cambodia depended on America for support, so when they withdrew their support, Cambodia could not continue the fight alone. The Khmer Rouge lied and said they wanted to negotiate, that we were all Khmer and shouldn't fight each other.

When all the artillery and big weapons were withdrawn and stored in the stadium in Phnom Penh, only the small guns were still being used. Those soldiers who were aggressive, not afraid, and wanted to continue fighting were brought into Phnom Penh and put to work in an office, like me. I never saw signs that the government in Phnom Penh was collapsing. I would look at the soldiers, and they were brave. But after the United States pulled out, some people cried, some people were disappointed, and the soldiers didn't understand what happened. When the Americans left, there were two million people living in Phnom Penh, including all the refugees who had come in from the provinces. There was not enough rice to eat. People were tired of war and were not supporting the military or the government of Lon Nol. Sihanouk was listening to Beijing, and the people heard Radio Beijing speak against continued fighting. Also, the people in the countryside who were already under the control of the Khmer Rouge were not allowed to listen to the Voice of America on radio, only the people in the city.

The Khmer Rouge had already indoctrinated the people in the countryside. They took all the valuables, like watches and radios, to give to *Angka*, the Khmer Rouge organization. The children were taught to call their parents *mit*, comrade or friend, not *mae* and *ow*. The children were also taught to kill. The people in the countryside learned to see that the Khmer Rouge were *tmil*, merciless, with no religion and no respect for life. They taught the children to love only Angka.

Lon Nol had support only from people who lived in Phnom Penh, and not all of them supported him, either. Of the fifteen million people who lived in Cambodia at the time, only two million of them were in Phnom Penh. Many villagers living far from the city, like the people of Chheuteal Kong up in the mountains of Preah Vihear, wanted what was best for their families. They trusted the ones who made it possible for them to have medicine and schools for their children. They just wanted to live happily and peacefully. They didn't care who was running the government in faraway Phnom Penh. There was no support from the people in the provinces, so when the Americans left, the government collapsed.

CHAPTER 6

Now We Will Have Peace

Because it was mid–April, the time of *Chaul Chnam*, the Khmer New Year, Kim and the children had gone to Pailin in Battambang Province, about sixty kilometers from the city of Battambang and close to the Thai border, to visit my wife's uncle. Back in Battambang, the American Consul General and his aides went to our house to take my family to safety, but they weren't there.

"Where is Bounchoeurn's wife and children?" the Consul General asked our neighbor.

"Oh, they went to Pailin to visit her uncle for *Chaul Chnam*," the neighbor replied.

The American Consulate radioed to Pailin, but the person receiving the call didn't have Kim's uncle's address and couldn't find them. The Consul General had to leave Battambang; I was stuck in Phnom Penh. When the Khmer Rouge entered Phnom Penh, I thought, "Oh, no...," and I cried.

My mother-in-law, Los Lan, asked, "Why are you crying?"

"Because I can't be with Kim and the children anymore."

"No, that's not true," *Mae* Lan told me. "The Khmer Rouge are coming, and now we will have peace."

"You don't know yet," I told her. I was separated from my family and didn't know where they were, but I hoped they were safe in Thailand. There were refugee camps there, but I wasn't thinking about the camps. I knew many people in Thailand, and I trusted they would help my family.

Three days later the Khmer Rouge soldiers came to our houses. "You must leave. The Americans are going to bomb Phnom Penh. You don't need to bring anything with you. Just prepare for three days," one of them ordered.

Some people trusted them; they didn't take anything, just a little food. Others didn't have enough food at home; in the morning before the Khmer Rouge came, mothers went to market, and fathers went to work as usual. Children were left at home with older brothers and sisters. They became separated from their parents.

I told my parents-in-law to stay home and not go anywhere.

"Why?" asked my father-in-law, Sak San.

"Because, *Pa* San," I told him, "the Khmer Rouge will not be friendly. I learned this when I went to Si Saket to train. They taught us about the people who had been treated horribly by the Chinese Communists under Mao Zedong." I remembered that.

Then I asked *Mae* Lan how much rice we had. "Only half a sack," she answered. This is only about twenty-five pounds.

"Hold on to it," I told her; "I will go find some more."

I went to a neighbor who had taken a great deal of rice from a warehouse that had been abandoned by the people who worked there. He and his family couldn't take all of it with them, so I borrowed some from them.

"When we return, I'll pay you back," I reassured him.

Back at the house, I took out the family's bicycle, which was a girl's bicycle, so I could carry the sacks of rice on the low bar.

"Why don't you take the Vespa?" *Mae* Lan asked.

"No, I don't want it; leave it here," I told her.

While *Mae* Lan and *Pa* San finished getting ready to leave, I went over to see what was happening at the Ministry of Defense, which was close to our house. I saw all those government workers being taken away by the Khmer Rouge soldiers. This frightened me. I went back home, took all the money to buy food to eat, and packed as much as I could onto the bicycle. Besides the center bar, which could hold sacks of rice, the bicycle had a rack to carry riders. I put a big board on it and tied it down so I could carry more. Because they were old, *Mae* Lan and *Pa* San couldn't carry very much, nor could my younger sister-in-law Kim Hai, who was able to use only one arm. Kim Hai had been paralyzed from birth and couldn't use her other arm and one of her legs. My brother-in-law, Sak Doch, could help a little, although he was young. Besides being old, *Pa* San had been wounded when he was in the army, so he really couldn't help. We had to take enough food to feed the five of us. We were able to take rice, salt, and soy sauce.

The Khmer Rouge evacuated the city in the morning. We walked, pushing the bicycle, from our house to Monivong Bridge, which wasn't too far, only about four or five kilometers. It took us almost two weeks, though, because there were so many people leaving the city. We would walk only one or two meters, then stop and wipe the sweat from our faces. April in Cambodia is the hottest month, and many elderly people died because of the heat. Thousands and thousands of people were being forced to leave on this road alone. People crawled and walked; children fell down, but no one picked them up. Many children and elderly people were sitting and crying on the side of the road because they lost their families and were scared and hungry. Pregnant ladies were being jostled back and forth; some of them fell, but I couldn't help. I couldn't stop. We had to keep moving and try to step over the people who fell down. Even the Khmer Rouge soldiers were trying to maintain order, but they could not. They knew only how to fight, not direct traffic, and there were too many people. About two million people had to leave the city, plus all the refugees from other provinces. It was terrible.

Children without their parents had no rice to eat. I looked at them, and they looked at me when my family stopped to eat by the side of the road. The children were crying, so I gave them rice to eat. Some parents died from heart attack or heat exhaustion, and their children didn't know what to do. I didn't know what to do. I still had my parents-in-law and the rest of their family with me. I kept thinking about my children and how sad they must be.

"I'm sorry," I said to the children, "I can't help you anymore." It was so horrible. I will always remember.

We had food to eat at first, so *Mae* Lan, who was a kind-hearted woman, would call people over to share with them when it was time for us to eat. I asked her not to call people over to eat because we would run out of food faster.

"No, Angka said only three days," she replied. I reminded her we had already been walking for one week and hadn't gotten very far.

When we finally reached Monivong Bridge, we walked along the Bassac River. I wanted to go on Highway 2, the road to Takeo; *Pa* San and *Mae* Lan also needed to go that way because their hometown was in Kompong Speu, a province west of Takeo. The Khmer Rouge told us the road was closed.

"Where do you want me to go?" I asked.

"Cross the Monivong Bridge and go on Highway 1," one Khmer Rouge soldier ordered.

"But I don't know anyone over there. I have no family there." Highway 1 goes to Prey Veng; I didn't want to go there. I had spent too much time as a soldier in Prey Veng.

A short distance away was a temple, Wat Russey Sros. I decided we should stop and camp near the temple grounds so I could think about what to do. We didn't have much rice left. We had also acquired our twelve-year-old neighbor boy Savoeurn and his grandmother. His parents had gone off to the market and to work that morning, so Savoeurn and *Yeay* were separated from the rest of their family.

I told Savoeurn I would help him since he didn't have any rice left either. I asked him if he could swim.

"Yes, I can swim," he replied, wondering why I had asked him that question.

During April the Bassac River was low, so we swam across the river back to the Phnom Penh side. Close to the river were many big warehouses of aid from the United States. All the workers had left their jobs when the Khmer Rouge evacuated the city, so hungry people were taking fifty-kilogram sacks of rice. In their haste, people pulled full sacks from the bottom of the stacks, causing the sacks on top to fall down on top of others. No one was helping anyone else, just scrambling for rice. Many people died from the falling rice sacks. I told Savoeurn to wait outside and not go in there.

As I was starting to go into the warehouse, a family came toward me with too much rice; they couldn't carry or pull it all. I asked if I could help them. They had a push cart, so I helped them load it. When we were finished, I told them I needed four sacks of rice. They gave me four sacks, so I didn't have to go into the warehouse. Many people were too greedy, taking more rice than they needed. Because they couldn't carry it all, they let some sacks of rice drop. I took one of those.

One man had a 100-kilogram sack of mung beans, which he couldn't carry, so I told him I could use some mung beans. He told me I could have half the sack; I found an empty sack that would hold fifty kilos of beans. Another family had a big can of lard, too heavy for them to carry, so I got their can of lard. Someone else gave me a sack of sugar. But now we had to get all of this food across the river.

"*Bong*, Brother, how can we take it across?" Savoeurn asked.

"Don't worry, I said. "Stay here and guard the food. Don't let anyone take it."

I went back to the warehouses, where I met a man, who asked me, "*Mit*, Friend, would you like some noodles?"

"Yes, thank you," I told him. He gave me a big box of dried noodles that weren't heavy to carry. Then I found what I was looking for: two empty barrels, some wall boards, and rope. Savoeurn and I tied the boards on top of the barrels, making a raft. We put all the food on the raft, slid it into the river, and pushed it upstream about one kilometer. We guided the raft by swimming and pushing, since the water was too deep to walk.

Mae Lan and Kim Hai were waiting for us on the other side and helped us carry the food back to where we were camped near the temple. After this we didn't worry about having enough to eat. We stayed there camping for about a month, as did many other people. We were waiting to go back to our families in our birth villages. Savoeurn and *Yeay* stayed with us. Our plan was to go to Highway 2 after all the people had come out of Phnom Penh. The Khmer Rouge were still not letting people go that way.

I decided I needed to make friends with the Khmer Rouge soldier who was guarding the Monivong Bridge. I talked to him and carried water for him, hoping he would let me cross to the other side. If he let me cross to the other side, I would walk along Highway 1 until I could hire a boat to cross the river at Takhmau and reach Highway 2. The Khmer Rouge soldier asked me what I did. I lied and told him I lived in Kompong Speu, the Lon Nol soldiers took me, but now I had escaped from them.

That made the soldier very proud. "Look at what Angka has done — helped a lot of people," he boasted.

When he said that to me, I was thinking the Khmer Rouge weren't helping the people. A lot of people had died because of them.

Suddenly one day my Khmer Rouge soldier was sent to a different area. "Oh, no!" I thought. "Now what am I going to do? I'll have to make friends with a different soldier."

Before he left, the Khmer Rouge soldier asked, "Do you need some rice? There are two sacks of rice. Go ahead and take them," he said. He had a big chunk of beef that he hadn't eaten yet, and also a chunk of pork. He gave them to me, saying, "Here, take them."

We had a big party with all that meat. It was wonderful.

We didn't have vegetables, though. I decided to find some, walking along the river until I found an island where people grew vegetables to sell in the market. The water had a strong current there and was dangerous for swimming, so I didn't let Savoeurn go with me because he was too young. Instead, a young man who was a strong swimmer went with me. He brought a big plastic bowl, which we took together, each holding onto a side. The water was deep, so we swam to the island. We filled the bowl with vegetables— cucumbers, eggplant and Napa cabbage. We also found lettuce, but we didn't take any because it wouldn't last long. We took only the vegetables that would keep. We didn't pay for them because no one was around, and we didn't know who owned them.

"Don't let any water get in the bowl," I cautioned the young man.

Luckily, we didn't get sick from eating these vegetables. Sometimes the farmers spray them with pesticides. These weren't sprayed, but I washed and washed them to make sure we wouldn't get sick. I went to get vegetables almost every day. *Mae* Lan used them to make pickles so they would keep longer, packing them with salt in a big tin petroleum can we had washed and washed to get rid of the smell of petroleum.

Another item we no longer had was salt. One day when I was walking around, I saw a man carrying two sacks of salt, but he didn't have any rice. I had two sacks of rice given to me by the Khmer Rouge soldier.

"Could you give me some salt," I asked the man.

"Not unless you have some rice to trade," he answered.

"OK," I said. "It's a deal." He gave me half a sack of salt, and I gave him half a sack of rice.

A month later, I had still not been able to get back to Highway 2. Then I remembered I had a Japanese Orient watch, which Cambodians really like. If you give an Orient watch, you will get whatever you want in Cambodia. I told one Khmer Rouge soldier (I called him *Samat Met*, best friend) that I wanted to go to Prei Pra village because my family and my children were there. That wasn't my village, but I wanted to get over there.

"No, you cannot," he said.

"*Samat Met*," I told him, "I will give you this watch."

"OK, you can go," he quickly replied. "How many want to go?"

I told him how many were in my family, and we were allowed to cross the river. I packed everything on the bicycle and on the raft I had made, which I tied on behind the bicycle. Again, the people in my family could carry very little. We had to go slowly and carefully so the ropes holding the raft wouldn't break. Savoeurn wanted to go with me, but I couldn't take him because his grandmother was so old, and they weren't going to Takeo. If he went with me, she would die. I felt really sorry about that. Savoeurn cried; he wanted to come with me because he trusted me. I told him I couldn't take him, and I wasn't going to stay in Takeo long. I had a plan to find a way to go to Thailand. He still wanted to come with me. I still see his face in my dreams.

CHAPTER 7

He's Just a Soldier

Eventually, I found a boat to take us across the Bassac River to the town of Takhmau. It was a typical Cambodian boat, shorter than the long-tailed boats of Thailand. It was big enough for only our family and my bicycle, plus the boat man, who stood in back with a long pole. We all sat on wooden benches and helped to bail water out of the boat when it leaked through the boat's seams. In order to cross in the boat, we had to pay two cans of rice for each person. Since one can was the size of a can of evaporated milk, it cost us a lot of rice, but we needed to cross the river. Once we crossed the Bassac, we spent the night past Takhmau, near the place where the road connects to Highway 2. In the morning we followed a dirt road over to Highway 2. When we reached the place where the roads separated, close to my village of Tang Russey, my parents-in-law talked about what they should do. Should they go to Tang Russey in Takeo Province with me, or should they go to Kompong Speu Province to their hometown?

"*Kon*, Son, I don't want to go to Takeo because we don't know anyone there. We don't want to inconvenience your family," said *Mae* Lan. "We want to go to Kompong Speu where we have family."

"OK, *Mae* Lan, if that's what you want to do," I told her. In my mind I was relieved because I wanted to go to Thailand. I knew it would be difficult to take them with me. We took a shortcut toward their village in Kompong Speu, until *Pa* San told me they could go the rest of the way by themselves. Before I left them, I tore boards off an abandoned house to build a kind of sled that *Pa* San could pull to make it easier to carry their possessions. They cried when we said goodbye. We knew we might never see each other again.

On the way to Takeo, I happened to meet my aunt-in-law *Ming* Sak, who had been married to a man from Tang Russey that wasn't really my uncle, but whom I called *Poo*. *Ming* Sak didn't know where to go because her husband, who had been a colonel in the national army, had been killed. *Ming* Sak was traveling with her children and her brother. They were hungry and without food, so I shared my rice with them.

"Where are you going, Choeurn?" *Ming* Sak asked.

"To my village of Tang Russey," I answered.

"I want to go with you," she said. "We have nowhere else to go. My birth village no longer exists. If we go to Tang Russey with you, at least we can stay with my husband's family."

Ming Sak's children were educated and could speak English. It was important that the Khmer Rouge not know these details about my extended family. Being the wife of a high-ranking officer put my aunt in a dangerous situation, but the English-speaking children were also a danger. I told them to let me do the talking when we reached the checkpoints.

We passed safely through all the checkpoints, where I talked to the Khmer Rouge soldiers. Each time they let us through without checking our things. Each time, I breathed a sigh of relief. I carried a first-aid kit, a military blanket, a military sleeping bag, and a hammock with me in a sack.

When we got close to my village of Tang Russey, we were stopped at the last checkpoint. I didn't know these young men, who were about fifteen or sixteen years old. They were looking for weapons. When one of the soldiers pulled out my military sleeping bag, he said, "Huh? *Poo*...."

I didn't know the one who called me uncle.

"Don't you remember me?" the young Khmer Rouge soldier asked. Then he told me the names of his mother and father.

"Oh, yeah," I said. "You've really grown up."

"Don't check him; he's my uncle. He's nice," the boy told the others, as I put the sleeping bag back in my sack.

I also had a photograph album of pictures from my parachuting days and certificates from my training. They were dangerous to have. They were memories, but I also thought that if something happened, I have my skills, and the album was evidence of those skills. Because this boy remembered me, the other soldiers didn't look further through my sack.

Finally, I arrived at my village; all the villagers came out to ask me about my family. *Ming* Sak and her family went to stay with her husband's people. *Poo* Yoeun, my mother's brother, and his wife, a Cambodian Vietnamese woman whom I called *Ming* Youn, came out to see me. My aunt cried because she knew how difficult this would be for me. She had lived with the Khmer Rouge since 1970 when they came into the village. *Ming* Youn had been there all the time, so she knew how dangerous it would be for me now.

The first thing *Ming* Youn did was make me dye my clothes black. I had been wearing my old army shirt since we left Phnom Penh. Now I took it off to change the color. Cambodians grew a special fruit they could use to dye cloth black. They put a lot of the fruit in a mortar, pounded it with a pestle, and put the crushed fruit in a big kettle. Next, clothes were put in the kettle and stirred; after the clothes were taken out of the kettle and dried, they were black. Now I could safely wear that shirt.

The people of Tang Russey were very poor, and they were hungry. I didn't know what to do with the food that I had carried with me. Because the poor villagers didn't have sugar, *Ming* Yuon buried my sugar in the rice storage area in her house. The can of lard was also buried in the rice, as well as anything that people didn't have and wanted. When my aunt saw the first aid kit, she told me I should give it to Angka. Then she took all the certificates, put them in a plastic bag, and buried them. But I still carried my pictures with me.

I spent several weeks in my old village of Tang Russey. I stayed with my favorite aunt, *Ming* Kith. Living with her was her son, my cousin Rin, his wife Sy, whom I called *Neang*, younger sister, and their two children. Rin was now a Khmer Rouge and the headman of that village. We argued back and forth, usually about whether the Communists were good or not. We always disagreed. At the time *Neang* Sy was sick, but Rin didn't care. He served Angka every day, his only concern.

"Rin, you should stay home and take care of your wife," I told him. "She's sick, and she still has to get water from the pond."

"I'm not a doctor," he replied and left the house.

I told *Neang* Sy not to go get water; I would get it for her. While I stayed there, I continued to carry water for *Neang* Sy, as well as *Ming* Kith, and catch fish for them in the lake. A lot of people in the village knew me, so I wasn't scared at first.

Then during the third week, a man came to me at night, saying, "Tomorrow Angka needs your help."

"Where?" I asked.

"In the temple," he answered.

"OK," I said, "What time?"

"In the early morning," he replied, and then he was gone.

In the morning my aunt was so scared, she was shaking as she cooked rice for me.

"*Ming* Kith, don't worry about me. I will take care of myself."

When I reached Wat Chambak Bethmeas, it was still dark. I saw many people waiting in the temple grounds for the truck to load them, including my uncle *Poo* Yoeun and my cousin Sok. They had been told they were going to build roads for Angka. *Ming* Sak, her children and her brother were also called to the temple. All of the people I recognized had been connected to the Lon Nol government in some way.

Then I recognized the man who was part of the Khmer Rouge interview team. He had been a monk. I lived with him when I stayed in the temple

Wat Chambak Bethmeas, the Buddhist temple near Tang Russey, where Bounchoeurn Sao's life was saved by the Khmer Rouge officer and former monk *Lok* Kel, 2010 (photograph by Rick Bird and from the personal collection of Karline and Rick Bird).

school. I helped him, boiled water for him, and took him places on my bicycle when he was asked to go to give blessings at people's houses. Now he was a Khmer Rouge in 1975. He was the one who took care of all the prisoners in the Khmer Rouge prison camp in Bati District. When he saw my name, he looked at me.

The other interviewer asked me, "What did you do in Phnom Penh?"

"He didn't do anything important. He's just a soldier; he didn't have any rank at all," my former monk quickly replied.

The interviewer quickly left me to question others. When we were alone, I said to my old friend, "*Lok Bong* Kel, Big Brother, he asked me. He didn't ask you. I know you; I won't say anything."

"OK," *Lok Bong* Kel answered, "Go over there and stay in the temple. When they call your name, come out. If they don't call your name, don't come out. Just stay there."

I went into the temple with *Poo* Yoeun and Sok. Even though *Poo* Yoeun had also been in the military, *Lok Bong* Kel had given similar answers for him when my uncle was questioned by the Khmer Rouge interviewer. We looked at all the stories of Buddha painted on the walls. It was still dark, and the tiles on the floor were cool. Since we were tired, we soon fell fast asleep. When we woke up, it was dawn and the sun was shining. All the people were gone, including *Ming* Sak and her family. All the trucks were gone.

"Angka did not need you," *Lok Bong* Kel told us. "You can go back home."

"Thank you, *Lok Bong*," I said.

Ming Kith was so happy to see me when I returned. "Don't say anything; don't talk," she advised me. She knew I liked to talk and argue with my cousin Sophi at night, as well as with her son Rin. She knew there could be *chhlop*, spies, around the house in the evening, listening to everything that was said.

Another man from our village named Sadee, whom I called *Poo*, uncle, was also called to the temple and taken away in the truck, but the Khmer Rouge released him. *Poo* Sadee was released because he fixed a jeep. He was useful. *Poo* Sadee had first belonged to Issarak, along with Papa. After that he lived in Phnom Penh, where he was a driver for the American Embassy, so he knew how to fix motor vehicles.

When *Poo* Sadee returned to our village, after being taken away in the truck, he told me what happened. The truck took all the people away to another temple grounds, including *Ming* Sak and her family. The people stayed and slept there, and each night several families would be taken out and killed. Luckily for *Poo* Sadee, a jeep would not start. The Khmer Rouge didn't know what to do, so *Poo* Sadee told them he could fix it. After he started the jeep, Angka decided *Poo* Sadee could live. He was told he could take his family back to our village.

The night before he left the temple ground killing field to come back to Tang Russey, he saw and heard what happened to *Ming* Sak and her family. Her husband had been a high officer in Lon Nol's army. For that reason alone, besides the fact that they were not originally from our village and were educated, they were killed. All of them. First the Khmer Rouge killed the children in front of *Ming* Sak. Then they stripped her of her clothes and beat her. *Poo* Sadee could hear her screaming. They beat her more horribly because she was crying loudly. It was so terrible, he almost fainted. When *Poo* Sadee told me what happened to them, I cried. I now understood what the Khmer Rouge were doing to Cambodia. I was afraid.

CHAPTER 8

If I Talk to You, You Will Die

In my village of Tang Russey lived a poor woman and her two children who didn't have any food. Sometimes the Khmer Rouge would force the mother to go and work in the rice paddies, so the little children, a boy and a girl named Lek were left to themselves. They were cute little kids, reminding me of my own children, but they were forced to eat like the pigs, anything they could find. I started to sneak food to them.

In front of my aunt's house were three palm trees. Every day I tapped juice from them, collecting it into buckets so *Ming* Kit could boil it down into palm sugar. And every day the children would come to watch, so I'd give them palm juice to drink and sugar to eat.

One night while my cousin and I were sleeping under the house in our mosquito nets, I felt a tapping on my foot and a little voice calling, "*Poo*."

"Who's that?" my cousin woke up and asked.

"I'm hungry," Lek answered. She wasn't afraid.

"Oh, no," I said. "What're we going to do?" Then I remembered we had some raw yams. We also had a fire to make smoke to keep the mosquitoes away from ourselves and the cows, so I put some yams in the fire to roast. When they were cooked, Lek quickly ate up the one I gave her.

"Can I take one for my mother?" she asked. "She doesn't have anything to eat."

"Go ahead and take it," I answered. Lek picked up the yam and ran back to her mother.

One day, I don't know what she ate, but Lek became sick, suffering from diarrhea for three days. Just like that she died. I was so sad; Lek was only five years old. Her mother cried and cried. I buried her by myself. The villagers were afraid to help me. The Khmer Rouge didn't encourage people to help each other. Now Lek's little brother was by himself. I vowed to myself to help him whenever I could.

Shortly after this, the Khmer Rouge told me I must move to another place. All the men who had been in the national army, and were still alive,

A Khmer Rouge soldier entering a Cambodian village, circa 1980 (photograph by Craig Faustus Buck).

were relocated. All the people who had remained in the village and lived with the Khmer Rouge since the beginning of the civil war were called the "old people." They were allowed to remain in the village of Tang Russey. Those of us who had left the village to live in Phnom Penh were called the "new people." We were also called the "April 17th people" because that was the date Phnom Penh fell to the Khmer Rouge and the city was evacuated. We were the ones not allowed to stay in Tang Russey. It didn't matter that I had been born in the village; I had left and then come back, so I was a "new person." I think the Khmer Rouge felt that those of us who were educated would question the way the Khmer Rouge were running the country. They didn't want us to cause the old people to question the Khmer Rouge, too.

The new people were forced to build our village, called Thnol Dach, in an abandoned cemetery that had become a mine field. Luckily, since we were all soldiers, we had been trained to clear mines, so it took us only about three days. After we had cleared all the mines, the Khmer Rouge told us to build houses for ourselves. My mother's youngest half-brother, Ti, was also a new person, so we built a house and stayed together there. At first we didn't have a roof, so my half-brother, Dorn, helped me get palm leaves and make one. My birth father, *Ow* Chham, and his son had also retuned to Tang Russey from Phnom Penh, so he and Dorn had been relocated to Thnol Dach, too.

We lived next door to each other, so I was able to see him again. When I learned he was my real father, I tried to call him *Ow*, but it was difficult. I still considered Papa my father. I remained in Thnol Dach with *Poo* Ti for about four months.

Every day we were sent out to work, and every night when we returned from working, we had a meeting. Then our Khmer Rouge leader would tell us what to do and where to go to work the next day. There was a leader for every twelve houses. Our new leader was a young twelve-year-old girl. That is what the Khmer Rouge would do — make a young girl be the leader of a group of men and tell us what to do, rather than someone who had experience.

One evening, our Khmer Rouge leader told us we had to clear the land from the village down to the lake. There had been a lot of bombing in this area, so there were a lot of unexploded cluster bombs. We knew this was dangerous work, but the area had to be cleared, and we were told to do it. Even though I wasn't the leader, I told the men to build a bunker. Then we took our *kramas* and carefully wrapped the cloth around our hands to very gently take the cluster bombs out of the ground and carry them to the bunker. We had to be very careful not to touch the cluster bombs with the skin or our hands, or they would explode. Then, I told the men to lie down in the bunker, and we quickly threw the cluster bombs to explode them away from where we were.

One day after we came back from clearing cluster bombs, I saw one of my old friends from school, Vanara, who was now an officer in the Khmer Rouge. When I saw him, I called to him in a friendly way, but he didn't answer me.

"I want to go to Battambang with the next group of people," I told him.

"No, you can't go," Vanara answered abruptly.

"I want to go in the truck," I told him.

"No, I don't want you to go. Stay," he ordered, as he turned and walked away from me.

Another day my Khmer Rouge cousin Sophi came to my village. He was now a commander of soldiers. He didn't talk to me, either, but he told one of his soldiers to give me some medicine that I needed. I wasn't sick, but I wanted to have medicine in case I needed it. There was no medicine in the village. I was lucky Sophi was my cousin. Even though he couldn't talk to me in front of others and had to treat me rudely, he was able to give me medicine.

Not too long after that, I was sent to help store medicine in another temple. My cousin, Sophi's sister Sokim, was a nurse for the Khmer Rouge, and she asked for me to help her. The Khmer Rouge were aware I knew how to read French, and they wanted to know what each kind of medicine or vitamin was. Most of the Khmer Rouge couldn't read. If it looked like the same letter, they would put them together. They didn't know. I saw a lot of medicine that was brought from Phnom Penh. Along with some other men, I helped to sort and store the medicine and vitamins. I liked working there because it was easy and I had food to eat. The Khmer Rouge had anything they wanted, including MSG that the villagers didn't have. When I asked if I could have some MSG, Sokim told me to go ahead and take it. After we were finished sorting and storing, I was sent back to my village of Thnol Dach.

After I returned, my old friend Vanara, the Khmer Rouge officer who wouldn't talk to me before, returned to my village at night. He came to talk to me alone.

"I'm sorry," he said, "I heard you were in Thailand. Why did you come back to Cambodia?"

"Because I'm a soldier," I answered, "so I must follow orders and do what my commander tells me to do."

"OK," he replied, "I know you want to go to Thailand. Now you can go."

"Why wouldn't you talk to me before?" I asked him.

"If I talk to you, you will die. I will die. They would not let me talk to anybody, so I had to be like that. But now you can go," he told me.

"Why do you want me to go now?" I asked.

I already knew that the Khmer Rouge had removed three different groups of people. First, they removed the military people who had fought in Lon Nol's army and their families. These people were killed, but my uncle and I had survived this tragedy. Then all the Chinese who did not belong to Tang Russey village were loaded into trucks and taken away. I asked what had happened to them.

"They were told they were going to Battambang, but all those Chinese were dropped off in rural Kompong Chhnang to survive on their own. They didn't have anything to eat, so they had to clear the land. They weren't used to that kind of work, and most of them starved. The last group had all the intellectuals, people who wore glasses and could read and write. These people were also told they were going to Battambang, but were dropped off in the middle of nowhere in Pursat Province at the foot of the Cardamom Mountains. There was nothing for them there, and many of them died from starvation, malaria, and diarrhea."

"Where are they going to take me this time?" I asked.

"This time they are going to take you to Sisophon, in Battambang Province. If you take this truck to Sisophon, you'll be close to the border with Thailand. I hope you find the way to go out," he told me.

"That's good," I said. "Thank you, *Met*."

When I went back into the house, I told my uncle what I had learned. I asked *Poo* Ti if he wanted to go with me or stay. He told me he wanted to go with me, but he needed to stay because his mother was getting old and needing care. I told him to go ahead and think about it and then decide because tomorrow I would leave.

That night, *Poo* Ti cried and said, "I'm not gonna go."

"OK," I told him, "I'm not going to force you. I'm going to Thailand. If it's safe, I'll live; if it's not, I will die. That's why I can't force you."

I prayed it would be safe.

CHAPTER 9

You Cannot Say No to Angka

Finally, after months of waiting, I had been given permission to go to Battambang. Although *Poo* Ti had chosen to stay behind in Takeo, the Khmer Rouge were forcing my other uncle, *Poo* Yoeun, to go. My uncle's name was on the list because he was married to a Cambodian Vietnamese woman. For this reason he was not wanted in the village.

When I got on the truck, the driver seemed like a nice, young man, so I talked to him, praising him and Angka, the Khmer Rouge organization.

"Where am I going to go?" I asked the driver.

He answered they were going to drop me off at the town of Pursat in Pursat Province, and then I would wait there for the train to Battambang Province. "If you want to go to Sisophon, you have to ask the people, like the conductor, and they will tell you what to do," he explained.

When we reached Pursat, a lot of people were waiting for the train. Some of them had been waiting for about a month. The Khmer Rouge didn't have enough transportation to move people from one section of the country to another. As we got off the truck, we were told to go stand in line to register and then get rice. *Poo* Yoeun wanted to put my name on his family list, but I told him no, I wanted to go by myself. It would be easier this way. In my mind I planned to escape, but *Poo* Yoeun had a family, and if there was trouble when I left, he would be involved. I decided to give just my name so no one would be punished on my account. When I signed my name, I said there were five people in my family so I could get more rice. If I said I had five people in my family, I would be given a half sack of rice rather than the meager single portion. Although I used my real name, I signed a fake signature.

We had to wait only five days until the train came. Then the Khmer Rouge announced, "All people going to Sisophon get on board."

We all carried what few possessions we had, including rice. My rice was in a big container of tightly woven palm leaves, now weighing about fifty kilograms. Since the train was a freight train, people sat in the boxcars. As we boarded, the Khmer Rouge didn't check their list, so they didn't realize I was boarding alone. I had learned that most of the Khmer Rouge weren't edu-cated and couldn't read. Some could read a little bit, so I had signed an illegible signature. There was no problem, however, and I boarded safely.

I found a place to sit in the doorway so I could face the section of Bat-tambang that went behind my old headquarters where I had left my family. I knew my family wasn't there, but I wanted to look anyway. I thought and hoped that my wife and children were in Thailand. I had talked to the Amer-ican Consulate, but they hadn't been able to find her, which led me to believe she might already be in Thailand. I hadn't seen Kim and the children for about five months. After the fall of Phnom Penh, I had been camped outside the city for a month and then had lived in my village of Tang Russey and the new village of Thnol Dach for about four months. I longed to see my family again.

The train stopped to let us off at the village of Mongkol Borei, about five kilometers from Sisophon. As we exited the train, the Khmer Rouge searched us. I was lucky, though, because they didn't find the pictures and clothing I had hidden in the rice container. They just assumed it was a container full of rice, but inside I had my pictures and an extra pair of pants. The Khmer Rouge didn't allow us to have more than one pair of pants; I had three pairs. I was wearing two pairs and had the third one hidden in the rice. The Khmer Rouge searched through all of my things, including the rice container, but they didn't find my possessions. I had buried them in a plastic sack, deep in the middle of the rice.

After we were searched, all of the people who rode in my boxcar were told we would be living in a specific village, and we were not to go anywhere else. Each person would live by himself, so I found an abandoned house, moved in with my possessions, and used whatever had been left behind by the previous owner. Besides *Poo* Yoeun and his wife *Ming* Youn, my half-sister Hoeung, Papa's daughter who had a different mother, was also in Mongkol Borei with her husband, but they were taken to live in a different section. Even though they were from Tang Russey, they came in a different boxcar on the train, so they couldn't live in our area. I didn't go close to my uncle or other members of my family. I wanted to protect them against the time when I would try to escape.

Poo Yoeun was fine in Mongkol Borei, though, because the Khmer Rouge liked him. His occupation had been a barber in Tang Russey, before he joined the military, and this new village didn't have one, so *Poo* Yoeun became the barber. He cut hair for all the Khmer Rouge and anyone else. When the impor-tant members of Angka needed a haircut, they would come to him. He didn't have to do any heavy labor, just cut hair, and he had plenty of rice to eat. When he arrived, he didn't have a razor, scissors, or clippers. When the Khmer

Rouge found out he could cut hair, and he was assigned that job, he told them he didn't have the right tools. The Khmer Rouge sent a driver to Phnom Penh to get new barber tools for him. Every day he cut hair, and when he moved from Mongkol Borei, he took his barber tools with him and continued to cut hair for everyone, but especially for Angka.

I waited in Mongkol Borei for three days until the Khmer Rouge announced the names of the people who would go to a new village. I was on that list. When the tractor came, the leader called, "Sao Bounchoeurn?"

"Yes, that's me," I responded.

"Get in; you have to go and live in my village," the leader said.

I got in the trailer that was pulled by the tractor and was taken to the village of Tep Prasa near the highway. The villagers had built huts for the new people who were supposed to live there. When I arrived, the Khmer Rouge asked again about my personal history. "Do you have a family?"

"No," I answered.

"Do you have good health?"

"Yes, but I am *waykanda*, middle-aged," I explained. In Cambodian, middle-aged means married, but a widower. This is what the Khmer Rouge called someone who had been married, but was now a widower or divorced.

I was given a one-room hut to myself, so I carried in the things that belonged to me. I had nothing then, only my clothes and rice and a cooking pot. At the time the Khmer Rouge seized power in April, they did not use money, abolishing currency when they proclaimed 1975 as Year Zero. People had thrown their paper money away or burned it.

The Khmer Rouge were tricky if they wanted to get something from someone. They didn't want us to have anything like watches, gold, rice, pots and pans—anything that was valuable. At night the Khmer Rouge would hold a meeting; everyone had to go, including the children. While we were at the meeting, other Khmer Rouge would search the huts and take anything they wanted. This search had yet to take place in Tep Prasa.

One day just after I had arrived, I went fishing because I had a fish hook on a string. I was lucky and caught some fish, so I walked alone back to my hut. On the way I saw a young boy named Suong. His father had been a Khmer Rouge soldier, but his parents had both been killed during the fighting with the Lon Nol army. The Khmer Rouge had kept Suong and raised him. He liked to threaten people. The Khmer Rouge gave him an American M-16, although it had only three bullets in it.

When Suong saw me carrying my fish, he ordered, "Give me one of those fish."

"No," I said.

"You cannot say no to Angka," he replied. The Khmer Rouge always used

 អ្នកប្រព្រឹត្តខុស... ម្យ៉ាងទៀតៗ ប្រតិកម្មប្រែប្រួមមិនបានទេ

៨. កុំយកលេសឆក្បាជាត្រាប់ប្ញាំងមុខមាត់ក្បត់ខ្សរបរសេរឆ្លងឆ្នូយអោះ៖

៩. ត្រូវបញ្ឈាខាងលើមិនព្រើតបត្ថូយម្ញ៉ូយសំបានខ្មែរក្រើងរាប់មិនបេះទេ

១០. ប្រទាំងធ៌ិយរក្សាម្ញ៉ូយបំណុយ ត្រូវរងឆ្នាត់១០រំពាត់បុកត់ខ្សរក្រើង ឆ្នាប់ ។

THE SECURITY REGULATIONS

1. YOU MUST ANSWER ACCORDINGLY TO MY QUESTIONS. DON'T TURN THEM AWAY.
2. DON'T TRY TO HIDE THE FACTS BY MAKING PRETEXTS THIS AND THAT. YOU ARE STRICTLY PROHIBITED TO CONTEST ME.
3. DON'T BE A FOOL FOR YOU ARE A CHAP WHO DARE TO THWART THE REVOLUTION.
4. YOU MUST IMMEDIATELY ANSWER MY QUESTIONS WITHOUT WASTING TIME TO REFLECT.
5. DON'T TELL ME EITHER ABOUT YOUR IMMORALITIES OR THE ESSENCE OF THE REVOLUTION.
6. WHILE GETTING LASHES OR ELECTRIFICATION YOU MUST NOT CRY AT ALL.
7. DO NOTHING, SIT STILL AND WAIT FOR MY ORDERS. IF THERE IS NO ORDER, KEEP QUIET. WHEN I ASK YOU TO DO SOMETHING, YOU MUST DO IT RIGHT AWAY WITHOUT PROTESTING.
8. DON'T MAKE PRETEXTS ABOUT KAMPUCHEA KROM IN ORDER TO HIDE YOUR JAW OF TRAITOR.
9. IF YOU DON'T FOLLOW ALL THE ABOVE RULES, YOU SHALL GET MANY MANY LASHES OF ELECTRIC WIRE.
10. IF YOU DISOBEY ANY POINT OF MY REGULATIONS YOU SHALL GET EITHER TEN LASHES OR FIVE SHOCKS OF ELECTRIC DISCHARGE.

Angka security regulations posted at Tuol Sleng Museum in Phnom Penh, 2001 (photograph by Rick Bird and from the personal collection of Karline and Rick Bird).

the word "Angka" when they wanted you to do something. They would say, "Angka wants you to do this." People were afraid of Angka because we didn't know who Angka was. We'd never seen Angka.

"You are selfish." Suong continued to explain the Khmer Rouge beliefs to me. "In the revolution you cannot be selfish. People are supposed to share everything. You even have to share your body."

"No," I told him. "I'm not going to share with you because you are young and rude."

"OK," Suong responded. "I'm going to report to Angka."

"Go ahead," I said, but I was scared. I didn't know what would happen, and this was the first time I had met this boy. I didn't know anything about him yet.

Suong liked to walk around the village, and he always walked by my hut. Two days after I had met him on the road, he passed by my hut to the house of *Kanak Phum*, the village headman's.

"Oh, no," I thought. "He's going to report me and there's going to be trouble."

Then Suong came to me while I was cooking rice. He sat down and put his rifle up against the wall. "I reported to *Kanak Phum* already," he said.

"What did he say?" I asked.

"He said he will call you. He will discipline you tonight," Suong replied. Then he walked away. But nothing happened. Suong really didn't tell *Kanak Phum*.

Then came the night when the Khmer Rouge called a meeting, and I was told to attend. Suong came to me and asked, "OK, do you have anything? Do you have gold?"

"No," I said, "I don't have any gold." I really had nothing except rice, a pot, and my clothes.

"Look at your rice," Suong pointed out. "Come on!" He helped me hide the rice in the bushes in front of my hut, explaining that they wouldn't see it. The meetings were always held at night because everyone worked during the day.

When I went to the meeting that night, Suong was the one who searched my hut, and, of course, he found nothing. When I came back to my home after the meeting, Suong came to me.

"Do you know what?" he asked. "I searched your hut, but you don't have anything."

"I know; that's what I told you," I responded.

"But you have rice," Suong replied. "You cannot put it in your house."

"Why not?" I asked.

"Because we all need to eat," he explained, "and Angka will cook for us." He went on to say that we will all eat together from one kitchen for the entire village. It hadn't happened yet, but it was going to happen. It happened as Suong said; the Khmer used me to build the village kitchen and rice storage.

About two weeks later, I was sent to build a dike, along with some other men. It was only about eight to ten kilometers away, but we stayed out at the dike. We still cooked separately, only one can of rice a day. After the Khmer Rouge found a big pot for the group, however, then we ate together. Actually, we could eat more by putting all of our cans of rice together. Besides rice, we would catch fish when we could, but we also cooked leaves that we knew were safe to eat, as well as insects, like the little red ants that bite. They were sour, but we could eat them.

After working out at the dike for a week, we came back to the village, and we were hungry. By then the entire village had started eating together, and everyone was ordered to give what he had to Angka. If you had a cow, you had to give it to Angka. All they gave us was rice and salt. Sometimes people would find things to put in the pot. *Kanak Phum* would send some people to fish, but the number of fish caught would be so small, it wasn't enough to feed the whole village. The Khmer Rouge said everyone would be equal and all would eat equally, but it wasn't true. When people went fishing, they gave the best ones to *Kanak Phum*, and the remainder would go in the pot for the village. We would have watery porridge with maybe a tiny morsel of fish in it.

Kanak Phum would say, "Go ahead and eat. When you are finished, we will eat the leftovers." But actually, they did not. The Khmer Rouge watched us eat, and then they would eat just a little bit. When they went back to their big Khmer Rouge house, they had good rice, big fish, and meat to eat. The people were starving, but the Khmer Rouge were fat.

When I went to Tep Prasa, I didn't know anyone except for my uncle and aunt, but I knew the others all came from Takeo Province. Those of us who had been in Lon Nol's army had not starved earlier because we were given plenty of food to eat. But now that we had been sent to live in Tep Prasa, no one had enough food to eat. I still had my container of rice, but other people didn't know about it. Angka took rice from some of the people, but they didn't take it away from me; they hadn't found it.

My next-door neighbor always talked to me, asking me if I liked Angka. At first I was afraid he was a *chhlop*, so I said. "Oh, yes, I like Angka." But after I worked with him in the fields and on the dike, I knew he didn't like Angka either. Then I told him the truth.

As we worked each day, the Khmer Rouge gave us only a little bit of rice to eat. It seemed to get less and less, and we were starving. When they made us work in fields far from the village or on the dike, we had to stay out there several days without going back to our houses, so I was unable to eat any of my extra rice. When my neighbor asked me if I would like some meat, I responded, "Of course, but how can we do that?"

"Do you see that little boy over there?" he asked, pointing to the "cow boy," the one whose job it was to guard the cows and calves. "Go over there and talk to him so he's distracted."

All the cows and calves were taken from individuals and held together in one place, now belonging to Angka. A guard was always on duty to prevent the cows from straying or people from stealing. I walked over and started talking to the boy, while my neighbor snuck around to the back, grabbed a young calf, quickly broke its neck, and carried it into the forest.

We had beef to eat, and we ate as much as we wanted. Then we buried the rest. The next day we dug it up and ate again. The meat wasn't wrapped in leaves or anything. We just buried it in the dirt. During the Khmer Rouge time, no one cared about dirt or anything like that. We were hungry, and we ate everything we could. The meat didn't spoil because we were so hungry and the calf was so little; we ate all of it in just two days.

At this time I had not yet asked my neighbor to join me in an escape. Before I could, he was sent to a new work camp, and I was sent to a different work camp. I never saw him again.

CHAPTER 10

You Must Be Like the Kapok Tree

The new village I was sent to was closer to the mountains, which also meant closer to the Thai border. I planned to escape, but I didn't know the geography around there, so I had to ask the villagers and the Khmer Rouge. I had to ask them carefully. My Special Forces training had taught me how to spy and find things out without people knowing what I was doing. I knew how to do it—carefully. I did exactly as I was taught.

First I had to praise them. "Why did the Lon Nol people want to get away from this village?" I asked. "Angka is good; now we have everything. We have houses and rice, but before we had nothing."

"Yes," one of the Khmer Rouge bragged, "and later on, we're going to have roads and electricity."

"That's right," I agreed. Then I pointed at the mountain. "Look at that mountain they call Dangkrek Mountain."

"No, that's not Phnom Dangkrek. Phnom Dangkrek is a big, long mountain range. That one is just a little mountain next to another mountain," another Khmer Rouge responded.

"Oh," I said. "There's a space in between the two mountains that looks like people can go up and down."

"No," the first one said. "They're far away from each other."

When I was alone, I wrote it down so I wouldn't forget, and I didn't ask them anymore. After two or three days, I talked to some different people.

"Look at that mountain. It looks like that's a good place for people to live and go up and down." I again pointed at the mountain.

"No," the villager replied, "They don't live there; they live on the other side."

"Why don't they live there?" I asked. "It looks like a good place to grow rice because of the soil."

"No," he explained, "There's only forest and a stream there. The people live on the south side."

"What about the north side? Why don't they live there?" I wondered.

"I don't know, but they don't," a second villager answered. "It's just forest and river."

"How far to the mountain?" I asked.

"Oh, not too far," they both replied.

Now I had the information I needed. When I was alone, I wrote it down. At that time people had paper and pencils. I got some when I arrived at Mongkol Borei and stayed in the abandoned house. The people who had lived there left many things behind, including paper and pencil. I took them and hid the paper in my rice sack in the rolled palm leaf container with my pictures. The pencil I kept in my pocket because it was short.

It was dangerous if the Khmer Rouge saw someone writing, but I wrote only when I was by myself. No one could see me when I was writing, and I wrote only briefly, just a short statement. For example, when I learned that it took three days to walk from my village to the border, I wrote only "3 days." If anyone would ever read this, he would wonder, "What is '3 days'?" But no one ever found my writings.

Once, someone stole my pencil. I never found another one, so I drew my map with candle wax. When I wanted to read it, I would burn paper and rub the ashes on the map; the picture would come out in the wax. I thought of this myself. Also, one day I found some paper in the village, so I took a feather and made a quill, then wrote with lime juice. When it dried, no one could see the writing, only the paper. When I wanted to read what I had written, I held the paper up to fire and the letters appeared. This trick I learned from Sokiang when I was in school. She taught me to write our messages like that so no one would know what we said to each other.

The leader of this new village, *Kanak Phum* Phol, was a kind man. He was a *khru* Khmer, a traditional healer, and didn't torture people. He would never report someone to Angka. When the new people made mistakes, he gave us advice. "Don't do like that," he would tell us. "It's not like before. You have to follow Angka. You cannot stop the revolutionary wheel. If you put your hand out to stop the wheel, they're going to cut off your hand. If you try to stop it with your foot, they'll cut off your foot. Just keep your mouth shut and do what they say. I know many of you are educated people from Phnom Penh, but you must be like the Kapok tree. Plant it in your mind and don't say anything; just keep your eyes open. *Deum-ko.* Be mute."

The new job the Khmer Rouge gave me was to watch the water buffalo. I was a cowboy, along with another man. At this time they weren't using the young boys to be cowboys. Boys eight to ten years old were used to collect cow dung to use as fertilizer. Strong married ladies worked in the village, sewing, weaving, and planting tapioca and rice. Young women and middle-aged men like me were sent to do hard labor, like building the dike. The old women stayed in the village to watch the young children.

Watching the water buffalo was not hard labor, but they liked to get into the water, and I was afraid of the leeches in the water. At first there were only four or five water buffalo, and it was easy to manage them. Later on there were twenty, thirty, and then a hundred. It became much more difficult to keep them out of the rice paddies. They wanted to go into the rice paddies because their skin is sensitive to the sun, and they don't have much hair to cover it. They like to lie down in the water, which destroys the rice plants. If the water buffalo decided to get into the rice paddies to eat the green shoots and lie down, I would have trouble. If I had trouble, the Khmer Rouge would take me to *kosang*, a disciplinary meeting. If I was sent there, the local Khmer Rouge would report about what I did wrong, and I would be reprimanded. If I was sent there three times, I would be sent to Angka to be killed.

I was never sent to kosang, but one day one of the Khmer Rouge said, "I saw you sitting on a water buffalo."

"I'm afraid of leeches," I explained.

"Leeches can't kill you; they're just animals," he told me, and he wouldn't let me sit on the buffalo. "The water buffalo is much better than you. It can plow."

Later another Khmer Rouge asked me, "Do you know how to plow?"

"Yes," I answered, even though I had never done it before. Although I was born on a farm, I had never learned to plow because I went to school and worked with my parents. I always responded yes, because if I said no, they would know I was educated. If I made a mistake, they would come after me and arrest me. I had to be careful.

The next day the Khmer Rouge gave me two large water buffalo and a plow. Earlier I had sat on a buffalo because of the leeches, but I really didn't like them because they scared me. A water buffalo can be very aggressive and prefers only one person, its handler.

"Plow in a straight line; don't let it *lewang*, weave from side to side," one of the Khmer Rouge instructed me. "Don't miss any parts."

"OK," I answered, but they didn't see how I was plowing. It was deep water. There were leeches in there, but when I plowed, the waves made by the plow and the muddy water swept them away. Still, when I first began to plow, I wore my pants long and tied them around my ankles to keep out the leeches.

About ten people were plowing the field, and when we were finished, we were told to pick up our plows and carry them over to the next field to be plowed. As we all started to leave the plowed field, Sadee, a man also from Tang Russey, so I called him *Poo*, said to me, "Choeurn, where is the point of your plow?"

"I don't know," I answered. "I didn't see that it was missing." I also couldn't see any plow point in the water, which was too muddy to see through.

"Angka is going to be angry with you," warned *Poo* Sadee.

"What am I going to do?" Angka could accuse me of destroying their property. I could be killed for that.

"Look over there," said *Poo* Sadee, pointing. "Somebody left that plow on the dike. Use it to fix yours."

I took the point from that one, using an axe to pull out the nail, and quickly nailed it to my plow. I didn't care if the plow worked well and dug deeply in the earth or not. I just wanted it to look like nothing was wrong.

I was allowed to have a small hatchet to be able to fix the plow if it broke. Since we didn't have spare parts, we needed to make them with wood, so the small hatchet was used for this. We were also allowed to have a small knife. Before I left Tang Russey to go to Battambang, my uncle gave me a piece of metal from a car part. I gave it to a blacksmith to make it into a knife and an ax for me. The Khmer Rouge allowed us to use knives and axes if we had them, but they didn't give tools to us. Not many people had them. Those who did never used these tools as weapons because people were already scared. They had seen torture and didn't want to risk being tortured themselves. They also thought of the safety of the people in their families. People were also weakened from hard labor and lack of food. Few felt strong enough to fight the Khmer Rouge.

After several days of plowing, the Khmer Rouge told me to prepare a paddy for sewing the rice seeds. They gave me three big bunches of rice straw and a rake. I was supposed to turn the dirt under and spread the straw, making the paddy smooth and even so the rice would grow properly. I did not know this was the way to grow rice.

After I made the dirt smooth, I was using my hands to pull the dirt out. A group of young women came over, carrying the rice seeds to spread. One of them asked me, "What are you doing?"

"Come on; help me so you can spread the rice seeds," I told them.

"We never planted rice like that," another woman said. I hadn't used the rice straw in the paddy; I had just given it to the water buffalo to eat.

"We never saw anyone do that," a third woman explained. "Probably you aren't a farmer."

"Where did you come from?" the first one asked.

"I came from Takeo," I answered.

"Oh, we did, too," they all replied. All those women came with me from Takeo, but I didn't know it. They were from other villages, so I hadn't seen them before. In Takeo they didn't plant rice like I had been doing. Probably no one planted rice like I had been doing.

"Do you have an axe?" one of the women asked.

"Yes," I replied, "I have a small hatchet."

"OK," she said, "Go cut that small bush and all its branches."

Then the women tied the branches together and attached them to the rake, turning it upside down. Next, the water buffalo dragged it across the paddy, making it smooth for planting rice. Also, the water buffalo was able to make a drainage hole in the paddy wall so the water could come in and out. We didn't have to dig the hole ourselves.

At the end of that day, *Kanak Phum* Phol came and saw the work I had done and called to me in an unfriendly way. "Come here. You don't need to do that work; give it to someone else to do. I know who you are. Come on."

He took me to the place where we had worked on the dike earlier and sat down. I was nervous about what would happen next.

"OK, *Mit*, I want you to read this for me. Tell me how much fertilizer and how to put it on, so we can make Angka happy."

The book he handed me was on agriculture, and it was written in French. I knew French, so I read it to him. I read out loud how much fertilizer to use and when and how to put it on. When I was finished, *Kanak Phum* Phol grabbed the book from me.

"You're not a farmer!" he shouted. "You're an educated person."

I had trusted him, but he tricked me. He also protected me, however.

"Don't read books," *Kanak Phum* Phol warned. "If anyone asks you to read, don't do it. Now, I don't want you to go anywhere. I want you to stay here and work on the dike again."

As it turned out, the Khmer Rouge gave me the job of building the dike, and *Kanak Phum* Phol put me in charge of twelve girls who were strong enough to work in the fields.

"What?" I asked, "Those girls are all from Phnom Penh. They can't do anything." And I had to take care of them. They gave us only one can of rice for everyone to eat — all thirteen of us. We had to cook the rice and add leaves from the bushes to have more to eat. I survived because of those girls; they did not eat so much and gave the remainder of their rice to me. Only one scoop of rice per meal with just a pinch of salt wasn't enough. Because they didn't eat it all, I received more.

"How can we eat only rice?" they asked.

I was worried about what to do because the girls did not have enough to eat. They were from Phnom Penh and were very pretty. One girl, Saron, was especially talkative, and she was educated, too.

"Saron," I said to her, "Are you willing to take a risk to get some rice from the Khmer Rouge tonight?"

"How?" she asked.

"I'll borrow the canoe from *Kanak Phum* Phol. When I land it on the bank, you can walk toward the Khmer Rouge place and talk to them. I'll sneak in and steal the rice from them while you're talking," I explained.

"Good idea," she answered. "Can I have some rice to take to my mother in the village? She doesn't have enough to eat."

"OK," I replied, and then I went to see *Kanak Phum* Phol. He usually went to other villages, especially back to his home village, to spend the night. "*Pook*, Father, may I borrow the canoe tonight to go to the other side to pick up one of my girls who went to visit her sick mother?" I asked. "She needs to come back this evening."

Kanak Phum Phol agreed. Soon after, I took Saron with me in the borrowed canoe to the landing place. She started walking and singing Khmer Rouge songs.

"Who's that? Who's singing those songs?" the Khmer Rouge asked.

"Oh, it's just me, Saron," she called. "I'm waiting for my leader to come and pick me up. I've been visiting my mother in the village because she's sick."

The Khmer Rouge came out and talked to her, hung a hammock, cooked rice, and offered her some to eat. Those men were dark-skinned, uneducated, and spoke Cambodian in a country dialect. Saron was a beautiful, educated girl from Phnom Penh. They smiled at each other and talked and talked.

By this time it was raining hard and making a lot of noise on the tin roof, so the Khmer Rouge didn't hear me, and their dogs didn't either. Since they had built a fire to keep warm and cook rice, the dogs lazily curled up around the fire. While they were talking, I snuck around, cut a piece of bamboo, and sharpened the end of it. I poked a hole in the rice sack with the bamboo, and the rice came out into my *krama*, which I had tied together to hold a lot of rice. I took the rice to the canoe, hid it under the seat, then paddled the canoe far away and came back singing a Khmer Rouge song.

The Khmer Rouge heard me, so Saron said, "Oh, my leader has come to pick me up."

"Why do you come at night time and not during the day?" one of them asked me.

"Because during the day time, I'm working," I answered.

"OK, goodbye; goodbye, Saron," they said.

"Oh, may I have some of those yams?" she bravely asked, looking at some roasted yams they had already cooked.

"Go ahead and take them," one Khmer Rouge told her.

"Oh, thank you, thank you," she sweetly replied. Then they gave her several cakes of palm sugar, too. So we had rice and yams and palm sugar to share with everyone in our group.

"That was a good idea," Saron told me on the way back to our camp. "Now we have food to eat."

When we cooked we had to be careful and not cook in a pot. We had to cook in a tea kettle instead. If we cooked in a pot, the Khmer Rouge would know that we had extra food, and this was not allowed. If we cooked in a tea kettle, they would just think we were boiling water.

Always thinking about food, I decided to get some fish. I used the hooks I'd been collecting, by now I had twenty of them, but I never caught any fish. The fish never took my hooks. Some people close to me, however, caught a lot of fish. One day I woke up very early. My neighbors were tired, so they didn't get up early. I took the fish from their hooks and put them on my hooks, discovering that the neighbors had better hooks. Then I went home and back to sleep.

After we woke up, my closest neighbor came to me and asked if I wanted to go look at our lines together. When we reached the water, he discovered he had no fish on his lines, but I had many. "Why?" he asked. "The bait is all gone, but there are no fish. And look at yours. You have a lot of fish."

"Yeah," I replied as I took my fish back to feed all those girls. They appreciated that I helped and looked out for them. They reminded me of Kim and made me homesick for my wife and children.

Angka and *Kanak Phum* Phol liked my team because we were healthy and could work hard. One day we were told to build two meters of the dirt dike, but the water was running very fast. When we put one shovelful of dirt down, the water would wash it all away. I asked myself what we should do; then an idea came to me.

"Come ... come with me," I called all the girls. I then cut a tree with lots of branches, they carried the tree over to the dike, and we planted it on its side. We used the branches and leaves to make a fence so the water couldn't go through. Three girls would help me make the fence, while the others would bring the dirt. We had to work fast, but it worked. The water went the other way. When the other teams saw what we were doing and the results, they started to do as we were doing.

This pleased me. I remembered my Special Forces instructor telling us, "You have to use your brains." I tried always to follow this advice.

One day after we finished this dike, *Kanak Phum* Phol came to me, saying, "OK, *Mit,* come with me."

I wondered why he called me to come with him at night. The moon was shining full as I walked with him along the dike we had made.

"You know, when I was a young man, I always went to Thailand. I was not always a good person. Sometimes I was bad; I stole cattle from another village, and I took it to sell in Thailand to the Thai people. It took me only one day if I walked fast. If I walked slowly, leading a cow, I'd arrive at the Thai border in one and a half days," he explained.

"But how could you do that? Look at that mountain; isn't that Dangkrek Mountain?" I asked.

"No, that's not Phnom Dangkrek. It's called Phnom Pakom," he answered.

There are villages on it," *Kanak Phum* Phol told me, "but only on one side. On the left side is forest; on the other side the people have their farms and villages."

Now I knew. Other people had already told me, but I wanted to make sure. If several people gave the same information, then I knew it was true. I knew *Kanak Phum* Phol liked me because he gave me rice, and when I didn't feel good, he gave me medicine. So I believed him.

"Now," *Kanak Phum* Phol went on. "You want to marry? Tell me who you love; I'll arrange it for you."

"No, I don't want to marry again. It would be too hard for me," I answered.

"That's right," he agreed. "If you're married, you can't do anything."

I understood what *Kanak Phum* Phol was really saying. If my wife and children were with me here, I could not escape. I think he knew what I was planning, and that's why he gave me all that information.

Just before we walked back to the village, *Kanak Phum* Phol advised, "Don't speak out. Angka doesn't trust anyone, and you shouldn't either. You can't trust anyone. You have to keep it inside yourself."

While we had been staying out at the dikes, I had been quietly planning an escape with *Poo* Sadee, the friend from my birth village of Tang Russey. He wasn't really my uncle, but I called him *Poo* because he was older than I. He had brought his family with him when we left Takeo for Battambang. When we were out working on the dike, the rest of the family was back at the village. As we planned our escape, we talked about whom we should take with us.

"Why don't you bring your son," I encouraged. "He's a strong, young man, seventeen years old."

"I wish I could," *Poo* Sadee answered. "But my wife is pregnant, so my son will stay in Cambodia with her. I want him to take care of her."

"I understand," I told him. *Poo* Sadee's daughter was sixteen and could have come, too, but he chose to go alone.

At the same time, my half-sister Hoeung, who was also in Battambang, but at a different village, came to visit me. I told her not to tell anyone, but we were ready to escape into Thailand. I asked her if she wanted to come with us.

"No," she replied, "I can't go. My husband is very sick, and his stomach is swollen from not getting enough food to eat."

"I'm sorry to hear that," I told her. "Please don't say anything, but we are leaving very soon." Even though *Kanak Phum* Phol had warned me, *Poo* Sadee and I had to tell the members of our families. We trusted them to remain quiet. *Poo* Sadee and I decided to take Chheang, a former monk from Takeo related to *Poo* Sadee, with us.

I had heard that usually when people try to escape at night, the Khmer Rouge would chase after them with horses as soon as they found out in the morning. The people would not know which way to go. I knew we would have to go north to reach Thailand. The sun came up in the east, so when I faced east, north would be on my left.

At night when we couldn't see, we planned to use the stars to guide us. We would have to find the North Star and follow it. When the North Star was directly overhead, we wouldn't know which direction was north, but once it had moved again, then we would know and could continue walking north. I had also learned in Special Forces what to do if we were in the forest and couldn't see the stars. We could touch the trees when it got dark to feel which side was hot and which side was cool. The hot side would be facing west, and the cool side would be facing east. Then we would know which way was north and go that direction. All this information we discussed with each other in preparation for our escape. We wanted to be ready when the right time came.

On the day we finished with the dike, we were told to move to another place to begin a new dike. *Kanak Phum* Phol said, "OK, *Mit*, I want you to wait here and show all the people which direction to move. Do you have rice to eat?"

"No, I don't," I answered.

"Let's go to my house, then," he replied.

We went into his house, he gave me a can of salt, and his wife gave me some rice. Before he left to move to the new location, he told me, "Take anything special that belongs to you so you will have it with you."

I knew he knew I was planning to escape. It would be easy to do at that time because everyone was moving, and they were moving in the right direction. All I had to do was tell the people to get food and point them in the right direction. It was time.

CHAPTER 11

Find the North Star and Follow It

Poo Sadee, Chheang and I left at night and walked toward the north. When we slept, we never slept far away from a village so we could hear and know the movement of the people. If we walked on the path in the daytime, we might meet some villagers who were going out to work in their fields, and they could see us, so we usually walked at night and slept during the day. We would sleep in the bushes close to the path —close, but not too close. I don't know if we were on the same trail that *Kanak Phum* Phol took or not. We just went in the direction of north, judging by the stars. It took us ten days.

As we were escaping, we didn't think about snakes and wild animals. We were taking a risk and couldn't worry about them. The wild animals had already been frightened away because of the fighting between the government forces and the Viet Cong earlier. We never saw any snakes or wild animals. Most of the poisonous snakes lived close to the bigger bodies of water. Even when we were building the dikes around the water, there were so many people who were looking for anything to eat that the snakes had been frightened away there, too.

There were wild banana trees growing along the streams up in the mountains, but when we got close to the border, there were mainly wild bamboo trees growing there. Wild banana trees need lots of water to grow. We could eat the wild bananas, but they weren't as good as the domestic ones because they had a lot of seeds. There were other wild fruits that we could eat, like a fruit from the mangosteen family. The wild fruit looks like the domestic mangosteen, but it's a different color. We could also eat the wild longan, but again, there wasn't much flesh, just a big seed. We ate whatever edible fruits and plants we found. *Poo* Sadee and Chheang didn't know about edible wild plants, but I had been taught about mushrooms and other edible plants when I was being trained by Special Forces.

When we got close to Phnom Chhat, we decided we couldn't cross it, so we went around it, following the path. It isn't really a tall mountain, but because that part of Cambodia is near sea level, it looked very tall to us. It was much easier to walk on the trail. We were too tired to walk through the forest bushes where there were big rocks, much brush, and streams. But we had to be careful of footprints; the Khmer Rouge patrol could follow us by our footprints. They also had mines and traps on the trail.

One day we had been walking in the woods and up the stream, so we were really tired; we decided to walk on the trail. *Poo* Sadee was first, I was in the middle, and Chheang was behind me. As we walked, my companions weren't looking at anything, just walking tiredly. I was looking around since we were on the trail. I knew we might find some traps. Up ahead, I saw a vine across the trail, and *Poo* Sadee started to kick it away.

"Stop!" I yelled. He started to turn around and come back, thinking I had seen some Khmer Rouge ahead, so again I called, "Stop! Stay still! Don't move. I think something is wrong."

"What happened?" Chheang asked.

"I don't know yet," I answered. "A vine never grows across a path unless it's been moved by someone to make a trap. I think this might be one."

I walked up, looked at the vine and saw a wire. I followed the wire and found a grenade. When he saw the grenade, Chheang, who had recently been a monk, started praying.

"Oh, thank you, Chheang. Thank you for praying for me," I said to him.

Usually, when the enemy makes a trap like that, he doesn't use just one grenade, so as I followed the wire, I found two grenades, stuck high up in the trunk of a bamboo tree. They looked like fish hanging from a line. I had learned to disarm grenades in both the Cambodian army and the U.S. Special Forces. When disarming two grenades, the second one has to be dealt with first, so that's what I did.

The Khmer Rouge had removed the pins, which made the grenades more dangerous for us. They had cut the bamboo and put the grenades inside the tree, tying them with telephone wire. If we would kick the wire, hit it or trip over it, the grenades would come down and explode. I took the second one and untied the wire, then set the grenade back in the hole to make it safe. I did the same thing to the other grenade, as well. If we had had the pins, we could have put the pins back to make the grenades safe. As it was, we each took a grenade to carry. Once we had the grenades in hand, I was no longer scared. We were now carrying the grenades, and if any Khmer Rouge came at us, we could hurl the grenades. We carried them on telephone wires. As we found more and more grenades, both *Poo* Sadee and Chheang helped to carry them. We all carried grenades on telephone wires; it was safe to carry them that way.

The Khmer Rouge wanted to kill or seriously hurt escapees, so they built and set many traps, including digging a pit in the ground and filling it with spikes, like a tiger pit. They made the spikes from bamboo and made them very sharp. So I cut a tree branch and tied my knife to it to use like a mine sweeper. If there was a pit, the knife would go through, and we would know there was a trap. Also, I learned the Khmer Rouge always built the pits in groups of three, but not in a straight line. If someone discovered one pit, then swerved to the right or left, he might hit a second or third pit. During our escape we came upon many tiger pits. Some of the pits had been washed through by the rain, so we didn't need to search for them. If the trail was flat, then we needed to search, but if the trail was steep, the rain would wash them away. The pits were always covered with branches, so if we saw branches on the trail, we would check so see if they covered a pit. This is why it took us ten nights to reach Thailand, even though it could have been done in about one day.

Another trap by the Khmer Rouge used a flat rock where someone might sit or lie down to rest. Above the rock, they would tie an 81-millimeter mortar, so when someone leaned against the tree, while sitting on the rock, the mortar would fall down, hit the rock and explode. When *Poo* Sadee and Chheang saw a big, flat rock, they wanted to go and sit down to rest.

"Stop; wait a minute. Let me check it first," I said.

"What do you think — there'll be a bomb under the rock?" Chheang asked.

"Just let me look," I told him.

When I found the trap up in the tree, I showed it to them. "See that? This one would kill you and they wouldn't even find your bones."

"Ohhh, yeah," they both responded. Now they believed me.

Then I looked for the wire. One thing I was afraid of was a bamboo arrow. Some tribal people set bamboo traps that would shoot bamboo arrows. But this trap didn't have that. From the Khmer Rouge work camp to the Thai border, we found thirty-five grenades and two anti-tank mines. The anti-tank mines were too heavy to carry, so we carefully rolled them down the ravine so they wouldn't explode. At least they were safely off the trail.

During the ten nights, we had enough rice to eat because we would gather it from the fields when we ran out of the rice we'd been carrying. One night when we were running out of food, we passed a village close to the mountains. Even though we didn't know the layout of the village, I decided to take a chance.

"Let's go get some rice from that village," I suggested.

"OK, but how can we do it?" Chheang asked.

"Come with me quietly; don't talk," I answered.

This village had its street in the middle, with the houses built on either side. The villagers planted papaya and banana trees and their gardens behind the houses. There was one big tree in the middle of the village. The Khmer Rouge soldiers were there. They had one rifle, and they had made a campfire because it was cold at night. We couldn't see where the rice storage was, so we walked behind the houses. I told *Poo* Sadee and Chheang to gather what fruit they could, and I would continue to look for the rice storage.

I came upon a water buffalo sleeping behind a house, so I took its wooden bell and walked around with it. Then I took banana leaves and tore and pulled them, acting the same as the buffalo when it eats banana leaves.

"Why isn't that buffalo tied? Who allowed it to walk around?" one of the Khmer Rouge soldiers asked when he heard me tearing the leaves. He took a dirt clod and threw it in my direction to chase the buffalo away.

When he threw the clod, I ran and rang the bell, "Dukh, dukh," like the buffalo would do. I didn't find the rice storage, so I picked some fruit, threw the bell away and joined *Poo* Sadee and Chheang. We went about one kilometer farther before we stopped to eat.

The next night, as we neared the mountains, we came to a field of sugar cane. We cut some canes and ate and ate. It was so good. It had been too long since we had eaten anything sweet. After eating the sugar cane, we lay down to rest. In the morning we could see that the rice was ready to harvest, so we cut rice, put it in our *kramas,* and carried it that way.

There are streams in the mountains, so we found one at night and built a small fire beside it. It was safe; people couldn't see the fire at night because we were deep in the forest, and there was usually fog near the water.

We had a military pot, so we put the rice in it and pounded it to remove the husks. As we pounded the rice, we made a hole in the pot.

Oh, no," said *Poo* Sadee. "Now we don't have a pot for cooking rice."

"Don't worry," I told him. "I learned how to cook rice without a pot in the army." I put the rice in my krama, soaked it in the water, dug a hole, put the krama full of rice in it, covered it up, and put coals on top of it, steaming the rice that way. It was regular rice, called *ang koa,* not sticky rice. It wasn't good, but it was better than nothing. We added anything we could find to our rice: leaves, insects, small birds and animals. I was thankful for the survival training I had received.

While we were in the mountains, we discovered what we thought was a Khmer Rouge camp. We didn't see them, but we saw their footprints; they were wearing sandals. I wasn't going to fear them because we had the thirty-five grenades with us. I told myself, "If I'm going to die, I'm going to fight the Khmer Rouge first." We found out later they were Thai *Dang,* Thai Communists, and they wore the same sandals made from recycled rubber tires that the Khmer Rouge wore. Usually, it was only the Thai Dang bands that camped out in the mountains. I don't know if they saw us or not. They never bothered us.

When we finally reached the border, we came upon farmers who were growing rice, tapioca, and corn, sleeping in their fields during the harvest season. They built little thatched huts on stilts when they slept in the fields, and they also built corn storages. Often times these people were cruel to the Cambodian refugees, raping and robbing them, especially if they were unprotected women. Even if the Cambodian refugees didn't have money, sometimes they were carrying gold. I wasn't carrying gold; I didn't have anything, nor did *Poo* Sadee and Chheang. But we were wearing our telephone wire grenade belts, with the grenades we had found on the path, so the farmers were scared of us. They couldn't speak Cambodian, because they were Thai *Isan*, Thais from the northeast. These farmers had come from Laos. They didn't have enough land to grow corn, so they came down to cut trees and grow corn here. After harvesting their corn, they went back to their home on the Thai-Lao border to grow rice. They spoke mostly Lao, but also Thai, so I spoke Thai with them. I told them the truth that we were escaping from Cambodia. They gave food to us and let us sleep in the corn storage. They also gave us homemade guns to keep with us during the night. They explained that the Thai Dang were in the area. That's when we learned the footprints had been Thai Communists and not Khmer Rouge. In the morning they pointed us in the direction of the closest village.

At that time the border between Thailand and Cambodia was closed. When we finally crossed the border into Lahan Sai District in Buriram, Thailand, there was just a big stone that said "Frontier Thai-Khmer." We were so happy. We knew the Khmer Rouge couldn't cross the border into Thailand and we were safe. But my feet were really swollen and infected, and it was difficult to walk. After we had gone about a kilometer from the border, we came to a big tree with garbage lying around under it. When I looked at the wrappers, I recognized them as food that the military groups eat; I had eaten the same in Special Forces, so I said, "This must be where the Thai border police stopped to eat lunch. I wish I could meet those men. I need to have some help for my feet."

It took us almost a day to walk from the border to the first village. We had to go through deep forest, and we couldn't even see the stars when it got dark. I was so happy; I sang and didn't fear anything. We came to a big stream filled with fish. Because we didn't have any fishing gear, we decided to use a grenade and throw it in the water, killing a number of fish that we could eat. We had just a little bit of rice and salt left, so I cooked that along with the fish and some edible mushrooms and leaves I found on the trees. *Poo* Sadee and Chheang were afraid to eat because of the mushrooms.

"Don't worry," I said. "You can eat them. These are OK." They ate just a little bit, even though they were hungry, but I ate a lot. We had to spend the night in the forest because we were up in the mountains, and the sun could not touch the trees. We weren't able to find out which direction was east or west by touching the trees as we had been able to do down on the plains of Cambodia.

Eventually, we arrived in the first village and were greeted by the Thai-Cambodian villagers who were living there. When I told them our story, they took us to the Thai Special Forces camp, rather than the police border patrol camp. This was a small camp set up near the border to get information from people who came out of Cambodia.

We were in the room where they send and receive Morse code, so there were paper and pencils there. I picked up a pencil and a piece of paper. While we were there, I heard one of the soldiers sending a message to the main station in Morse code. As I listened, I wrote down the dots and dashes. I didn't know the translation, but I did know Morse code. When the men were finished, I handed them my piece of paper, saying, "Here, did I do it right?"

"How do you know this?" one of them asked.

So I told them I was Khmer Special Forces and trained in Morse code in Hua Hin. I asked them if they knew *Phu Kong* Sang, the Thai soldier who was the captain on the border in Preah Vihear.

"Oh, yes," the leader answered. "But now he's *Phu Phan* Sang, a colonel at headquarters. How do you know *Phu Phan* Sang?" They were surprised.

"When he went to Phnom Penh to meet with the prime minister, I was the one who translated for him. He took me with him from Preah Vihear to translate. He's my friend," I explained.

"What's your name?" the leader asked.

"My name is Bounchoeurn, Sao Bounchoeurn."

After writing my name down, one of them used a two-way radio to call headquarters to talk to *Phu Phan* Sang. I couldn't hear what they were saying, but the result of it was they were told to take care of me.

A school building was next to the outpost, so *Poo* Sadee and Chheang were sent to stay there; I was allowed to sleep with the Thai soldiers. I also ate with them while the soldiers took the same food, only less of it, to the school building for *Poo* Sadee and Chheang. They cooked ordinary food, like regular rice and grilled chicken. They also gave me a mosquito net, but none to my companions. I felt uncomfortable with this situation.

"This isn't right," I said to the soldiers. "My companions shouldn't be treated this way."

"This is the way it has to be," one of the Thai Special Forces soldiers told me. "We trust you because you're a friend of our colonel, but he doesn't know your companions. We can't trust them."

This made my companions angry. They assumed I had said something bad about them in Thai to the soldiers, but I had not. The Thai soldiers asked me many questions, and I told them everything I knew about the movements of the Khmer Rouge. At night they gave me a rifle to use in case the Thai Dang came. They were in the area and could easily attack. There were only a few Special Forces men at the outpost, so I would make one more man during an attack.

Soon the Thai border police learned *Poo* Sadee, Chheang, and I were in the Special Forces camp, so they came to arrest us. "You shouldn't have these men," one of the border police said to the Special Forces. "Give them to us."

We were supposed to check in with them first; instead we had gone to the Thai Special Forces outpost. But it turned out that I was very, very lucky. The captain of the border police, *Phu Kong* Rean, was also a friend of mine from Preah Vihear, and he just happened to be in the area to check on this border patrol outpost.

When I saw him, I said, "*Phu Kong.*"

He turned to look at me and then answered, "Bounchoeurn! *Nong*, Little Brother!" He came and hugged me and asked me about my mother, my wife, and children. When he was in Preah Vihear, he liked to come to my house for my mother's cooking. Now he asked me to sit down and eat with him while his policemen cooked his meal, and he gave me five hundred Thai baht, which was a lot of money at that time. We talked and talked. *Phu Kong* Rean asked me where all the other Special Forces Cambodians were. I told him I was the only one who had escaped, as far as I knew.

Phu Phan Sang couldn't come to eat with us because he had much to do at Special Forces headquarters. He told his soldiers to give me two thousand Thai baht, so the Thai military and the Thai border patrol both gave me money. The border patrol police treated me very well, giving me sandals and clothes to wear. It didn't matter whether the clothing fit or not. In order to buy anything at a store, they would have to go into Lahan Sai city, so they shared what they had.

Our feet were dirty from not being able to wash them, swollen, and cracked, but not bleeding. The border patrol medic looked at my feet and treated them, giving me a shot and antibiotics to cure the infection. They took good care of me. I had to stay there for a week until my feet healed. But for *Poo* Sadee and Chheang, who also had infected feet, they just treated them with antibiotics and did not care for them as they did me.

The border patrol policemen also let me eat with them, but they didn't invite *Poo* Sadee and Chheang. When the border patrol interviewed us, they did it one by one, and they didn't let me sit in on the interviews with *Poo* Sadee and Chheang. They wouldn't let me translate for them, even though my companions didn't speak Thai. Instead they brought in a man from the village who could speak Cambodian. He wasn't a good translator, though. When they let me listen to the tape afterwards, several times I would stop the tape, saying, "No, that's not right." When *Poo* Sadee was answering the questions, the border patrol couldn't find the places he gave on the map because the translator didn't know how to translate those names. So they had to interview *Poo* Sadee again, and this time they let me translate. The Cambodians living on the border weren't educated, and they spoke only country dialect.

Because the border between Thailand and Cambodia was closed, we didn't have official documents to show when we entered the country. According to Thai law, when refugees arrived at the border, they had to spend three months in jail and then go before the Thai court before they would be sent to the refugee camp. Because the refugees have no passports or immigration papers, the Thai government has to find out who the refugees are — criminals or Communists or good citizens. My companions and I didn't have to do this. They let us go after one week when our feet had healed, and they sent us from the border camp into the Lahan Sai city station, where we stayed for only three days. We were allowed to sleep on the outside with the police, not inside the detention center with the prisoners. We were fed, but it was only the single bowl of regular rice that the prisoners were fed.

We were hungry, so I told the guard that we didn't get enough to eat. He asked, "Are you Cambodian?" When I told him I was, he told me his wife was also Cambodian, and she was the one who cooked the food for the prisoners. The next evening she brought us a big bowl of food, but we weren't allowed to eat it in front of the prisoners. The guard took us to another area to eat.

Since I had money in my pocket, I was able to take *Poo* Sadee and Chheang downtown to eat at one of the local restaurants. Also, in the evening the police would bring back bowls of fried noodles and share them with us. It was a good feeling to be free and able to buy food for my friends and myself.

I had left Phnom Penh three days after its fall on April 20, 1975, and I arrived in Thailand in January of 1976. *Poo* Sadee, Chheang, and I were allowed to go to the refugee camp in Surin Province after only a short time because I was friends with the head of Thai Special Forces and the Thai Border Police. Once again, I was fortunate to have been with the U.S. Special Forces.

CHAPTER 12

I Can't Find My Wife and Children

At the end of the three days, *Poo* Sadee, Chheang and I were sent to the Lum Pok Refugee Camp in Surin Province. At first we lived together, but we didn't get along. They didn't trust me anymore. *Poo* Sadee wasn't really my relative, but we're from the same village, and my parents had known his family for years and years. Actually, he is related to *Ow* Chham, but very distantly. When we escaped from Cambodia to Thailand, we didn't have any other family, and since we were from the same village and our families were so close, it was almost the same as being related. Even though Sadee was like an uncle to me, and we both came from Tang Russey, he no longer felt close to me. Chheang came from a distant village in Takeo, so we had never been close. I had not met Chheang before we were in the Khmer Rouge work camps. He came from the same village as *Poo* Sadee's wife; Sadee and Chheang now trusted each other more than they trusted me.

In Lum Pok Refugee Camp, Chheang, a big, strong man, quickly got the job of butchering pigs for pork for the refugees. At first I didn't have a job, but then I was approached by a man named Tep that I had known since 1970. We had worked together before, and now he worked for the U.S. Central Intelligence Agency as a translator because he spoke good English. He lived in Si Saket Province and was Thai-Cambodian. Several times I met Americans who were CIA when *Lok* Tep, Mr. Tep, came to talk to me. Thai intelligence would also come to talk to me. Both groups asked what I had seen and knew about the Khmer Rouge after their takeover. They wanted to know about the Khmer Rouge military, their movements, and where they were located. They also wanted to know if the Khmer Rouge had radios, what kind of weapons they had, where their camps were, and if they had any forts. Other concerns were how we were treated by the Khmer Rouge, what they did for sick people, and what happened to the children who lost their parents. I told them what I knew.

Soon, I was asked to be a part of the intelligence team. When new refugees arrived at the camp, my job was to go ask them questions as a friendly neighbor, not in an official capacity. I would talk about many different things and slip in the questions that we wanted to ask, without writing anything down. Then when I went back to my barrack, I would write down what I remembered. After writing down the information, I took it to a place in town and dropped it in the mailbox of the man who was collecting it. The camp authorities didn't know I was working for the CIA or Thai intelligence, but *Lok* Tep had told them to treat me well and not let anything happen to me. If I needed to go outside the camp, I was allowed to go.

After the fall of Phnom Penh to the Khmer Rouge in April 1975, the people who had been living there were sent in all directions to the provinces. Many of them were sent north to Kompong Thom and Preah Vihear. Those who survived the journey that far north were able to easily cross into Thailand at Si Saket and take refuge in the camps there. Eventually, there were too many refugee camps for the United Nations to manage, so they sent the refugees in the northern camps to the big camp in Surin. Because of this, all my friends from the outpost in Preah Vihear ended up in Lum Pok Refugee Camp with me.

Lum Pok was considered the best refugee camp in Thailand. The refugees were allowed to go out and work, as long as they had refugee identification cards. Those who went out to work in the morning had to be back in camp in the evening. Sometimes when foreign visitors and UN observers were expected to visit camp the next day, refugees were told to stay in camp and not leave. In the morning before the arrival of the visitors, everyone had to quickly clean up the camp. This was a United Nations refugee camp, as were the others in Buriram, Surin and Si Saket Provinces. These were the best camps for the Cambodian refugees because the people who lived in the border region and worked in the camps were generally Thai-Cambodian, so they could speak Cambodian with the refugees and treated them like neighbors. Most of them still had family members living in Cambodia.

At this time I believed my wife and children were in Pailin, Cambodia. The Cambodian chauffeur who worked for the American Consulate had left Battambang along with the other consulate people when they all left Cambodia for Thailand and had ended up in Lum Pok. When I talked to him, he told me that Kim had gone to Pailin. The wives of the Special Forces soldiers, who had been with us in Battambang, confirmed that Kim and the children had gone to Pailin. The chauffeur told me the Special Forces that had stayed behind in Battambang were told by the American Consul General to get packed up because everyone would be leaving. One of my co-workers asked, "What about Bounchoeurn's family? They went to Pailin for *Chaul Chnam*." That's when the American consulate tried to call to see if Kim had checked in with the American office in Pailin. They were hoping that when she heard the news about the fall of Phnom Penh, she would have gone to the American office to see what to do. But because people were happily celebrating the New Year and also celebrating the end of the war, Kim didn't check in with the Americans. They didn't know her uncle's name or have his address; the consulate was unable to find her.

I heard from those who had been in Preah Vihear that my mother had gone to Siem Reap to buy items to take back to sell to the tourists who had been coming from Thailand to visit Preah Vihear temple. There was still Thai tourism in the north, despite the fighting. After the Khmer Rouge took over Phnom Penh, however, they cut the roads, so my mother had been unable to return to Preah Vihear. If she had been in Preah Vihear, she could have easily escaped to the refugee camp in Si Saket, but if she was in Siem Reap, she was stuck there.

I tried and tried to locate my wife and children. I wrote many letters to all the refugee camps on the border between Thailand and Cambodia, especially to Kamphut Refugee Camp in Chanthaburi Province near Pailin. If Kim had been able to escape across the border, she would have seen one of my letters posted on the information board, or someone who knew her would have taken the letter to her or written to me to tell where Kim and the children were. This didn't happen. For two years I had no word about my wife and family. Frequently, the UN people would go from camp to camp, carrying letters and information, even announcing over the loudspeaker that certain individuals were looking for family members. Church World Services was doing the same thing. I finally gave up. I didn't write letters in search of my mother because I had already heard that she was in Siem Reap at the time of the Khmer Rouge takeover. Because she was old, she would not have tried to escape into Thailand. It was no use trying to look for her in the camps.

I wished to immigrate to the United States, but when I asked to be allowed to leave, *Lok* Tep told me "not yet." I was still needed to interview refugees, and the system was not in place for large-scale immigration to America, only to France and Canada. Those Cambodians who had been working for the American Embassy were allowed to go in 1975, as well as anyone who had a mother, father, sister or brother living in the United States. Most of them chose to stay because they believed, like my mother-in-law, that now Cambodia would have peace.

When President Jimmy Carter signed the agreement to accept twenty thousand refugees from the refugee camps in Thailand into America, two-thirds of them were Lao and Vietnamese refugees and only one-third of that number was Cambodian. The first category was those refugees who had a relative in the United States who would sponsor them. The second category was those refugees who had worked for the United States. The third category was those refugees who had been Lon Nol soldiers. I fit into categories two and three and had a higher priority than many people.

Poo Sadee had first worked for the French government as a soldier in the French-Cambodian army. After the French left Cambodia, he went to work for the American Embassy. He applied for an immigrant visa to France, since he had priority with the French government. He was allowed to take two or three people with him.

"Choeurn, would you like to go to live in France with me?" *Poo* Sadee asked me one day.

"If you really want me to go with you, I will go," I told him. "I would rather go to America, but if you want, I will go with you."

When it came time for the interview with the French people, I discovered that *Poo* Sadee had erased my name from the list. I knew that he was getting back at me for how I was favorably treated by the Thai Special Forces and the Thai Border Police.

"You know what?" I said to *Poo* Sadee. "You've forgotten everything. When we agreed to escape from Cambodia, we said, 'We go together. If we die, we die together. If we have something to eat, we eat together.'"

Poo Sadee replied, "Don't worry; when I go to France, I will send you money."

"Don't worry about the money," I told him. "I don't need it. Good luck in France." As it turned out, *Poo* Sadee and Chheang didn't do well in France. It did not work out for them.

It was at this time that I chose to move from Barrack 5, where I had been living with my two companions, to Barrack 11, where many of my friends from Preah Vihear were staying. After I moved in with my friends, I started noticing a beautiful, young lady that walked by our building every morning on her way to the pond to carry water. I asked one of the older women what her name was. I was told her name was San Bounriem.

Part II

San Bounriem: Village Girl

CHAPTER 13

The San Family of Thirteen

My childhood name is San Bounriem and I'm the last child in a family of eleven children. I was born in the little village of Sam Rong, Svay Chek District, in Battambang Province, now called Banteay Meanchey Province, on January 15, 1960. In Cambodia a person's family name comes first and the given name second. My brothers and sisters and I were born into the San family. First came my brother San Bounroeurn, then brother San Bounrien, brother San Phong, brother San Pha, sister San Samphao, who died when she was only two years old, brother San Phath, sister San Rieng, brother San Phan, brother San Phin, brother San Pheav, and finally I came. I called all of my brothers and sisters *Bong* because they were older, and they usually called me *Neang*, Little Sister. My parents called me *Mii Own*, a term of endearment that my brothers and sisters sometimes used, as well as *Neang*, which also means daughter.

My father was named San Here, but I remember everyone calling him *Ta* Here, Grandpa Here. All eleven of us called him *Ow*, the Cambodian country word for father. My mother was named Nem Yan, and we all called her *Mae*, Mother. She came from Chub village in Battambang Province, now Banteay Meanchey, near Siem Reap Province, where the world-famous Angkor Wat stone carvings are still made. My father came from Thmar Puk, a village very close to my mother's.

During the beginning of World War II, in the very early 1940s, there was fighting between the Japanese, Thai and French in Cambodia. During the Japanese occupation, the Thais actually seized the provinces of Battambang, Sisophon, and Siem Reap. My mother and her family moved to Thailand and settled in the village of Makak. At that time in Cambodia, the men were being drafted into the French-Cambodian army, and the women were not safe from the French or Japanese soldiers. My mother and grandparents escaped into Thailand to get away from the soldiers. They became refugees, living in Makak, Thailand.

My father was always a farmer and a business man, never in the military.

He would go in and out of Thailand, trading food and animals whenever he had something to sell. One day my father was in the village of Makak and saw my mother for the first time. This was about 1940. He followed her to see where she lived. When he found out, he asked around to see who her parents were. Since my grandparents had relatives in that village, they soon learned that someone was asking questions about the Nem daughter. The relatives told my grandparents to watch out because someone was interested in their daughter.

My grandmother, whom we called *Yeay* Lay, began to hide my mother. *Yeay* Lay never wanted my father to marry my mother. Because my father traveled around, my grandmother didn't know who his family was or where they came from. *Yeay* Lay told my father she wouldn't let her daughter marry him. "I don't know your family history," she said.

"I come from Thmar Puk village near Svay," my father replied. "You have relatives over in Svay, so if you don't believe me, you can go visit Svay and find out where I come from. My parents have already passed away, but my brothers and uncle still live in Thmar Puk."

My grandmother continued to hide my mother with friends in different neighboring villages, but my father was persistent. He knew everyone in the villages, and soon *Yeay* Lay had nowhere left to hide her daughter. At that time a young girl had to marry whomever her parents chose for her. It didn't matter if she loved him or not.

When my father came to my grandparents' house, he asked, "Where is your daughter?"

"Oh, here and there," *Yeay* Lay replied, not telling him the village or house where my mother was hiding.

"*Min aiy te.* If I can't see her today, I'll see her another day," my father told her, and he went off to do his job. He was smart and followed his heart. He had a lot of friends in the villages, and they told him what they knew.

"Hey, San Here, your future mother-in-law took your girl to another village," one friend said and then told him the village and house where he could find my mother. He was lucky he had friends who wanted to help him.

This was very exciting for my mother to have a man so in love with her that he searched until he found her, against her mother's wishes. I think she went willingly with him when he finally found her. I don't know where they went, and *Yeay* Lay didn't tell me, but they didn't do anything wrong. Later that day my father brought my mother home to my grandparents.

"Why did you come home with him?" *Yeay* Lay asked my mother, implying that she thought my mother had already lost her virginity.

"We didn't do anything wrong," my mother responded. "We just went to visit one of my friends, and then I came home nicely." My grandmother was angry, but she didn't say a word.

"You know," my father said, "I truly love your daughter, but if you try to hide her again, I'm going to steal her away."

"OK," *Yeay* Lay sighed. "I tried to keep her from you, but you found her; this is what she really wants, so you can get married." She realized that my father really loved her daughter because he was so persistent. He had passed her test.

My grandfather *Ta* Nem didn't care if they married. He had a very easy-going personality, so it was fine with him. I think my mother took after her father and had the same easygoing personality. She never got angry or punished us or tried to make us feel bad. She was always a sweet and loving person. I loved my grandmother, too, and she loved me, but she was very strong-willed and tough. I think I take after her!

My parents were married in a small ceremony in my grandparents' house. A monk performed the ceremony, and the village headman brought official papers for them to sign. My grandparents invited other elders of the village to come as witnesses.

When my parents married, they became Thai citizens. My grandparents also became Thai citizens. After my parents married, they lived in Kuk Plom village in Ta Phraya District, in what is now Sa Kaew Province. Kuk Plom is located just next door to Makak village, so they lived close to my grandparents.

But my parents had to leave Thailand about ten years later and move back to Cambodia after my father's friend came to stay with them in Kuk Plom village. This friend was a thief who stole a neighbor's calf. The Thai police accused my father. He told them he was innocent, but they replied, "If someone stays in your house, you are responsible."

My father didn't want to go to jail, so they picked up and left Kuk Plom in the middle of the night to go back to Cambodia. They left everything behind, taking only themselves and all the children. My grandparents didn't go with them. They were free to go wherever they chose, but my father had to leave Thailand to escape going to jail, even though he was now a Thai citizen.

My family went back to the village of Sam Rong. First, they had to build a shelter to protect them from sun and rain. One villager especially helped my family, *Ta* Mukh, who became a family friend. When my parents told us stories about the past, they always mentioned *Ta* Mukh. He gave *Ow* Here wood that he didn't need so my father and brothers could build the family shelter. Then they gathered grasses to weave and make a roof. It was big enough to hold eight children and my parents.

Because my parents brought nothing with them, the villagers shared what they could. If one person had an extra old pot, she gave it to my family.

If another person had an extra bowl or spoon, he gave it to my family. It didn't matter if the items were old and used. My parents were grateful for the generosity of the villagers. Immediately, *Ow* Here and my four oldest brothers went to work, building our shelter, hunting and gathering food in the fields and forest, taking care of a neighbor's cattle — whatever needed to be done. The villagers could see that even though my family had nothing, we were willing to work hard.

The first shelter was just a little lean-to, made of thatch, but after a time, my father was able to barter for enough building materials to build a bigger house. In the beginning it was only two rooms— one bedroom for the present eight children, and one bedroom for my parents and the three future babies, with an open-air kitchen out back. The two sleeping areas were separated by a curtain, and everyone slept on mats on platforms raised off the floor. The front of the house had walls with steps leading up, but the back of the house had no wall, so it was open to the kitchen area. The house was raised up on round posts, so animals could live underneath, while the people slept upstairs. The roofline on the back of the house extended down to cover the kitchen area. We were not allowed to play in the bedrooms with the pillows. This was the rule. We could play outside around the house or in the fields, but not in the sleeping area. My family ate sitting on the floor at a low, hand-made table, just a plank of wood, really, in the living area off the kitchen, never in the sleeping areas.

Because my parents had so many children, it was difficult to feed everyone when they first returned to Cambodia. People in the village gave them food, but they had to work for it. My father and older brothers went out hunting and fishing and brought back meat that other people would want. There were many streams in the area and ponds in the fields for catching fish. *Ow* Here and my brothers hunted for birds, rabbits, snakes, all different kinds of animals that people can eat. They would bring these back to the village and ask the old people if they wanted to trade for rice or vegetables. The villagers helped my family by trading things that we needed for things they wanted. My family didn't just hold out their hands and ask for help; they had to have something for exchange. They bartered for what they wanted and needed.

When our family returned to Cambodia, my father had no weapons, so he made his own bow and arrows. He made three sets so he and my brothers could hunt at the same time. They used the bows and arrows at night so they wouldn't scare away the birds and animals with a loud noise. When they hunted at night, they had to be careful of snakes. Cobras, banded kraits, and Russell's vipers are among the most dangerous snakes in Cambodia, and they lived in our area. Snakes rarely go into the rice fields, but they are found in the dense forests.

Cambodian village children, 2001 (photograph by Rick Bird and from the personal collection of Karline and Rick Bird).

Ow Here and my brothers borrowed battery-powered flashlights from neighbors and wore them on their heads so they could see where they were walking. They had to be careful about the very poisonous banded kraits that lie on the ground. If you don't see the banded krait and step on it, it will bite you. A bite from the banded krait will kill you within seconds. *Ow* Here knew how to find protective herbs that grow in the forest. He and my brothers picked the herbs, dried them, and tied them in small pieces of gauze. They put these herb packets in their pockets, which protected them against snakes. The scent of the dried herbs calmed the snakes, so when my father and brothers walked by, the snakes wouldn't attack. *Ow* Here and the boys had no protective clothing or boots; they wore their regular clothes and everyday sandals. Our neighbors were willing to lend the flashlights and batteries because our family had nothing at first and asked for help. It wasn't long, though, before my father could buy batteries, and eventually they could buy their own flashlights.

My father also used a gun that fired a single ball after putting gunpowder in the barrel, a flint-lock musket. He didn't have the musket when he first came back to Cambodia, though. He had to wait until he could afford to buy the materials needed to make one. The bows and arrows were fine for shooting small animals and birds, but he needed the musket in order to shoot larger animals, like wild boars, deer, and wildcats. *Ow* Here and my brothers also made and used slingshots to kill lizards during the day when they could see them running.

Eventually, *Mae* Yan was able to plant a vegetable garden around the house, and the younger children would help her, but the older boys and *Ow* Here would go out to the fields to work and gather wild fruits and vegetables to bring home for my mother and the rest of us. In the beginning the neighbors gave us some seeds to plant, and then *Mae* Yan saved seeds from that harvest to plant the next year. The villagers and my parents helped and benefited from each other.

Mae Yan planted squash, string beans, cucumber, watermelon, zucchini, garlic, chives, corn, and a bitter melon vegetable called *mariah*. My mother also planted fruit trees around the house when she could. She would save money to buy fruit trees. When she wanted to buy a little mango tree, a kind seller gave her a couple of extra ones because she had a lot of children. When *Mae* Yan wanted a coconut palm tree, she first bought a coconut and planted it, and after six years, she would be able to gather coconuts. Soon we had banana, papaya, and mango trees growing around our house, too. We didn't grow oranges because they were hard to grow in our area. My family also grew sugar cane and pineapples. Tamarind trees grew wild in the forest, so people didn't have to grow or buy them. The pods dropped from the trees; my family gathered wild tamarind to use for cooking.

My parents didn't raise coffee or tea; they drank only water. On a special occasion, when they went to a larger town, they would save some money or trade a large squash to buy an orange soda or another kind of soda, but that wouldn't happen very often. Soda pop was expensive, and there were many children to feed. The family drank herbal teas only for medicine, not regularly. Our farm, like most, didn't have a well. Water had to be carried from the streams or rivers. Houses kept water reservoirs or large water jars to save water. Rain water was considered number one for drinking, so if you could collect rain water, you were better off. When we were out working away from the house, we went to the ponds in the fields and drank the water there.

The villagers boiled water only to give nursing mothers with newborn babies. The rest of the time, we drank the water without boiling it, as long as the water looked good. Sometimes we got sick and maybe had diarrhea, but when that happened, people gathered herbs from the forest, boiled them in water, drank the herb tea, and felt better.

When my parents first returned to the village of Sam Rong, my father had no land. But at that time, there weren't many people in the village, and they didn't have to buy land. It was free. Once my family built our house, my father went outside the village and found the land that he wanted to have. As long as it didn't already belong to someone else, it didn't matter. All the houses were in the village, and the farms were outside to the north of the village. My father took the village headman, who eventually became his best friend, out to show him the land he wanted — how many hectares — and the headman approved. Instead of driving stakes in the ground, they tied a string around the trees to show the property line. My father chose three pieces of property.

Ow Here eventually ended up with a large herd of cows, but he didn't have to buy his animals; he worked to earn them through bartering with his neighbors. One of the jobs he had was taking care of villagers' cows. If a neighbor had five cows, my father would arrange to take care of them, and when the cows had calves, *Ow* Here would take two and the neighbor would take two. He said to the neighbor, "The fifth calf is yours. When you sell it, you keep half the money and give me half because I'm taking care of your cows." The neighbor agreed. Another neighbor had fifteen cows. The farmer came to my father and asked him to take care of them — take the cows to the fields to eat wild grasses and water them. When the cows had calves, *Ow* Here got half of the calves and half of the money from the one that was sold.

The village of Sam Rong was small, with only about forty houses. When my parents first came back from Thailand, everyone was richer than my father. But since *Ow* Here worked so hard, with the help of my brothers, over the years our family became one of the ten wealthiest families in the village. It took about ten years for my father to go from having nothing to being secure. We had a total of three houses; the last three children — my brothers Phin and Pheav, and I — were born in the first tiny house after my family returned to Cambodia.

After that we built the second large house, with our cows living under it, and the family living on the second floor. This happened about ten years later. We no longer had to work for people. We had our own land, animals and comfortable house. As my father's herd of cattle grew, they would no longer all fit under the house at night, so *Ow* Here and my brothers built a corral close to the house. When the cattle returned from the fields, my brothers put them in the corral for the night.

At that time my three oldest brothers, Bounroeurn, Bounrien, and Phong, were planning to get married, so my father sold three pieces of property from our family land to the wealthier parents of their brides. Even though my father had gotten the land for free, it was now his to keep or sell. He wanted his sons to have part of the family land, and their parents-in-law were willing to buy the land so they could help my parents. By buying the property, the new brides and their parents all became part of our family. My brothers each got the land, and my parents got money to help pay for the weddings.

My father was a smart and successful man, but he always remembered what it was like to be poor. That's why I want to help the people now when I go back to Cambodia. The villagers helped my family, and now I can help them. When I visit Cambodia, it's difficult for me to eat. The food sticks in my throat because I think about how little my parents had back then and how hard it was for them to take care of eight children when they had nothing. Today I see how little the villagers have, and how difficult it is for them to take care of their families. I can't make them rich, but at least I can give them one meal. I do this to honor my parents and remember the kindness of our neighbors long ago.

CHAPTER 14

A Spiritual Child

The last child in any family is usually spoiled, and I was a cute little girl, so I got to do whatever I wanted. From the time that I knew who I was, what I could do and what I could not do—from the time of my first memories, my father, my mother, my brothers, and sister never said, "No you can't have that," to me. I never heard the word "no" from any of them. They all loved me and tried hard to find what I wanted so they could give it to me.

I was what you may call a spiritual child. When I was born, I had memories of my past life. My father wanted to know more about me — who I was and where I lived in my past life. Because of this, *Ow* Here, who was a *khru Khmer*, traditional healer, never let me eat the yolk of an egg or liver. Traditional beliefs were that if I ate egg yolks or any liver, I would forget my past life. This started when I learned to talk at about the age of two. I told everyone — my family and friends— about my past life. *Ow* Here kept track of my stories. When I told things to my brothers and sister, they would say to my parents, "Why does she say things like that? No one around us talks like that." My parents cautioned them to never let me eat egg yolk or liver and to never hit me with a barbecue skewer. In fact, they were never to hit me at all. My brothers and sister listened to what *Ow* Here told them because he had learned about traditional medicines, herbs, and practices from the old *khru Khmer* in our village.

My brother Phath remembers that I told my family the name of my past village and the names of my past parents. I told them I lived in Bango, a village located close to the border of Vietnam. I told them that both my sister and I drowned.

Up until the time I was about five, I thought about my former life every day. Because I knew that I had drowned when I died, when I was with my friends and they wanted to go play in the water, I said, "I'm not going to go with you because I'm afraid I'm going to die again."

My friends replied, "Why are you afraid? We need to learn how to swim so we can play and work in the water."

97

"No," I said. "I'm not going to go." I tried to talk them out of going into the water. I never learned to swim, and I never played in the water when I was a child. I did, however, go to the fields with my brothers during the rainy season with my bucket to scoop up water to catch crabs or little fish to bring home to eat.

My parents cared more that the boys were educated than the girls, but when they lived in Thailand, all the children went to primary school. When they moved back into Cambodia to Sam Rong, the village school wasn't always open and running. Our village had a school, but it had a teacher only off and on. Because Sam Rong was far from the city, teachers would refuse to come. A teacher would come for a few months, and then he would leave. It would take time before a new teacher would come. When I went to school, an army teacher was assigned to teach in our village. He didn't last long. The teacher was mean and hit the students. I had never been hit before. My parents didn't hit me, and my brothers and sister never hit me. I started school when I was about six, and I already knew that no one was supposed to hit me. You can tell me what to do, but you can't hit me. If the teacher told me to hit myself, I would do it, but he shouldn't hit me with a stick on my back. At that time Cambodian teachers hit the students with a switch when they were naughty or did something wrong, but in my mind, I could not be hit. Children whose parents hit them at home could deal with being hit at school by the teacher, but not me.

I went to school for about two years before I quit. It was the beginning years, kindergarten and first grade, so I learned to read and write only a little bit — simple words like *slaapria*, spoon; *trey*, fish; *mae*, mother; *ow*, father; and my name. I know the alphabet, but I can't read or write in Cambodian.

On the day I quit school, my friend Asuan had been called up to the front of the room to write on the chalkboard. We were studying the Cambodian alphabet, and the teacher asked him to write the letter *kha*. Asuan just stood there and didn't write the letter. Everyone in the class tried to help him, saying, "It goes like this, and then like that."

When he still didn't write the letter, I picked up my book to show him, calling out, "Like this! Go ahead and write it!"

Asuan just stood there and looked at everyone. He didn't pay attention to our help. The teacher took his switch and hit Asuan because he wouldn't write the letter, and then he hit me because I was his partner. When your partner makes a mistake, both of you are punished.

After the teacher hit me, I cried. I grabbed my things and went home. I didn't wait until break time or after class. When my father saw me walking home, he called, "*Mii Own*, why are you crying?"

"The teacher hit me," I sobbed.

"Why did he hit you?" my father asked sternly.

"Because Asuan did something wrong, and the teacher didn't just hit my friend; he hit me, too," I told him, still in tears.

My father picked me up, put me on his shoulder, and walked to the school. Then he called the teacher to come out of the class. *Ow* Here told the teacher, "Look, even my wife and I and my children cannot hit my daughter. You cannot hit my daughter. If you want to teach her or not, you tell me right now."

"You know, I had to hit her; her partner got hit, so I had to hit her, too," the teacher explained.

"OK, if you say you had to hit her like that, it means you would hit her again. Forget it. You can take my daughter's name off your class list." And with that he picked me up, put me on his shoulder, and walked home.

"Well, *Mii Own*," he said to me. "I don't think I need you to go to school anymore. If you want to go, or if you want to stay home, it's up to you. If you get hit by the teacher, then I can hit you, too."

Of course, he would never hit me. Since that day I never went back to school. All my brothers and my sister went to school except the last three boys. All the rest could read and write Cambodian, but I can't. If I had chosen to accept being hit by the teacher, then I'd be able to read and write Cambodian, today.

I often wonder why I never went back and talked to the teacher. I don't think my father was that serious about what he had said, but at that time, it wasn't as important for village girls to go to school, or the boys either, for that matter. If I had lived in the city, it would have been different. I would have needed to go to school. I wouldn't have had anything to do without school in the city. But because I lived in the village, I could ride my cow to the fields and pick wild fruit from the trees to eat and bring back home. I could go with my brothers to catch fish in the ponds to bring back home for the family. That time of my life was easy, and I could do the things that I wanted to do. I had complete freedom.

My brother Phan went to school for a while, but he quit because it was too difficult for him. My older sister Rieng used to do homework with him, and she'd hit him when he couldn't put sentences together. He frustrated her, and she was modeling their teacher. "What's the matter with you?" she'd shout at him, and then hit him. He got tired of that and stopped going to school. Much later when *Bong* Phan was a young man, he learned to read and write Thai well. I don't understand that.

Brother Phin went to live with a family in a neighboring village to help take care of their cows, so he never went to school. At that time we were no longer taking care of people's cows in order to build our herd by getting new calves. This family wanted someone to help take care of their cows because they needed more people to work. They paid money for *Bong* Phin to take care of their cows, so we had money coming into the family. My father chose *Bong* Phin to work outside the home rather than *Bong* Phan because my brother Phin was physically bigger and stronger. He could walk every day following the cows and not tire out. He was about fourteen years old when he went to live with this new family, so my mother didn't worry about his going. This family lived in a village about thirty kilometers away, so we saw him only on special holidays—*Chaul Chnam Khmer*, our Cambodian New Year in April, and *P'Chum Ben*, our Festival of the Dead in September.

My brother Pheav went to Cambodian school, but he didn't pay attention. When it was time for school, he just left the house and went somewhere else. A lot of kids were not interested in school; they were more interested in helping their parents work. *Bong* Pheav had a lot of friends and they had fun playing in the fields or wherever they went. It didn't matter if they worked hard first, they had fun playing together when they were finished with their work. I don't know what my brothers played with their friends because they went to different places from where I went with my friends. I do know that after school, the teacher went around to the home of the boys who skipped school and told their parents. The boys were punished, but we don't know what they really did because they never told our parents the whole story. My brother Pheav started school when it was time, but he didn't finish the first year. I guess my parents were not pushing my brothers to attend school.

Some of my friends didn't go to school. In our village the oldest girl in her family was needed to take care of the younger children. Many of my friends were the oldest girls in their families, so they often didn't go to school. However, my older sister Rieng went to school in Thailand about the same time as my brother Phath. They completed primary school, which was four years, and were finished by the time I grew up. They could read and write, as could all of my older brothers. But my last three brothers and I could not.

Equal numbers of boys and girls went to school when *Bong* Phath and *Bong* Rieng went to school. After I quit school, my friends stayed and completed elementary school. At the time they were jealous of my freedom, but I think it was good for them to stay because now they know how to read and write, and I don't.

The knowledge of my past life we mostly kept within our family, but one time when I was about nine, an old traveling monk and his family — a brother monk, a nephew monk, two old sisters who were now nuns, and their children — came to our village of Sam Rong. My father talked to them and told the story of my past life. The old monk, whom I called *Lok Ta*, told my father which direction they were going and that eventually they could travel to the village of my past life. I wanted to go with them, and my parents decided to allow me to leave home. I went to live with the monks and the nuns at the temple on the mountain of Svay Sisophon for more than a year without my family. I was taken care of by *Lok Ta* and one of the nuns, whom I called *Mae*, the mother of my new best friend Mii La, one of the children. It's true that monks and nuns are not allowed to marry and have families while they are officially in those positions, but after monks retire, as three of my brothers did, they are then free to marry and have children. My friend Mii La's mother didn't become a nun until after her husband died. Then she became a nun and entered the temple where her family members were living and brought her daughter with her.

The temple was far from Sam Rong, and during that time I never went home, but my grandmother would go to visit my parents and then bring my mother to visit me. My mother and father allowed me to live in the temple far from home because I wanted to find my past family and see if they would remember me. My parents wouldn't do anything to stop me. They just wanted to make sure I was safe.

While I lived with the monks and nuns, we traveled around in a pickup truck with covered benches in the back, collecting alms of fruit, vegetables, and raw rice. As we collected alms, I told the villagers the name of my past village and my past parents' names. No one ever knew the village or heard of my past parents. We traveled far from Sisophon, but we never found Bango. I think the monks and nuns were really trying to help me, and we kept searching because they didn't want to disappoint me or make me feel sad. During the almost two years I lived with them, I was happy and never homesick for my family in Sam Rong. Instead, I thought about my past life every day, and I missed my past family. I wanted to find them. The monks and nuns never went straight to the place I wanted to go, however. We came close, but we never went to where I believed my past village was located. Something was never quite right, and I never felt, "This is the place." I still believe and I'm still looking for any of my family from my past life. That's one of the reasons why I go back to Cambodia and travel all around, looking to find anyone who remembers me from my past life.

My parents worried about me, and eventually my father became ill worrying. When I had been gone for almost two years, my grandmother and mother came to the temple and told *Lok Ta* that my father was sick and I needed to go back home to Sam Rong to see him. Over time he had become an alcoholic and was suffering from alcoholism. Worrying about me made it worse. Whenever he drank, it made him sick. My mother asked me, "*Mii Own*, do you want to go home to see your father?"

I thought about it. I knew that my father loved me, and his love was a good thing for me. I remembered that when he had been drinking, and my brothers and mother would get in trouble, I was never in trouble with my father. He always held me and carried me, and it calmed him down. I decided it was time for me to go home and be with *Ow* Here and *Mae* Yan.

I remembered what happened shortly before I left to live in the temple. I had been playing over at my friend's house. When I came back home, my brothers and sister told me that our father had verbally abused our mother, and she ran away from home into the forest. One of them said, "You know, *Mae* Yan tried to hang herself because of *Ow* Here." And then we hid ourselves. Whenever our father was drunk and angry, we hid, and we hid anything he could use to hurt someone. If he found any object he could use as a weapon, we had to be ready to run. That's how wild he would be.

He wasn't like that every day, but it would happen after he had friends over for drinks. I think my father was jealous. My mother was the hostess during these get-togethers; she would offer drinks to the guests, and they would talk with her. That made my father jealous that she was talking to other men. But my mother never considered being unfaithful to my father. There was no reason for him to be jealous. She was always honest and never raised her voice to him. He always put blame on her, though, even when she was completely in the right. When he verbally abused her, she wanted to die because she didn't know how to make him happy and how to make him understand her.

When our parents fought and *Ow* Here yelled at *Mae* Yan, our neighbors knew and could hear them. They would tell my brothers if they saw them out getting water or wood. "Hey, *A Nga*, Little Brother, you need to get home; your parents are fighting."

Then all the children would go home and try to make the situation better. This wasn't the only time our mother tried to commit suicide. She tried several times because my father wouldn't stop abusing her. Every time he got drunk, he would verbally abuse her. He never physically abused our mother; he just beat my brothers. I know of three times that my mother tried to kill herself. If it happened more than that, I didn't know about it.

When *Mae* Yan would get to the point of wanting to kill herself, she just cried and took a long piece of cloth and walked into the forest. She didn't shout or scream, just cried softly and left. She probably just wanted to end her pain that she couldn't do anything to change. No one stopped her. But each time *Mae* Yan reached the place in the forest where she planned to hang herself, she would remember her children. Our mother loved us more than anything and anyone, so she stopped herself each time. She couldn't bear to leave us without a mother. As she walked away from the abuse of her husband, she was able to think about her children and realize that we needed her to take care of us and protect us from our father.

Later in the evening, when the villagers got together after eating dinner to talk about their day, *Mae* Yan would go to visit her friends. "Where did you go today after the fight with your husband?" they would ask her.

"I wanted to kill myself; I went out to hang myself. But the more I walked, the more I thought about my children. I couldn't do it," our mother told them.

She had support and comfort from her friends. They always listened and gave her good advice when she was depressed and needed them. "Next time you're feeling this way, let us know, and you have to let your children know when you're feeling depressed. Next time you might not come to your senses and think about your children; they'll find you hanging there, and it'll be too late," one friend advised her.

But our mother didn't talk to us about when she was sad and depressed. *Mae* Yan didn't want us to be against our father. At least she could tell her friends, and they helped her. They told her the next time it happened, she should come to one of their houses. "Come and hide in my house," a friend told her. "Even though I can't fight your husband, I can protect you and tell him to leave you alone."

One of *Mae* Yan's friends was the wife of the village headman, *Ow* Here's best friend. Everyone in the village was afraid of our father when he got drunk and mean. But the village headman was older than *Ow* Here, and our father respected him. Sometimes when *Ow* Here got drunk, *Mae* Yan would go to their house, if they were home, and ask her friend if her husband would help her and talk to our father. I don't think any other women in our village had this problem or were so depressed that they tried to commit suicide. Our father wasn't the only one who drank, but he was the one who became mean. The other men went home and fell asleep when they were drunk.

This happened when my brothers, sister, and I were younger. None of the boys were old enough to protect our mother against our father. *Ow* Here had absolute control over all of us at that time. After *Mae* Yan tried to kill herself, I never heard my father apologize for making her feel so bad. But he backed off and quietly showed his love for her. It was not the Cambodian way in our village for the head of the house to apologize. Husbands didn't apologize to wives and fathers didn't apologize to children. We didn't hate *Ow* Here for treating *Mae* Yan this way. We were upset because our mother was sad, but we didn't hate. Our parents gave us life. We didn't know any other kind of behavior. We knew this was the way it was, and no one ever told us our father was wrong to treat our mother like this. His rule was law in our family, and we were taught to respect our father and mother. No child could talk to the parents about what they should or should not do. It was part of our culture to not speak to our elders in a disrespectful way. Even *Mae* Yan couldn't tell *Ow* Here what to do. She was the wife, and in Cambodian culture at that time, her husband had the power, and that was that.

I didn't start working until I was fifteen. Until that time I was free. If I wanted to go out in the fields with the rest of my family, I did. If I wanted to go play with my friends, I did. I didn't help cook. I didn't work. I was free to do whatever I wanted to do.

Among my father's cattle, he had a steer, a castrated bull that had been trained to be ridden. Because it was castrated, it wasn't dangerous. I always rode that steer, and I was the only one who ever rode it. My brothers didn't ever ride my steer. They didn't ride the other cows, either. They generally went with the cart and helped take care of it and the oxen that pulled it. If I didn't ride the steer, it would go along with the rest of the cattle to wherever they wanted to go and eat. If I wanted to ride out to the field, I would tell my father, "*Ow*, tomorrow I want to ride my steer out to the fields."

Early in the morning, *Ow* Here would have one of the boys tie my steer up to a house post by its reins, so it would be ready for me when I got up. After I woke up, I would go out and get on my steer to ride the long distance to the fields. I didn't want to get up so early to ride out in the cart with the rest of the family. *Mae* Yan said, "Let her sleep in. She's not going to work in the field anyway, so it doesn't matter when she comes." I was really spoiled.

Ox cart in rural Cambodia, 2001 (photograph by Rick Bird and from the personal collection of Karline and Rick Bird).

In our village we had no electricity, so when the sun went down, everyone went to bed. In the morning when the sun came up, that's when I woke up. My father, however, wanted to get up at 4:30 so he could be all ready to go at sunrise. I would stay in bed until seven or eight in the morning. Often, I would go out to pick up wild fruit, which I really enjoyed. If I didn't go out to the fields, then my father would bring some home to me. He gathered all kinds of wild fruits. He also caught crickets because he knew I liked to eat them. He would catch four or five crickets, clean them, and roast them on a skewer. Then he tied them up in a cloth — one side would be fruit, and the other would be crickets — and then bring home the treats for me. When I saw the treats, I wanted to go with him to the fields and catch crickets with him.

"Thank you, *Ow*, for the treats! Tomorrow morning can I catch crickets with you?"

"OK, *Mii Own*, but you can ride your steer out, so you won't have to get up so early."

I always slept with my parents in their bedroom, my brothers were all in their one bedroom, and my older sister Rieng had her own room after *Ow* Here built the big house. Even though I got along well with my sister Rieng, I wanted to sleep with *Mae Yan* and *Ow* Here. Traditionally, the youngest child sleeps with the parents.

I got along well with all of my brothers, except oftentimes *Bong* Pheav and I would fight; we were only three years apart in age. My brother Pheav had the habit of eating very slowly. When we were given something good to eat, the rest of us would eat quickly, but *Bong* Pheav would take his time, leaving it there, making us want to take his food from him. When it was something good, I ate fast, and then I wanted my brother to share his with me. Usually my father would say, "*A Nga*, give her some!"

Bong Pheav wouldn't want to do that, so I'd scream, "*Ow!*" Then he'd share with me. I was about ten then.

When I was young, I didn't always arrange with my father to have the steer ready for me to ride. Sometimes I would get up in the morning and feel lost, alone and frightened, because my mother would have gone to the field with my father and brothers. She would have heard that some vegetables were ready to be picked, so she would have gone to gather them.

"Did they go and leave me?" I would ask myself. Then I would walk around and listen to see if I could hear my mother out feeding the pigs or chickens or picking vegetables in the garden around our house. If *Mae* Yan wasn't there, I would go to the bakery in the village, where they had just baked some cookies or Cambodian cupcakes. I would eat that for breakfast or a snack. *Mae* Yan often left me some money, so I could buy my breakfast at the food stand in the village. She wouldn't always prepare food before she went to the fields because *Ow* Here would leave so early. They often cooked breakfast and lunch out in the fields.

When our mother went out in the fields, she usually left the house at around nine or ten o'clock, carrying a pot of soup and a pot of rice hanging from a bamboo pole over her shoulder. It took her about twenty minutes because she walked quickly. When I walked out to the field, it might take me an hour because I always stopped to look at things, pick fruit, or chase lizards. When *Mae* Yan reached the field, our family ate their breakfast. What they had in the morning, they also ate for lunch later. It wasn't two separate meals. Sometimes she went with my father and brothers at dawn, walking with the cart, which was small, so the boys pulled and pushed it. Sometimes our mother took the wagon pulled by the oxen, and sometimes she walked, carrying the food. It depended on what she fixed that day. She had to carry the soup because otherwise it would spill if she put it in the wagon as it bounced along over the bumpy path. If the boys caught fish, birds, or small animals, then *Mae* Yan would cook the meat out in the field, along with steamed rice and vegetables.

If I wanted to eat something else, or if my mother hadn't left any money, I would go to my brother Phong's house and eat breakfast or lunch there. He and his wife never said no to me. *Jae*, Sister-in-law, never said, "You need to cook for yourself." I don't know why my brother and his wife never told me I needed to learn how to cook. No one ever taught me how to cook until I was fifteen. As a child when playing with my friends, we sometimes pretended to cook, but I never did the real thing until I was fifteen. Maybe my spiritual side made me special to all.

After I ate breakfast at my brother's house or at the food stand, I usually went to play with one of my friends. They called me *Gnep*, Tiny Person, because I was tiny, skinny, and smaller than most of them. Sometimes, my friend would say, "Oh, *Gnep*, I can't play today; my mother wants me to prepare some vegetables," or she might say, "Today I have to take care of my younger brother." Then I would go to the next friend's house to see who was free. We would go together to pick fruit or catch some crickets or lizards— whatever we wanted to do to have fun.

One activity my friends and I especially liked to do was go to the fields after the dry season was over, when the rains came. We took our buckets and scoops to catch crabs or little fish and brought them home with water in our buckets. Anything we could see in the water that could be eaten, we caught and took home.

When my friends were jealous of me because they had to go to school or work taking care of younger brothers and sisters, I tried to make them happy. I would say to them, "Why don't you ask your mom if you can take a day off from school or work so you can go play with me?"

"Oh, *Gnep*, I can't ask my mother; why don't you come with me and ask her if I can go?" my friend would say.

Then I would usually ask my friend's mother if her daughter could stay home from school, or work, to play for the day. I think the parents of my friends respected my parents, so they usually allowed their daughters to have a free day once in a while. In order to have a free day, though, the next day my friend would have to work harder or longer.

"See, *Gnep*," my friend would complain, "If I ask to have free time, then I have to work harder."

"*Min aiy te*," I answered. "As long as you have your own time once in a while, never mind." If I knew how to do the work, I would help my friends. Most of the time, however, it was work I didn't know how to do, so I just kept them company while they worked. They all knew that I was the one who didn't work.

There were some things, though, that I could do for my friends. Sometimes I had money to buy a special treat at the village food stand. If my friend complained, "Oh, I never have any candy; we can't afford it," I could make her feel better.

"If there's something that you want — a cookie, a cupcake, a chocolate bar — you let me know," I would tell her. "I will get some for you. Not right now, but sometime when it's something you really want."

That's how I made it up to them for being free and not going to school or working. Because my family was wealthier than most, I had everything I needed around me. I could share with my friends.

Even when my mother was working in the vegetables around the house, she never asked me to water the garden. I watched many kids watering the vegetables for their families, but *Mae* Yan never asked me to do it. I never asked her if I could water the vegetables, either. Cambodian children do what their parents tell them to do. They aren't supposed to ask if they can do this or that. I learned by watching; I watched my mother work. When I was younger, I usually followed her everywhere she went, but she never asked me to help. I don't know why. I think *Mae* Yan didn't let me water the vegetables because she was afraid I would slip down into the pond if I carried water for the garden. My parents didn't want me to be near water because of my former life. I never planted rice in Cambodia, but I watched my brothers and sister plant it. If I wanted to plant rice now, or if I wanted to grow a vegetable garden, I could do it. I learned by watching.

CHAPTER 15

Lightning Strikes

The beginning of my teenage years was not quite as carefree as my younger years, but I still had an easy life. I remember the day the traveling salesman who sold six-battery radios brought them to sell in our village. A couple of families already had radios, so we knew that every afternoon you could hear good stories and music on the radio. When the salesman came to our house in the afternoon, we were all home when he turned on the radio so we could listen to it. I was so excited to hear a radio playing in my very own house. I told my parents I wanted that radio. It must have really upset my parents when I told them this because they didn't have that kind of money. In the entire village, maybe only three houses had radios, while the rest of the villagers didn't have enough money.

"*Ow, Mae*, I really want that radio!" I excitedly told my parents.

"*Mii Own*," my father answered, "We don't have the money to buy it."

"Well, if you don't have the money, then I'll sell all my chives and green onions every day so I can buy it." This was the money I used every day to by a cookie or a little cake. I didn't know it wasn't enough money to buy a radio.

That evening my parents talked it over between the two of them; they wanted to find a way to be able to buy me what I wanted. They also probably really wanted to have a radio, too. The next morning *Ow* Here said, "Today we aren't going to be home; we're going to the next village to find a person who wants to buy two of our cows."

The next day the person who wanted to buy the cows came to our house. It always took at least two days to complete a sale like this because people generally traveled on foot. It took a day for the seller to go and come back, and it took the same amount of time for the buyer to come and go back. The buyer came early in the morning while the cows were still in the corral. "Which cows do you want to sell?" he asked.

My father answered, "This one and that one — we just need enough money to buy something for our daughter."

At that time the price of a cow wasn't very much — only two to three hundred riels, but it was a lot of money for the villagers then. The radio cost six hundred riels, so my parents needed to sell at least two cows. When the buyer heard that my parents wanted to buy something for their daughter, he wanted to help. The sale was made, I had my radio, and I was happy.

Every Friday evening the radio played stories for several hours, so all our friends and relations would come to listen. People brought food and drinks, men brought their tobacco, and everyone sat around, eating, drinking, smoking, and listening to our radio. It was a friendly, sharing time. If people had fruit, cigarettes, or drinks, they brought them. Some women made dessert from potatoes or bananas for everyone to eat.

Besides listening to the stories, music, and the news, the older people especially liked to listen to King Sihanouk when he spoke on the radio. The villagers didn't know the king's politics or what he planned to do. They loved and respected him and thought of him as their father. They trusted him and believed whatever he said. When he spoke on the radio to the people who were farmers, he talked to them about the best way to farm. He told them to work hard, to save their seeds from year to year, how to plant their fields, and the best way to raise a garden. When he learned that a better kind of seed came from China, he told the farmers how to get the seeds, and once they had the new seeds, how to save them and keep them to increase their yields and make more money for their families.

Because few of the farmers could read and write, the king taught them about agriculture through the radio, not through pamphlets or books. He also asked those who had radios to spread the word to the families who didn't, so all the farmers would know how to improve their farms. My father would talk about what the king said to other farmers when he saw them. In this way the people in the countryside learned from the king. This radio program was boring to me as a young person. I was interested in stories, comedies, and music — not agricultural lessons from the king. It was like the king was teaching a class. The purchase of the radio benefited not only me and my family, but also our friends and relations.

Another exciting event that happened when I was a young teenager was the ordination of my brother Phath to become a monk. Since most Cambodians are Buddhist, and most young Cambodian men spend some time as Buddhist monks, their ordination days are causes for great celebration. When a young man or boy becomes a monk, even for a short period of time, he makes great merit for his parents in their afterlives.

After a Cambodian male becomes a monk, we then call him *Lok Bong*, a term of respect because he is or was a monk. When my third brother Phong became a monk, I was very small, so I don't remember it, but my brothers and sister and I have always called him *Lok Bong* or *Lok Bong* Phong for as long as I can remember. I was a young teenager at the time my sixth brother Phath became a monk, however, so I attended his ordination ceremony along with the rest of my family. *Bong* Phath became *Lok Pheuk*, which means he was at least eighteen years or older. I was about twelve years old at the time.

The closest temple to Sam Rong village was in Svay Chek, and that's where the ordination ceremony for all the young men in the neighboring villages would be held. Because Svay Chek was too far from our village for us to make all the preparations at home, we had to find a place to stay near the temple during the days of celebration. We stayed at the home of a family who did business with my father. Because *Ow* Here had a lot of cows, they produced a great deal of manure. When people needed manure to improve their gardens, they came to my father. The people of Svay Chek did this, including the family who lived close to the temple. When it came time for my brother Phath to become a monk, my parents asked this family if we could stay there during that time.

Everyone had a task to do. Some people prepared the food in the kitchen, while another person borrowed the horse to carry my brother to the temple on the appointed day. Still other people prepared the clothing my brother would wear, and a respected elder in the community shaved *Bong* Phath's head and eyebrows. Cambodians believe that the head is the most sacred part of the body, so only mothers, fathers, grandparents, monks, or respected elders can touch a person's head.

About fifteen young men were planning to become monks on the same day. They needed to be at least twelve years old, old enough to read and write and learn the teachings. They were all bathed, shaved and dressed in new, white robes. The sarong and the wide sash that went diagonally across their bare chests showed they were novices. At the scheduled time, the novices rode horses, or if small boys, they were carried on the shoulders of strong men, from the houses to the temple to begin their ordination. They slept in the temple dormitory for three days, and the head monk placed a variety of small objects under their sleeping mats. When the novices woke up in the morning, the head abbot asked them to sit up and reach behind under their sleeping mats and pick up one of the objects. They gave the objects to the abbot, who then told their fortunes from the objects chosen. If my brother Phath chose a blade, the abbot would tell him what the choice of a blade meant for his future. This continued for three days.

During the three days, *Bong* Phath was taught how to be a monk. He and the other novices sat on mats on the floor in front of the abbot in the temple and prayed, meditated, and listened to the abbot's instruction. The rest of the families sat on mats behind the novices to hear the teachings and prayers. We were free to come and go as we pleased, but the novices had to

Buddhist monk shaving head of young novice prior to ordination, 1970 (photograph by Rick Bird and from the personal collection of Karline and Rick Bird).

remain seated and attentive. They couldn't take part in the family activities outside. I was bored during the time we had to spend in the temple.

When it was time to eat, the family went outside to eat the special foods we had prepared. Chicken curry, stir-fried vegetables and fish, and a big pot of Cambodian beef stew were among the dishes enjoyed, along with steamed rice, of course. At night time we ate desserts to keep us awake — sticky rice with coconut milk and a dessert made from potatoes. We didn't have to stay awake and could go to sleep if we were tired, but we were all excited and wanted to stay awake. Besides, the person who made the desserts served them in the evening, so we looked forward to that time. *Bong* Phath did not join us for the special meals; he ate like a monk, only twice a day.

The second day was like the first; we sat on mats in the back of the temple, listening to the prayers and teachings, and came and went when we wanted to enter or leave. We prepared and ate the same special foods. On the third day, my parents formally presented my brother Phath to the monks, the monks gave him the saffron-colored robes, and he became an official monk. Once my brother became a monk, he could not do the things he normally did or come home to visit us if he became homesick. We could talk to him, but we had to address him in the special words reserved for monks. At the end of the third day, we had to pack everything up and go back to our village and home.

Lok Bong Phath remained a monk for more than two years and lived at the Svay Chek temple during that time. While he was there, he studied the Buddhist scriptures, prayed, meditated, and chanted. When people in the villages needed monks to come to pray for them or perform ceremonies, *Lok Bong* Phath was part of the group of monks that went. Because there are different prayers for the different ceremonies or occasions, he had to learn them all. He needed to know the prayers for a funeral, a wedding, a house blessing, the opening of a family *stupa* (the dome-shaped Buddhist shrine where ashes of deceased family members are interred), and *P'Chum Ben* (the Khmer Festival of the Dead), among others. Each prayer was unique, and they all had to be memorized.

My parents were supportive when my brothers Phong and Phath decided they wanted to be monks for a time, but they had already passed away when brothers Phan and Pheav became monks. Having sons become monks makes merit for the parents, hopefully shortening the number of times they will have rebirth. Because four of my brothers eventually became monks, my parents should be very lucky in their next lives.

One evening after my brother Phath had returned home from spending his two years as a monk, we heard our father coming home drunk from the village. He was shouting, screaming, and cursing about everything and everyone. *Lok Bong* Phath was embarrassed that our neighbors and his friends would hear *Ow* Here. All of us were embarrassed, especially my older brothers. I think my brothers were also worried about what our father might do.

Lok Bong Phath called, "*A Nga*, Phan, go get the rope!"

My brother Phan looked at him and asked, "Why, *Lok Bong*?"

"*A Nga*, go get the rope," my brother Phath repeated.

Soon my father was near the house, still screaming and cursing. When he reached the stairs, ready to climb up, *Lok Bong* Phath called to him in a loud voice. "*Ow!*"

"Why are you calling me like that? You have no right to call me like that!" shouted my father.

That's when four of my brothers — Phath, Phan, Phin, and Pheav — grabbed our father. Because he was drunk and his skin was slippery like oil, it was difficult to hold on to him, but my brothers managed to loop the rope around his arms and legs. Then they carried our father over to one of the house posts and tied him to it so he couldn't get away. *Ow* Here screamed and cursed even louder. He roared his anger.

Two brothers went to the pond in front of the house to get buckets of water, throwing it on *Ow* Here from head to toe. Finally, our father called, "*Kon*, Son!" to *Lok Bong* Phath. "*Kon!*" he called again.

"Have you had enough, *Ow*?" my brother Phath asked him. "Are you sober now?"

"Yeah," our father answered. "I'm not drunk anymore. Untie me." He was now speaking in his normal way, so my brothers released him.

Later, my father said to my mother, "Probably I'm going to have to stop drinking. Our sons are grown up now and embarrassed when I drink in the village. I'm not going to drink like that anymore and get out of control."

Our mother never said a word against him. He didn't realize how lucky he was to have such an excellent wife. My father was able to cut way back on his drinking and never got out of control again until after my mother's death. After she died, he started drinking heavily again.

I was fourteen when my mother died. My family was all out in the field, except for me. I didn't go with them that day. My father was digging a dike with a hoe, one brother was plowing the field with the ox, and everyone was working. A storm came up, the wind began to blow, and soon lighting started to strike. My mother and our three dogs went to sit under a tree, and my brother Phath came to sit next to her. Another brother was sitting under a big tree across the field. Lightning struck my mother and knocked *Lok Bong* Phath unconscious.

My brother Phan ran home and shouted at me, "*Neang! Neang!* Go to the little store and buy a bottle of wine and some white cloth!"

"Why, *Bong* Phan?" I asked. The storm had hit the village, too, and I was afraid to run to the village in the middle of it.

"*Mae* Yan has been hit by lightning," my brother answered. "That's what *Ow* Here asked for, so you have to go find it so we can save *Mae*!" he explained as he ran back to the field and the rest of the family. My mother was still alive.

By the time *Bong* Phan had run back to the field, my father and the others had already picked up *Mae* Yan and placed her in the cart. Because everyone was so panicked about *Mae* Yan, they weren't attending to *Lok Bong* Phath, but he was able to snap out of it and help the others. My brother Phath had been unconscious for only a few minutes before he was up and walking. To this day, though, he has a dark scar on his side from the lightning strike. They all walked back to the house beside the cart. Because it was raining and blowing so hard, and the lightning continued to strike, my father and brothers brought our mother home instead of waiting for me to bring the wine and white cloth. She died half way home. By the time my brother Phan had reached them, *Mae* Yan's body was already cold.

In the meantime, I ran to the little store to buy wine and the white cloth and met them back home. Because my father was a *khru Khmer*, he performed this traditional medicine to try to bring my mother back to life. He covered *Mae* Yan's body with the white gauze-like cloth, put the wine in his mouth, and blew it over her, through the white cloth, from head to toe. He did this several times, but it was too late. She had already passed on and could not come back to us.

When I realized my mother was dead, I was devastated. Even though I was fourteen years old, I still slept with my parents and always went to sleep holding *Mae* Yan. That night *Ow* Here placed my mother's body in the room where my sister Rieng used to sleep before she got married. I couldn't go to sleep without my mother, so I spent the night holding her body. I cried and cried and couldn't sleep. This made everyone wake up, and they cried, too. They were sad for me and for themselves. During the time we were all mourning the loss of *Mae* Yan, my brother Phong and his family came to stay with us. At night when I cried, *Jae* came to where I was trying to sleep to comfort me. We sat up for a while talking, and finally I was able to fall asleep.

In Cambodian tradition the body is kept in the house for three days, open to the air, but surrounded by burning incense. Waiting for three days gives the relatives a chance to hear about the death and come to the funeral. Also, there is always a chance that the person could wake up. The lightning strike was an accident. It was possible my mother would awake, just as *Lok Bong* Phath had awakened. My father performed the ceremony several more times, trying to wake *Mae* Yan by blowing wine through the white cloth over her body. It didn't work. Even though many people told him it wouldn't work, he didn't give up hope and had to try. I stayed with her body for those three days and nights. Everyone loved our mother. *Mae* Yan was a really good woman, she was kind, she never had arguments with people in the village, and she never said unkind words to her children. *Mae* Yan's death was a tremendous loss for our family.

The traditional Cambodian funeral ceremony took place in our house. We invited the monks to come. Four monks came in a wagon from the temple in Svay Chek to Sam Rong, a distance of about five kilometers. They spent the day at our home performing the ceremony. Each monk held onto a white string, which was tied to my mother's wrist, while they chanted the Buddhist prayers for the dead. Their blessings would travel through the string from the monks to my mother's body, releasing her soul and helping it leave her body to fly up to heaven. Our family and friends sat on the floor in front of them and listened to the monks' prayers.

The next day the family and friends prepared *Mae* Yan's favorite foods and presented them to the monks to bless. After their blessing everyone ate the prepared foods. Friends who wanted to help bring food to the funeral would ask what our mother liked to eat. *Mae* Yan didn't like sweets, so no one prepared desserts. She liked fresh fruit, so many people brought different kinds of fruit. She also really liked noodles cooked in a soup with chicken or fish, as well as slices of raw potato dipped in sugar.

Traditionally, bodies are cremated after death in Cambodia, but my mother was buried in the small cemetery next to the village. The head monk told us that a body struck by lightning should not be cremated; it had already been burned.

After our mother died, I slept in the room that had belonged to my sister Rieng. When she married and moved to her husband's village, the room became mine. All my brothers slept in the big room next door, and my father continued to sleep in the bedroom where he always slept.

My sister Rieng and her husband came for my mother's ceremony, but they weren't able to spend any more time with us. They needed to go back to their home to take care of their property.

Our house was always protected, even if the family was out in the field and I was playing at my friend's house, because we had dogs. Our dogs would never let anyone in the house if one of us was not there or if the dog didn't recognize the person trying to enter. The dogs didn't go out to the fields with the family unless they were needed for hunting, so they wouldn't leave the house in the morning unless they were called to go. The dogs preferred to stay home and sleep in the shade. But *Bong* Rieng and her husband didn't have a dog, and they didn't have a fence. It was important to have a fence around the house; the dogs stayed inside the fence and kept strangers on the outside. My sister's and her husband's house was open to the street, so anyone could enter it.

After our mother's death, my brothers cooked for the family because they knew how. My older sister Rieng was living with her husband in his village, so she didn't cook for us. I was not asked to help; I guess because I was the youngest child, but also because of my special, spiritual place in the family. Our father would tell my brothers what he wanted to eat, and they would all help each other with the cooking. My brothers learned how to cook by helping our mother, but they also learned out in the fields from our father. *Ow* Here taught them to do the work of the fields—chopping, cutting, digging, and planting—but he also taught them cooking in the fields. After they hunted for small animals, they learned how to clean them, build a fire, and roast the meat over the fire. Our father taught my brothers to survive on the land.

After our mother passed away, when my brothers came into the kitchen, they cooked the way our father had taught them, not *Mae* Yan's kind of cooking. If they wanted to cook like my mother, perhaps make a curry, they needed to ask *Jae* or a neighbor woman which ingredients to use. They learned quickly and were good cooks.

I wanted to start helping after my mother passed away, but when I tried, it usually didn't turn out well. One day I decided to cook a chicken and surprise *Ow* Here and my brothers. I didn't ask *Jae* or a neighbor lady what to do because I had already seen them cook chicken, and I wanted to do it all by myself. I went outside and looked at the chickens, trying to decide which one would be the easiest to catch. Once I caught a chicken, I had to kill it. I tried wringing its neck, as I had seen others do, but it didn't work, and I only succeeded in making the chicken squawk with fright, fighting and clawing me, trying to get away. I didn't know what to do, and I couldn't put the chicken down, so I started swinging it against the house post, again and again. It took too long, but finally the chicken was dead, and I felt terrible.

Next, I had to pluck the chicken, which looked easy when watching our mother do it, but it was impossible when I tried. Eventually, I remembered that *Mae* Yan always dunked the chicken in scalding water before she began plucking it. Of course, I didn't have any boiling water, so I had to stop and build a fire, and then carry water to fill the big kettle. After waiting and watching for the water to boil, I dunked the chicken in the scalding water. I must have left it in the water too long, because not only was I able to pluck the feathers, but I also managed to pull off the chicken's skin. To make matters worse, the scalded chicken feathers smelled terrible. By the time my father and brothers returned home from the fields, I had finished plucking the chicken, but I was nauseated and in tears. I was relieved and grateful to let my brothers finish cooking dinner.

As a young teenager, I really didn't have any male friends. This would have gone against Cambodian tradition. One of my brother's friends became my friend. If he came to the house and my brother was not there, he would talk to me. It was scary for me, though, because if my father ever heard me talking and laughing with a boy, I would be in trouble. Talking and laughing with a boy does not look or sound good. None of the young Cambodian girls could behave this way.

It was OK for my brother's friend to ask, "Where is your brother?" or "What are you doing?" He could ask simple everyday questions like that, and I could answer the same. But we couldn't talk and laugh and sit down and smile at each other, nor could I call him by name. I called him *Bong* because he was older than I, and he called me *Neang*, just like brother and sister.

If all of my family were out in the fields, he couldn't come to my house. It would not be proper. I don't know if he was interested in me, and I didn't have those feelings for him. If he asked polite questions to me, I would answer, but if he joked, then I was frightened and would turn my head. My father never said anything about him, but I was very careful and respected tradition. I never got in trouble with my father over a boy.

Once I got in trouble with my father when I was fourteen, not long after my mother passed away. Early in the morning, *Ow* Here got up and said, "*Mii Own*, are you going to go somewhere today?"

I didn't think I was going anywhere, so I answered, "No, I'm not going anywhere today, *Ow*."

My father replied, "OK, if you're not going anywhere, then you stay home. I'm going to go visit my friends and have a drink." He didn't have to work at this time because the harvest season was already finished, so he was free.

In the afternoon *Jae* came over and said, "*Neang*, do you want to go to the rice fields and pick up snails with me?" Rice field snails are small, not big like the pond snails, and they come out on the fields. We all loved to eat these little snails, so I went with my sister-in-law, and I didn't think I'd get in trouble because I was gathering food with her.

When I came back to the house with a full bucket of snails, I found my father sitting at the top of the stairs by the door, already drunk. He had come home and found me gone, not watching the house as I had said I would do. As soon as I reached the stairs, I showed him my full bucket, saying, "*Ow*, I've got a lot of snails!"

He was so angry; he was ready to kill me. I don't know where he got it, but he whipped out a knife and came toward me. In my whole life, this was the first time my father ever scared me. I was afraid he really would kill me. "I asked you and you said you weren't going to go anywhere. But you went to pick up snails with *Jae*. You aren't honest; you didn't keep your word."

"*Ow*," I explained, "I just went to pick up snails with *Jae*!"

But he wouldn't listen to me. He just held out his knife and walked slowly toward me, shouting, "I'm going to kill you because you aren't honest with me."

"*Ow*," I cried, not believing what I was hearing. "I just went to pick up snails! There's nothing wrong with that!"

"See!" he continued to shout. "That's what happens with a girl. She isn't honest, she breaks her word, and then she's not a good girl anymore!"

I was so frightened; I dropped the bucket and ran to my brother Phong's house. I told my sister-in-law what had happened. "*Jae*, my father is so angry; he wants to kill me with a knife!"

Jae didn't believe me, but then she saw my father following me, coming to her house with the knife.

"*Mii Own!*" my father called. "*Mii Own*, where are you going? You have to come back, *Mii Own!*"

But I was too scared — he still had the knife in his hand and he had said he would kill me. I stood there for a moment and then I ran. I escaped out the back of *Jae*'s house, and I ran to the house of an old family friend, but no one was home. I then ran to my friend's house. "I want to hide myself here, so if my father comes, don't tell him I'm here, OK?" I explained. My friend assured me my father wouldn't find out I was hiding there.

I think my father must have stopped to talk to my sister-in-law. I managed to get safely away. I was too scared to go home that night. I stayed overnight at my friend's house.

The next morning, my father was afraid he had lost me. He asked *Lok Bong* Phong and *Jae* to come and talk to me and bring me home. They took me to *Ow* Here; he was no longer drunk. He didn't apologize — Cambodian parents never apologize to their children. Instead, he said to me, "Next time, *Mii Own*, if you want to go somewhere, you have to tell me first. Even if I'm over visiting my friends, you have to go there and tell me before you go with someone else."

The reason why he was so angry with me is because I didn't go all the way to his friend's house to tell him where I was going to go. After all these years of having complete freedom, now that I was a teenager, he wanted to know where I was going. When our mother was still alive, I could go wherever I wanted, and she usually knew where I was. Probably because he had lost our mother, he was afraid of losing me, too. I still had my freedom, but I had to tell *Ow* Here where I was going. Because I was now fourteen, he was worried about protecting me.

Even though I now understood what my father expected of me, I was still afraid of him. I no longer stayed in the house alone with him. Every day my brothers would go work in the fields, or pick vegetables, or go hunting for food somewhere. If our father didn't go with them, I would go to *Lok Bong* Phong's house or a friend's house. I no longer trusted *Ow* Here. I think he just wanted to scare me so the next time I wouldn't do that again. But I decided I didn't want to die just because he got drunk and mad.

During the day my brothers were away working, but they always came home at night. Our father could still work, but once my brothers became teenagers and knew how to do all the work, *Ow* Here could relax and not work so hard. The boys would say to him, "Don't do that job, *Ow*; we can do it."

"I'm glad you boys can do the work now like I always did it when you were small," he told them. He had a lot more free time now that the boys were older. During the rice planting season, starting in May and going into August, our father was always out working in the fields. He never wanted to be home. Although he no longer worked as hard as he once did, *Ow* Here continued to go out and oversee the boys, making sure that everything was done correctly.

During the growing season, after the hard work of planting rice was done, my brothers still needed to go out to the rice fields to manage the water and the dikes. If the water level rose too high, they needed to open the gate in the dike and let some of the water out. In September when the rice was getting ripe, my brothers continued to watch to make sure that the rice fields had the right amount of water, so the grain quality was the best it could be. By November the rice was ready, and then the water needed to be emptied from the fields so the rice could dry.

The harvest season went from November until January. If there was a lot of rice, it would take that long to harvest all of it. When our father and brothers harvested rice, they used hand scythes, grabbing a hold of several stalks, cutting and laying them on the ground on top of the straw. When a certain amount of rice had been cut, *Ow* Here and my brothers took the stalks, gathered them into bundles, and tied them with lengths of rice straw.

The next day they collected all the rice bundles, put them in the cart, and took them to the threshing area. Once all the rice was in the threshing area, piled around the cleared area in a circle, my family put the rice on the ground and had a cow walk on it. When the cow walked on the rice stalks, the grains of rice fell to the ground. This was the way the grain was separated from the stalks when there was a lot of rice to thresh. Sometimes, when the amount of rice was small, or my family wanted the rice to be especially clean, as with Jasmine rice, they would thresh it by hand and let the grains fall onto a mat. Either way, the rice still had the husks on it and was still mixed with the chaff.

The next step was to separate the rice from the chaff. Two people worked together to do this task. The grains of rice were placed in a large bamboo tray. The person holding the tray would move it up and down, letting the rice rise and fall back into the tray. A second person took a palm leaf and fanned the air back and forth as fast as possible to blow the chaff away from the grains of rice. I never did any of this work because I was too young, or I didn't have to work, but I always watched my family as they worked. The family grew several kinds of rice, including the very special Jasmine rice, our favorite.

From February until April, there was not as much work to do, but my family worked to put everything away, including the rice and its straw. They bagged the rice and stored it in the rice storage building, and they brought in the straw for the cows to eat during the hot season. In April there was no grass for the cows to eat because it was too hot and dry, so *Ow* Here and my brothers prepared straw for the animals in the morning, often times putting some water on it to soften the straw to make it easier for the cows to eat.

After the harvest was finished, the men my father's age would get together and play cards or just get together to drink and talk. My father didn't play cards, so he and his friends drank and talked. They usually talked about business—how they could get more help, a better yield from their fields, a better profit, and more animals to raise. They always talked about work. The two groups never met together during their free time. The card players were in one place, and my father and his friends were in another place. If a man

Young woman threshing rice in rural Cambodia, 2002 (photograph by Rick Bird and from the personal collection of Karline and Rick Bird).

wanted to play cards, he went to the card group. If he wanted to talk and drink, he went to my father's group.

When the men drank, they always had a meat dish to eat — roasted, grilled, or stir-fried. Usually, my father and his friends went to a little stand where they could buy alcohol, and there were tables where they could sit, drink, and talk. The owner of the bar had some kind of meat or dried fish prepared for them to eat with their drinks. They never ate rice when they drank because of the saying: "If you eat rice with your drink, you're not a man — you're a chicken."

Rarely did the men go to someone's house to drink because they would feel uncomfortable with the wife there. They used to occasionally drink in each other's homes, but after my father became so jealous when my mother was hostess, the group decided it was better to go to the village stand.

Our father was known for his temper. Our mother never beat her children, but our father did. He just beat the boys, though, never the girls. This isn't tradition; it depends on the person. Some of the fathers in the village beat their daughters, as well as their sons. *Ow* Here was a very honest and serious person, but he was mean — maybe because he had so many children. My brothers were afraid of him because he swore at them and beat them. Before I was fourteen, I wasn't afraid of him, even though my brothers were, because he had never sworn at me or beat me. I had never done anything to make him unhappy or angry, until the knife incident.

Our father was strict with my brothers. If he said, "Pheav, go get that knife for me," and my brother Pheav replied, "Wait, *Ow*, just a minute," our father would be furious. Never mind if my brothers were busy with a project. If our father said to do something, they got up and did it right then. They didn't say, "Wait, I'm doing something." If they did, they couldn't even turn around quickly; they'd be hit already. My brothers could do what they were doing after they did what our father asked them to do, but not before. Also, the children could not look at his face when he was talking to them. We had to look down and never look him in the eye. *Ow* Here usually didn't ask me to do something, but the few times that he did, I never argued with him.

My brothers tried to see what they could get away with doing. If one of them said, "*Ow*, I want to go play with my friend," our father would answer, "Well, if your work is done, if everything you were supposed to do is finished, then go ahead and go." But if *Ow* Here said, "No, you can't go; you need to stay home," even if my brother's work was finished, he couldn't go. He couldn't argue with him. If our father said, "No, you can't go," and my brother decided to sneak out, he would be punished when he returned. The boys generally did what they wanted to do because their friends would be waiting for them. They took their chances. Sometimes they thought they wouldn't be beaten, but they always were. And sometimes they were beaten really hard, but they had fun in spite of the beatings. They paid for their own freedom with the beatings.

CHAPTER 16

The Khmer Rouge Are Coming!

It was early April 1975, and the Khmer Rouge were trying to take over Cambodia. It was almost the end. I had heard news on the radio about the Khmer Rouge fighting the Cambodian army around the country and had overheard people in the village talking about it, but I didn't really understand or think much about it until the fighting came close to Sam Rong. Day and night the Khmer Rouge had been shelling the town of Svay Chek for a week. We could hear the shells explode; we could hear the people cry; and we knew people from Svay Chek were escaping to Thailand. I was fifteen years old.

Late one afternoon shortly after we first heard the shelling, our brother Phong came to our house to ask us to flee with him. "*A Nga* and *Mii Own*," he said, "you have to think about your lives. I know that *Ow* Here has a lot of land, animals, and food for us right now. I accept that we have everything we need — except our safety. We have to worry about our lives. We need to all leave now and escape the Khmer Rouge. We can come back later after the war is over and pick up this life again with all of these possessions. I'm going to take my family and escape into Thailand to live. I want you to come with me."

"How can you ask your younger brothers and young sister to go into Thailand?" our father cried. "There will be no one to take care of *Mii Own* and the boys. They're still young; they don't have a family like you do."

"Well, they're old enough, *Ow*," answered *Lok Bong* Phong. "If you want them to live here ... you never know because.... You hear that? Shelling and shooting and killing every day!" My brother couldn't say much to our father because he was afraid of him. "OK, it's up to you. You can make them stay, or you can let them go; it's up to you, *Ow*. I just want to let them know that I will leave tomorrow morning with my wife and children. I'm going back to my house now to get ready."

After *Lok Bong* Phong left, we talked and argued about what to do. My three brothers, Phan, Phin, and Pheav, were afraid to say much to our father, also. At first we didn't all agree. Our older brother Phong didn't have the wealth that our father did; he didn't have much land, many animals, or possessions. It was easy for him to decide to leave everything, take his wife and children and go. He could forget about his small house. But it wasn't easy for my other three brothers and me, who were living at home. We had to think about what was going to happen to our possessions when we left. What would we do if we came back and everything was gone?

Then *Bong* Phan said to us, "Either way you look at it, we lose. If we want to save our things, we gain our possessions, but we may lose our lives. If we save our lives, we may lose our possessions."

It took us almost four hours to decide what to do, but finally my brothers and I decided to flee. It was especially difficult for us because our father was not going to go with us. He didn't give us a hard time when we made our decisions to go. "If you want to go, you can go," our father told us. "I'm not going to go with you right now. I know the way better than you do; I can come later."

I went over to *Lok Bong* Phong's house and told him, "*Lok Bong*, I want to go, too."

My brother said, "OK, *Mii Own*; if you survive this war, you can come back, and if *Ow* survives, he will have everything for you." He knew what I had living with our father — land, house, animals— everything.

When I went back to our house, I told my father, "*Ow*, I need to go." My father cried and cried. "*Ow*," I said, crying, too, "if I survive, I will come back to you. I can't promise, but I will."

"*Mii Own*," my father told me, "I've worked hard and tried to give you everything. Now if you decide to go to Thailand to save your life, I just want to know that you're safe and still alive."

"*Ow*, I will have four brothers with me," I told him. "I'll be OK."

"Well, I know you want me to go with you, *Mii Own*," he replied, "But I don't want to go. I know the land; I know the way to Thailand already because I've been back and forth. If I need to go see you and your brothers, or if I decide I want to go live with you in Thailand, it will take me only about two or three hours."

I believed what he said to me. I thought he would follow us. But he didn't. He knew he would not come later, but he didn't want us to worry about him.

The next morning *Lok Bong* Phong and his family, my brothers Phan, Phin, and Pheav, and I left for Thailand. Our brother Phong didn't invite our sister Rieng and her husband to go with us because they lived too far away. He couldn't contact them in time before we left. Our brother Phath and his new wife were living in our village of Sam Rong at the time, but they were unable to go with us. He was now a part of his wife's family, and her parents, his brothers-in-law, and his sister-in-law didn't want to go. The same was true of our oldest brothers, Bounroeurn and Bounrien. They lived in Sam Rong with their families and extended families and didn't want to leave. Our older brother Pha lived in Svay, another village, too far away to contact.

Just as we were setting off, our father said to my brothers, "It doesn't matter if your sister is good or bad; if you can't handle it, you have to bring her home to me. Take care of *Mii Own* or bring her back."

"Goodbye, *Ow*," I cried. "I'll see you in Thailand."

"OK, *Mii Own*," my father whispered, then turned his face away. He sounded sad, but he didn't show us tears.

We all cried, and I cried until we got close to Thailand. We all missed home and everything that we had. On the way we had to pass by our rice fields, so we paused to have one last look. "OK, all this land belongs to us," my brother Phan said. "We will come back to protect it." Then we left.

We took twelve bags of rice, a couple of cooking pots, and a bowl and spoon for each one of us, as well as a few pairs of clothes. These few possessions went into a wagon pulled by two oxen. All of us walked alongside the wagon, except when one of us became too tired, that person rode in the wagon. We followed a trail that was wide enough for our wagon.

We left at the same time as the villagers who were going out to their fields, not rushing, because we wanted to look like we were doing our normal routine. We took our time and knew how long it would take to reach our aunt's house. We just needed to arrive before dark, so we were able to have several breaks. When we came to a pond, we stopped and picked wild plants, caught some fish or small animals, and cooked them with rice. We also timed our arrival at our aunt's house so we could follow along with the Thai farmers as they went back to the village at the end of their work day. We knew where our aunt's village was because before the war, we traveled back and forth to visit her. I never went by myself; I always went with our mother and brothers. *Mae* Yan and her younger sister Muth were close, so she often went to visit her in Thailand, and sometimes our aunt and uncle would come to visit us in Cambodia.

There was no sign that told us we were in Thailand, but we knew by the way the Thai farmers made their fields and houses. On the Cambodian side, there was only forest and brush, but on the Thai side, the farmers had neat fields and little shelters out by their fields for harvest time. There were no border patrols here and no one checked for documents.

The Khmer Rouge didn't come after us; they had not yet come into our village of Sam Rong, so they didn't know people were going to leave the country. We were the first people from our village to leave Cambodia. We left at four o'clock in the morning and arrived at *Ming* Muth's house in Ta Phraya,

Thailand, at about four o'clock in the afternoon. It took us less than one day. We left Cambodia in early April, before the fall of Phnom Penh, before I ever saw a Khmer Rouge face.

Sadness followed sadness. We had just left our home and half of our family in Cambodia. As soon as we started on our way, we realized that *Lok Bong* Phong's oldest daughter Sa Luan was sick with fever. She had been sick for a couple of days, but our brother didn't tell us. Although we questioned whether or not we should travel while she was ill, our brother Phong felt strongly that we should cross the border into safety.

Our first night at our aunt's house in Thailand, my little niece said to me, "*Ming*, I don't want to sleep by myself." We were all sleeping around her, but she was afraid to sleep alone. Her father held her in his arms, and I sat next to her, holding her hand and talking to her. By morning we discovered Sa Luan had passed away. She was only four years old.

We were all so sad, especially *Lok Bong* Phong and *Jae*. They feared they shouldn't have left Cambodia, but the Khmer Rouge were coming. Our brother Phong buried Sa Luan by himself without ceremony, except the words he spoke in his heart, because she was a child. Children cannot be buried in the cemetery, and they can't be cremated or given an official ceremony by the monks. She was little, though, so her soul could easily leave her body. Traditionally, we would honor and pay respects to the dead in September on *P'Chum Ben*. That's when we would pray with the monks for little Sa Luan and any other children who had died.

Several weeks later, after the Khmer Rouge takeover, our grandmother *Yeay* Lay went to our village of Sam Rong to visit us. Our father said to her, "Your granddaughter has gone to Thailand with some of her brothers."

When *Yeay* Lay heard that, she hired a driver and a cart and told him to take her all the way to Ta Phraya, Thailand. I was special to her, more than any of her other grandchildren, so she came to be with me. She often went back and forth across the border to visit her daughter and son and their families. Whenever she wanted to go somewhere, she hired the cart and driver to take her. This time she left her second husband in their village of Phnom Chub to join us. Either the Khmer Rouge didn't care or didn't know she was leaving.

First we stayed in *Ming* Muth's house with her and her four children, but then my brothers built a smaller house of bamboo and thatch next to the big house. My brothers, my grandmother, and I lived there, *Yeay* Lay and I sleeping in one room, and my brothers sleeping in a second room. My brothers also helped *Lok Bong* Phong build a second little house for his family and him.

After I arrived in Thailand, I decided I had to go to work. My brothers

Cambodian men building a bamboo house in a forest clearing, 1981 (photograph by Craig Faustus Buck).

worked to make money, gathering wood for charcoal in the forest or working in the tapioca fields. Even though my brothers were working, they told me, "You don't have to go to work; you don't have to do this or that." But I knew I couldn't live like before. I was fifteen years old, and I had nothing in Thailand.

I earned money for some of the jobs I did. I carried water to fill up the water jars and was paid by how many trips I took. I also washed clothes. People would come to our house the day before and ask, "Can you wash clothes for me tomorrow?"

If there were too many clothes, or the clothing was heavy and would take a long time to dry, or it was the rainy season and would take even longer to dry, I would tell the person, "If I don't get it all done today, it will be done by tomorrow." I would need to haul water from the well before I could wash the clothes. It was difficult for me to go from being the spoiled, youngest child who never had to work to being independent and having to work to make money in order to live. Ta Phraya had a village well, so it was safe for me to go get water, as opposed to going to the river. My hands became blistered and chapped from hauling the bucket up from the well by rope, carrying the water in buckets hanging from the end of a bamboo pole, and washing clothes. I used powdered detergent and cold water; I spread the clothes out on a board and scrubbed the stains with a brush. I didn't have a washboard. It was hard work.

Other jobs that I learned to do were planting and weeding tapioca and harvesting rice. If I didn't want to go all the way to the tapioca or rice fields to work for money, I went fishing with my grandmother, or we gathered grasses to dry and weave into mats for the floor. *Yeay* Lay taught me how to weave. We gave the mats away to new refugees who had just come in from Cambodia and didn't have any. *Yeay* Lay also taught me how to cook.

Also living in the same compound with us was my mother's younger brother *Mia* Leiy, Uncle Leiy. *Mia* is another word for uncle, just like *Poo*. He, his wife *Ming* Sok, and their children lived next door on the other side of *Ming* Muth's house. *Ming* Sok was jealous of my brothers and me because we were getting jobs and making money. She complained to her children that they were lazy. "Those jobs aren't hard for you to get, but you never get them. Your cousins can get those jobs— why not you?"

When she accused us of taking jobs away from her children, I said to her, "*Ming*, it's not my fault if someone wants to hire me to work. When someone sees that I work hard, then I am asked to work at another job. It's not my fault if your children aren't hired for these jobs."

We're lucky that our cousins weren't jealous of us; they were really good to us. They didn't take it out on us when their mother complained that they didn't get enough jobs. Our cousins never said it was because of us that their mother yelled at them.

Each of my cousins and friends could swim. One day we were down at the river, and they all jumped in and started swimming across the river. "Come on! Come on!" they called to me. "We'll watch, and if something happens, we'll catch you."

Since I was no longer in Cambodia, and my parents and brothers weren't there to watch me, I decided to go across the swift moving river. I tried carefully walking through the water, but when I got to the middle, there was a drop-off. It was deep; I sank down and it felt so comfortable. I didn't panic; I just thought that this was the time I was going to drown again, as I had in my former life. When my feet touched the bottom of the river, I pushed myself up to the surface so my friends could see me. They didn't know where I was; the current had pushed me downstream. When my cousins and friends saw where I was, they all swam out to get me. Some swam farther downstream to catch me if I continued to be swept along. Some came straight to where I was. If they hadn't saved me, I would have been swept out of sight. I was frightened and shaken.

When I got home, my grandmother, my aunt Muth, and my brothers were very upset. "What would we do if she died?" they asked each other.

"*Ow* would kill us," said my brothers.

"My son-in-law would kill me," *Yeay* Lay added.

"From now on, *Mii Own*," *Ming* Muth ordered, "You are not going to go to the river."

That was that — the first and only time I ever went in the river. My brothers continued to try to stop me from eating what I wanted, like liver and egg yolks. I knew they were only trying to protect me, but I didn't want to live that way anymore. I started to eat the forbidden foods after I almost drowned in Thailand. "*Min aiy te*," I told my brothers. "I'm going to eat what I want." I just promised them and myself that I would stay away from dangerous water. I remembered how I felt when I sank down to the bottom of the river. It wasn't difficult or uncomfortable, but I didn't want to die the same way as before. My brothers honored my decision.

By the time of the rice harvest season of November 1976, many, many Cambodian refugees had fled across the border to escape the Khmer Rouge. Some of the Thai people who lived on the border did not have good hearts and took advantage of the Cambodian refugees, raping the young women and robbing the men when they came back from working all day at a job. Just as in Sam Rong, the houses were all in the villages, and the fields were on the outside. In order to get to the fields to work, to pull yams, for example, we refugees would have to go along a path through the forest, where evil-hearted people hid in wait. It was dangerous to go alone. We wouldn't know who these people were, or whether or not they were from the same village. The evil ones were dressed as soldiers or policemen or even beggars. They wanted money, gold, jewelry, and nice clothes. Teenage girls would be taken and raped, even if they were walking in small groups. The other refugees would run and hide to protect themselves and their possessions, abandoning the young girls.

The Cambodian refugees were powerless to stop the violence. The people who wanted to take advantage of the refugees could attack them anytime, anywhere. Fortunately, I was never attacked, nor were my brothers and cousins. I always stayed close to the village and didn't go very far. When I did go into the forest, I made sure I was always with a large group of people, including my brothers. It was a frightening time for us.

Soon the village leaders reported to the Thai provincial authorities what was happening to the Cambodian refugees in the border villages. But the Thai government had grown more and more fearful of the Khmer Rouge among the refugees and didn't want to prosecute the local Thais. They decided that all the Cambodian refugees had to be sent to the United Nations refugee camps so they would be safe and the Thai border would be free from violence.

When the Thai authorities decided to send all the Cambodian refugees to the camps, the Thai village headmen went from house to house in every village to find out which houses had relatives from Cambodia living there. The headmen wrote down the names, making lists of all the people who did not have Thai citizenship papers. Then the village headmen reported the names to the Thai authorities, and on the designated date, all the people whose names were on the lists were taken to Lum Pok Refugee Camp in Surin Province. First they were going to take us to Aranya Prathet Refugee Camp, but that camp was already full. Five buses had gone to Aranya Prathet before ours, so there was no room left there. The rest of the refugee buses were sent to Surin.

We had come into Thailand with a wagon and a pair of oxen, which my brothers used in Ta Phraya, but before we left for the refugee camp, my brothers Phan and Phin took it back to Cambodia. They took the wagon and oxen only as far as our rice fields, where our father was already working when they arrived. *Ow* Here wanted them to bring me back to him before they left for the refugee camp, but they told him they couldn't do that. The Khmer Rouge were already in the village, so my brothers couldn't enter it. As it was, they were seen and chased by a Khmer Rouge soldier, so Phan and Phin split up and ran in different directions. Fortunately, they both made it back safely into Thailand to Ta Phraya. When they told the rest of the family what had happened, we were so happy they were safe. It had been very dangerous and foolish for them to take the wagon and oxen back; they could have been killed.

When we left for the refugee camp, my grandmother wouldn't go with us because she couldn't stand to ride in an enclosed vehicle like the bus. It was too frightening for her to be so confined. *Yeay* Lay was very sad to lose us and worried about her grandchildren going off without any parents. The Thais left her alone because she was so old.

Because we were traveling on a bus, we couldn't take anything except our clothes on our backs and what we could carry. We didn't have much. Besides a change of clothes, I took only my gold jewelry that my parents had given me, which I wore. I felt like my life had ended. First, when I left my home in Cambodia, I lost part of my life, leaving behind my father, some of my brothers, my sister, and their families. Now as I was leaving my aunt's compound in Ta Phraya, I felt I had lost my life a second time, leaving behind my beloved grandmother, as well as my aunts, uncle, and cousins. I was miserable.

CHAPTER 17

We Arrive at Lum Pok Refugee Camp

Lum Pok Refugee Camp isn't that far from Ta Phraya; we should have arrived in the late afternoon. Unfortunately, the bus broke down in the middle of the road, just as we were starting up Lahan Sai Mountain. The driver tried and tried to get it to start again, but the engine wouldn't turn over. We all got out of the bus to see what was going to happen. It would soon be dark, and we all knew that it was unsafe to be out on the road at night. There were Thai *Dang*, Thai Communist insurgents, in the area, and we were afraid we would be attacked. There was also the danger of robbers at night.

The last bus came up behind us, and our driver flagged it down. He told the other driver his problem and asked if he would take as many people as he could fit into his bus up to the army base at the top of the mountain. The driver agreed; half of the people on our bus climbed into the other bus and rode up the mountain, standing in the aisle, but there was no room for us. Our bus driver told the other driver to ask for help, and he told the rest of us to start walking as quickly as we could. It was a long, hard climb up the mountain, but luckily we made it to the army base before dark.

In the meantime an army mechanic went down the mountain and helped the driver get the bus going again. On top at the base, the soldiers gave us food and water and a place to rest. Finally, the bus arrived and we were on our way again. When we finally arrived at Lum Pok Camp at eleven o'clock at night, we were so relieved.

All the people from one bus were housed in two barracks, the next bus dropped its people off at the next two barracks, and so on down the line. We were dropped off at the last one, Barrack 44. The refugee camp didn't have a common kitchen, so the camp authorities arranged to have food cooked by host families for five hundred people arriving that day. When we got off the buses, we were each given a sack of food — whatever the host families had prepared. The host families were told we were arriving at dinner time — five o'clock in the afternoon. We were lucky the food was still good and the rice wasn't soggy when we arrived at night. The camp authorities also provided bedding for us. We were each given a sleeping mat, a mosquito net, a light blanket, and a pillow, in addition to our food.

Lum Pok Refugee Camp had a guard station at the gate, which was large enough for cars and trucks to drive through. A large ditch went around the entire camp, marking the boundary, but there was no fence around the camp. During the rainy season, there was lots of water in the ditch, but during the dry season, the water was gone. It was easy for refugees to leave the camp by just crossing the dry ditch. There were no guards along the perimeter of the camp. There were several rows of barracks, ours being the last one in the last row.

When we entered the barrack, which looked like a long warehouse, about the width of a tall double-wide trailer, each family was given a small area. The barrack was built up off the ground, and our sleeping area was on the upper floor. Beneath the barrack was dirt, cool and shady, so when it was hot, refugees could hang a hammock under the barrack to be cooler. There wasn't enough room underneath to stand up, but you could sit down or lie in a hammock.

Upstairs was one big room, and we were each given a space from one post to another. There was only one wall to the cubicle, the outside wall. We had to make our own walls, which we began putting together the very next day. Some people built bamboo walls that reached up six to eight feet, not to the ceiling. Others built walls made from twigs or thatch. Still others bought blankets or curtains to hang for walls and the door. My brothers and I just bought blankets to hang for our walls and the doorway. The people who lived in the barracks trusted each other, just wanting privacy when sleeping.

I shared a cubicle with my brothers Phan, Phin and Pheav, while *Lok Bong* Phong and his family were given one several cubicles away in the family section. We put our possessions down, and then we all sat down on the floor together to eat, sharing what we had in our dinner bags—rice, fish or meat, and fruit. Each bag also contained a sweet with a hand-written note, like a fortune cookie, which we set aside until later.

After the meal we washed our hands, drank water, and whoever smoked or chewed tobacco did that. We all brought out our hand-written notes and asked the older people who knew how to read what our notes said. Those who could read said, "Don't throw it away. You keep that note until you find the person who wrote it."

"*Lok Bong* Phong, will you read mine for me, please?" I asked.

My brother took my note and read, "If you are the one who will be my wife, contact me at —," and gave a number.

"What?!" I questioned. "Is that really what it says?"

"Keep this one," *Lok Bong* Phong told me. I did keep my note, but I never really looked for the person who wrote my fortune, and I don't remember what any of the other notes said. It was a fun way to be welcomed into the camp.

When I woke up the first morning in camp, I asked myself, "Where am I? I don't know this place." Even though there were thousands of refugees there, I felt like I had been dumped in the middle of nowhere.

Every morning, groups of people, mostly young men who were bachelors, or those who had been married but were now alone because of the war, came walking by the barracks — looking. They were looking to see who the new people were and if there were any young single women. In my barrack there were only three teenagers; the rest were the elderly, married couples, and children.

When the young men came by, five or six at a time, they stopped and asked, "May we have some water? We're thirsty."

"Yes," I would answer, not happily, because I had to carry the water a long way from the pond to fill our water jar — water for the whole family, for my brothers when they came home from working all day.

A group would always stop and ask, "May we come in? May we have some water, *Neang*?"

I always looked at them and said, "Yes," the first time. When they asked again, I told them, "You need to turn around and go back to the pond and get your own water. I have to carry water all that way from the pond. If you want to be nice to me, you'll carry water back and fill up that jar. That's what I have to do." I didn't want them to just come and look at me, to see if I was available and drink my water.

Some groups of young men were polite when they came to visit, and they would ask how I was doing and how I liked the camp. Those men made me feel comfortable. But the groups of men who just wanted to look at me and ask for water made me feel uncomfortable. I didn't want to meet them again outside the barrack, though some asked me to meet them in the camp market. Even though my brothers were out working during the day, I was safe inside the barrack. There were other people there, and the walls of each little cubicle were thin, not reaching to the ceiling, so everyone could hear what anyone was saying. Help was available if needed.

During the day my brothers went out of the camp to the closest village to look for work. Refugees were allowed to leave the camp during the day. Sometimes my brothers would dig ditches or a pond, sometimes they would cut down trees to clear a field or make charcoal, and sometimes they would do work around a house — whatever Thais would pay them to do. My job was to carry water each day from the pond, the only source of water for the camp, except for catching rain water in a jar, which was never much.

Lum Pok Refugee Camp was about one square kilometer in size, and our barrack was at the very end of the camp on the side opposite the pond, which was outside the gate. Each family had two buckets hanging from a bamboo pole that we used to carry water from the pond to our barracks. That's how I carried water every day. I had to walk one kilometer to the other end of the camp with the two empty buckets to get the water and then bring the full buckets back again another kilometer. Half way back I would have to stop and rest my shoulders. Every day, twice a day, I would carry a total of four buckets of water for our family.

People also bathed at the pond. Many people took a bath when they reached the pond before carrying the full buckets back. We carried a bucket of water about twenty-five feet away, up a little rise, where the ground sloped down to a rice field. When we poured the water over ourselves, the dirty, soapy water ran down the slope to the field. It didn't drain into the pond. No one bathed in the pond or stood in it. The water was clean enough for us to drink.

In Cambodia and Thailand, people bathed by dipping a bowl or cup into the water, then throwing the water on themselves. Women would wear a sarong and men would wear their *kramas* while bathing. We were able to buy bar soap for bathing, including our hair, and powdered laundry detergent for washing our clothes, which we did back at the barracks. Women wore the sarong under our arms while washing our hair, face, arms and legs. Then we put our arms inside the sarong, tying it under our chin, so we could wash the rest of our bodies modestly.

I didn't like to bathe at the pond before carrying the water back to my barrack. I got sweaty again carrying the heavy water. Sometimes I would walk back to the pond a third time just to take a bath. Sometimes when it was too hot, I went to the pond only once a day; one of my brothers would carry water after coming home from work. There wasn't enough water in the water jar for us to bathe at the barracks. That water was used only for drinking, cooking, and washing dishes and our few clothes— not for bathing. To fill the entire jar would take five trips to the pond, but it was such hard work for me, I never carried more than four buckets of water a day.

I also cooked rice for my brothers when they came home in the evening, and they usually brought something with them, like fish or vegetables, to eat with the rice. We weren't able to bring cooking utensils with us on the bus, but we could buy them in the little store inside the camp. We brought money with us, since my brothers had been working in Ta Phraya, so we bought two pots— one for making soup and one for cooking rice. We also bought soup bowls, spoons, and plates for each of us, plus one small, plastic water bowl to share for drinking.

We cooked on a small bucket stove that was made of clay, about two inches thick, and covered with metal. It had a rectangular hole cut in one side for air circulation, and the cooking pot sat on top with a charcoal fire in the bucket underneath. We bought these bucket stoves in the camp market, as well as a rectangular pan with a grill on top that we used for baking. When we baked a whole chicken or large fish, we wrapped it in banana leaves, placed it in the pan, and covered it tightly. The pan was placed on the fire and it had to be watched carefully so it wouldn't burn. We didn't use this type of oven very often — only for special occasions. We also grilled using a green stick split halfway down to hold the meat and long grass wrapped and tied around to keep the chicken, fish or frog in place.

Once a week, the United Nations organization provided some kind of meat for us, as well as rice. One week they gave chicken, the next week fish, the next week pork, the next week beef, and so on. The amount given was less than a pound for our family of four — just enough for one meal. Sometimes the UN would give vegetables when they gave out meat and rice. When the UN truck came, we had an assigned time for each barrack, so we didn't have to stand in a long line. An announcement would come over the loudspeaker, "Number 44 barrack: Time to come and get food." When that happened, someone from each family would go stand in a short line and wait for the UN agent to call the family name to get the weekly rice, meat, and whatever else they had that week, like vegetables, cooking oil, or fish sauce. It took all day for people from forty-four barracks to go get food, so our time was usually in the afternoon, since we were the last barrack.

There was no electricity back in our home village of Sam Rong, so we didn't have refrigeration. We were used to having no refrigeration at the refugee camp. When we got fresh meat in Cambodia, after slaughtering a cow, we had to deal with all the meat that day. We would boil whatever meat that wasn't going to be used that day just enough so it wouldn't spoil. Then we would cut the meat into thin strips, marinate it, using black pepper, salt, garlic, and green onion, and let it dry in the sun. The other way we dealt with a lot of raw meat was by fermenting it in a large jar with cooked rice, salt, and fresh ginger. The ingredients were mixed and pressed down tightly together, and then the jar was completely sealed. As long as the jar wasn't opened, allowing air in, the meat would keep without rotting for a long time, even up to a year. The result was a sour meat mixture that could later be grilled, stir-fried, or made into a sour soup. Once you opened the jar, the meat mixture had to be used within one week.

In Lum Pok Camp, since they gave us enough meat for only one meal, there was no problem with spoilage because we cooked it that evening and ate it. During the week, I would go with my brothers or friends from our barrack outside the camp and into the neighboring rice fields to hunt for fish, snails, crabs, frogs, lizards, and eels. When we caught something, we would bring it back to cook for dinner. There was also a forest near the camp, so sometimes we would go there to find wild, edible plants.

We learned from our family which plants we could eat, information that had been passed down from generation to generation. Some trees and bushes had edible young leaves or flowers. If the leaves or flowers were bitter, we would dip them in hot sauce. We also knew which mushrooms were edible, so during the mushroom season, we went to the forest to gather them. When we escaped from Cambodia into Thailand, it had not been difficult for us to find food on the way. The only time it would have been difficult for us to survive in the forest would be in the dry season. It's true there are still birds and small animals during the dry season, but you have to be fast and accurate enough to shoot them with a crossbow. We could also gather wild fruit, like plums and berries similar to blueberries and raspberries. The wild mango tree has fruit that we can also eat when it is green to make the Cambodian sour soup, and when the mangoes are ripe, they are really sweet. They are just like domestic mangoes, only smaller. We usually didn't eat the wild bananas because they had too many seeds. Instead, we would use the leaves as plates or to wrap food for carrying.

In front of each barrack at the refugee camp was an area big enough to build little bamboo cooking shacks for the families who wanted them. We cooked outside of the barrack on our little bucket stoves in the cookhouse built by my brothers of bamboo with a woven grass thatch for the roof. If we cooked inside the barrack, it would be too smoky. Each family built a little cookhouse, or else they just cooked outside without any protection from the sun and rain. *Jae* had her own cookhouse, which *Lok Bong* Phong had built for her, so we didn't cook together.

In addition to the vegetables the UN might give us once a week, which was not enough, we were also able to buy vegetables at the refugee camp store, and, eventually, grow our own in the open area behind and around our cook shack. One of my brothers prepared our garden so we would have enough vegetables. We grew lemon grass, squash, cucumbers, string beans, and tomatoes. During the rainy season, it was easy to grow vegetables, but during the dry season, we would have to water the vegetables by hand.

Some people were lazy and didn't grow their own vegetables. Instead, they would come at night and steal vegetables from other people's gardens. In the morning when I would go to water the vegetables, if I saw something missing, I would raise my voice against the thief, who was probably smiling, knowing he had been successful. "If you want some of my vegetables, why don't you ask instead of just taking it?" I yelled out as loudly as I could.

I spread the word, and soon people started talking about the stealing. Most people decided to grow their own gardens. Several people came to ask for seeds or a piece of lemon grass root to plant in their own areas. It wasn't hard to grow a garden in the camp. We could buy seeds in the village market or save seeds from the vegetables we grew.

During the day if I was hungry and wanted to eat something, I would go to the camp store, which also included a little food stand with several small tables and chairs around it that offered rice soup or noodles, to buy something to eat—cake or cookies, or a snack of some sort. Other refugee camps also had a small store and noodle stand inside the camp. This was something new for the rural Cambodians. Villages like Sam Rong were too small to have noodle stands, but the town of Svay Chek had one because it is a district town. Country people usually didn't eat noodles because they weren't available in the village markets, they didn't know how to cook them or have the money to buy them if they were available. They were usually subsistence farmers, cooking and eating what they could raise and gather themselves or barter with a neighbor. They preferred to cook dishes that were quick, easy, and didn't cost money.

Refugees who had been in camp for a while usually went to the camp store and noodle stand to meet and greet the new refugees. My brothers were working, so they always gave me more than enough money to buy whatever I wanted. Lum Pok Refugee Camp was called "Number One Camp" because refugees could go out and work or go to the village market and come back every evening. Thus they were able to make money to buy extra food and necessities for their families. If refugees were not able to go out and work, then they could trade things that they had for the items they wanted or needed. Many people traded their extra UN rice, mosquito nets, blankets, cooking oil, and fish sauce with people outside the camp for more meat.

My parents had always been very protective of me, but when we were in the camp and my brothers were working, they couldn't watch over me. My brothers counseled me, though. *Bong* Phan said, "*Neang*, you can't go by yourself outside the gate, except to carry water. I don't want you to go to the market in town unless you are with the three of us. It's too far from the camp." All I was allowed to do alone outside the gate was carry water. My brothers also told me that if I had enough water for the day, I didn't need to carry water. I could wait until they got home from work, and then they would carry water for me.

I didn't have a job inside the camp, other than carrying water, gardening, and cooking in the evening. Occasionally, I washed clothes, but I didn't have many, and my brothers washed their own clothes. During the day I visited the friends I made who lived in the same barrack. They would tell me their life stories, and I would tell them mine.

My first friend named Kantuoch was really pretty. She lived with her parents and was the oldest daughter. Everyone was attracted to her, but she wasn't lucky. Kantuoch was beautiful, but she didn't have a beautiful personality. She was too judgmental. As her friends we understood her, but probably when she talked to men, they didn't appreciate her personality. When she saw someone, she criticized that person: "Oh, he's too dark; he looks old; he smokes."

When men heard her talk like that, they didn't like her, saying, "Yeah, she's pretty, but she's not very nice. She's not polite."

Kantuoch did marry, although her husband was first interested in me. He reminded me of my brother Pha, and he had the same name and the same walk. He asked me to marry him, but I told him, "*Poo*, to tell you the truth, I'm not ready to get married yet."

"Why not?" he asked. "You're already a teenager; you're ready to get married."

"If you want to be my brother, *Poo*, OK," I said, "but not my husband."

"I don't know why I'm not lucky," Pha replied. "Probably someone will be lucky and marry you, and I hope that he takes good care of you." He was very sweet and worried about me.

"If I accept and marry someone and he doesn't take care of me," I said to him, "you know me, *Poo*."

"Yeah, I know you now," Pha told me. "That's why I like you; you're honest. I don't know how you'll be when you have a family. If you have a hard time, then you'll know how difficult it is to get out or stay in your marriage."

A few weeks after we had this discussion, and Pha understood that I wasn't going to marry him, he married Kantuoch. She was the one who decided she was going to marry him. She went to his room, which is not done in Cambodian culture. If a girl goes to a man's room first, it's not good. Her parents were so angry with her. "Why don't you be like Bounriem?" her mother asked her.

"I'm not like her, and I'm not going to be like her," Kantuoch answered. At first she didn't even say that she loved Pha. She continued to say negative things about him when she talked to me, but decided to marry Pha anyway. They got married without a traditional ceremony in Pha's barrack. Her parents didn't attend because they didn't approve of what Kantuoch was doing. Only the elders in the barrack were there to give the couple their blessings.

My other friend Karien was darker than I am and on the chubby side. She had a much nicer personality than Kantuoch, though. Karien married my brother Phan's best friend. She didn't have parents, so they didn't have a traditional wedding either. After they married, she and her little sister moved into her husband's barrack, so I didn't see her much after that.

One man living in my barrack with his two teenage sons said to me, "You know, your father and I lived in the same district."

"You know my father?" I asked.

"Yes, I know your father. Probably we're relatives," he replied.

I didn't ask him anymore. He had two sons, and I didn't want to talk to them. If my father had told me these people were part of the family, I would have talked to them. I was afraid this man was trying to trick me. I found out later that my brother Phong talked with this man often and found out that he did know our extended family, but not our immediate family.

The next time the man spoke to me, I told him, "OK, you have two teenage sons, so I'm not going to talk to you anymore about family."

Inside Lum Pok Refugee Camp, the UN enforced the camp rules; Thai policemen enforced the rules outside the main gate. When people wanted to come in or go out of the camp, they had to go through the main gate and sign in and out with the Thai police. We didn't have any identification cards to show, and when we went out, we went out the main gate. The police at the main gate got to know us and knew we belonged in the camp. If I wanted to go to the market in the village, after my brothers felt comfortable with my going, I went with a group of people from my barrack during the day. It was dangerous to go alone, so we always went in a group. While I lived in the camp, the Thai policemen were very polite and good to us, and I felt safe in the camp. One older policeman even treated me like I was his daughter and always looked after me. After I left, though, things changed. People who left the camp later said the Thai police became mean and started beating up people, including women who were pregnant.

The camp had a curfew set at sundown, usually about seven o'clock. People were tired then, and it was time to go to bed. After sundown, if anyone was outside the barrack building, he would have to go through the refugee barrack guard to enter. The older men in each barrack took turns being on guard duty for their own barrack. The barrack guard would demand to see permission from the refugee barrack leader in order to allow a person entry to the barrack building after seven o'clock. The seven o'clock curfew was all week long, including on weekends. When the camp showed a movie after dark, each barrack leader knew how many people from his barrack went to the movie. Usually, all the people from the same barrack came back from the movie together, so the barrack leader could keep track and make sure everyone had returned. The UN camp authorities chose the men who were the barrack leaders and the barrack guards. Eight men were chosen for each barrack—

seven to take turns guarding the barrack each night, and one to be the barrack leader. If a man was sick the night he had guard duty, the leader took his turn for him. I didn't feel unduly controlled by the camp rules; I liked having strict rules. They were designed to make us feel safer and protected.

People were usually free to come and go, but occasionally, the camp directors would shut down the whole camp for three days. No one could come inside the camp, and no one could go outside it. There were various reasons for a lockdown, but usually it was caused by the arrival of an important person in the area, like the king or queen, or the prime minister of Thailand visiting the province. During that time the Thai authorities didn't want refugees out wandering around. They wanted them safely inside the camps. It was then forbidden to go out, and if a refugee was found outside during a lockdown, that person was in trouble. The camp authorities wouldn't help someone who got caught on the outside; they had given fair warnings. If you disobeyed, it was your problem. If a refugee was caught outside during a lockdown, he was beaten up by the Thai guards or the Thai police in town. No one I knew ever got caught on the outside during a lockdown.

Shortly after we left Ta Praya for Lum Pok Refugee Camp, our grandmother passed away. We found out about *Yeay* Lay's death when a new man and his family moved into our barrack. He moved around a great deal, and since he had relatives living in Ta Phraya, he knew our aunt. I don't remember his name because in Cambodia, names are not important. Relationships between the people are important. We called him *Poo* because he was much older than we were. I think his name was Puy. That's what I heard the old lady call him who lived with him in the barrack. He took care of her like she was his aunt, although they weren't related.

After we left Ta Phraya, *Poo* Puy stopped to visit our aunt before taking his family to Lum Pok Refugee Camp. When *Ming* Muth learned that he would be going to the same refugee camp, she told him, "If you meet my niece and nephews, please tell them of their grandmother's death. She became sick with worry when they left for the refugee camp, and she couldn't go with them. I think she died of a broken heart."

It was a coincidence that this man and his family moved into our barrack, met us, and learned who we were. When *Poo* Puy told us that our grandmother had passed away, I cried to myself, "We're not going to see *Yeay* Lay again. When we go back to that village, she's not going to be there."

We sat quietly and thought about our grandmother and our loss, and then each of my brothers went somewhere quietly by himself. *Bong* Phan and *Bong* Phin went to the temple in the village outside the camp to light a candle and some incense and to pray. *Bong* Pheav went out to work in the field outside the camp. I chose to sit quietly in our cubicle. I didn't want to go to the temple because it was such a long way to walk in the heat. There was no way that we could go back to my aunt's village to attend *Yeay* Lay's funeral. We didn't have the papers that would allow us to take a bus to go back. I missed not being at my grandmother's cremation.

On *P'Chum Ben* in September, we pay respects to all the people who have passed away in our family, all the way back seven generations. After we had been living with *Ming* Muth in Ta Phraya for half a year, we had this celebration. Then we were able to have the ceremony for our brother's little daughter Sa Luan who had died as soon as we reached Thailand in April. On *P'Chum Ben* we honor all those who have passed away with food, gifts, prayers, and the calling of names of all the members of our extended family. If we can't remember all the names of those who have died back seven generations, we say, "We pray for all the members of our family for seven generations. These gifts and prayers are for all of them who are related to us."

I waited to honor my grandmother until *P'Chum Ben*. The camp directors invited Thai monks, who used the same language of Buddhist prayers that the Cambodian monks did, to come inside the camp to celebrate the holiday. I made some special food that I knew *Yeay* Lay liked, and bought a dessert to take to the monks when I asked them to pray for my grandmother's soul. The monks were sitting inside the central meeting room on a raised platform, and the old people were sitting on mats on the ground in front of them. In front of the building, the organizers set up tables so the people could bring their offerings and place them on the table. It was well organized and ran smoothly, even though thousands of people took part.

After I placed my food on the table, I went inside to the monks and gave them the list of names of the people I wanted blessed. Then I left and went back to my barrack. Only the old people stayed, sitting on their mats and listening to the monks and talking. People helped each other get ready for the ceremony; a person who could write would help those who couldn't by writing down the names. *Lok Bong* Phong wrote the names for me. Loud speakers were set up so people would know it was time for the ceremony to start and everyone could hear the monks praying.

I know there were westerners working in the camp or visiting, but I never saw any walk through my barrack. Probably the westerners worked for the UN or were religious missionaries. The camp had a church at the other end of the grounds, but I never went there, so I'm not sure if it was run by westerners or not. I heard the people singing songs in the church and having Sunday school classes there, but I never went. I don't know why. I guess I wasn't old enough to think about whether or not I should be attending church or English or French classes at the school. I never thought about that. No one came to my barrack to invite me to go to church or school, and I didn't have my parents to guide me and tell me what I should be doing. The camp was so large, and the church was so small, it was probably too full to bring any more people in.

One night the camp had a party with a Thai movie and dancing, so I went with my three brothers. The movie was outside with a big white sheet for the screen; some people stood and some sat on the ground. Even though we hadn't studied Thai, we could all speak and understand much of it. We had picked it up the year we lived with our aunt in Ta Phraya, so we could understand enough of a movie. I stood in between my brothers Phin and Pheav, holding hands so we wouldn't get separated, and Phan stood behind me because young men were always looking at me.

That night a man came over and stepped on the side of *Bong* Phan's foot, wanting to get our attention. It wasn't just an accident. He didn't ask who we were, or who the young men were who were with me, but he wanted to reach me. This was before the movie started, when people were walking around, getting food and meeting friends. My brother Phan was always calm and easy-going, so he just moved away when it happened, saying, "OK, let's go, you guys."

"Why? The movie hasn't even started," we all asked him.

"I don't want to stay any longer," my brother Phan explained. *Bong* Phin, who had a more aggressive personality, would have wanted to stay there and fight for his space. This man was lucky he didn't step on my brother Phin's foot instead. We didn't stay to watch the movie that night, and we didn't ask any questions. If our older brother told us it was time to go, that's what we did.

The next morning we all talked about what happened the night before. My brother Phan didn't tell us who the person was that stepped on his foot only that it happened. "Why didn't you tell your two brothers to fight?" I asked him. "Three against one — you could have beaten him up."

"Oh, I didn't want to cause problems," *Bong* Phan answered. "We're new here; we just wanted to go and have a good time and then come home. *Min aiy te.*"

My brother Phan also told all his friends about the incident, and they all wanted to know who the person was. They wanted to fight. But *Bong* Phan didn't know who it was. Because it was dark, he hadn't seen the man's face. We found out later that man was Sao Bounchoeurn.

Part III

*Sao Bounchoeurn
and San Bounriem*

CHAPTER 18

Bounriem: How Can I Marry Her Tonight?

The first time I remember seeing Bounchoeurn, he was sitting in front of his barrack, watching me carry two heavy buckets of water hanging from the long bamboo pole over my shoulder. As I stopped to catch my breath and lean against a tree in the shade, he called out to me, "*Neang*! Want some help?" But I didn't reply. Instead, I picked up my bamboo pole and buckets of water and hurried away. Since young women were very desirable at the refugee camp, we were continuously pursued by the single men. Not only was I shy, but I was also tired from all the attention the men paid me.

Several days later, my two friends, Kantuoch and Karien, and I went to the noodle stand close to Bounchoeurn's barrack to eat breakfast. He saw us arrive and decided to join us. At the time I thought he was interested in the beautiful Kantuoch, so he wanted to sit next to her at our little table and talk while he ate.

Kantuoch was not interested in Bounchoeurn. "I don't like him," she whispered loudly to Karien. "He's so dark-skinned," she complained.

"OK, if you don't like him, then I'll marry him," I said softly to Kantuoch, just joking. "But he'd have to ask me in the traditional way." I didn't really mean it, but Bounchoeurn heard me say it.

Whenever my friends and I ate breakfast and lunch at the noodle stand, Bounchoeurn came to eat, too, but he always flirted with Kantuoch and Karien. I was shy and didn't talk to him. I felt that Kantuoch was much prettier and taller than I was and had lighter skin; I thought Bounchoeurn was attracted to one of my friends. After he left, Kantuoch talked about Bounchoeurn, saying, "Oh, he's not handsome; he's too dark; he's not my type."

"Oh, shut up!" I said jokingly. "If you don't want him, leave him for me," only half serious. I *was* only half serious, but the more I thought about it, the more I wondered if perhaps it was time for me to get married. After all, I was now seventeen years old. I was tired of the men hanging around my

145

barrack, and I didn't feel safe when my brothers were away at work. Besides, I disagreed with Kantuoch; I thought Bounchoeurn was handsome.

Shortly after that, when I was again carrying water, one of Bounchoeurn's friends stopped and asked me if I was sure that I'd marry Bounchoeurn.

"What do you mean? Why are you asking me that?" I answered, surprised.

"Bounchoeurn heard you say at the noodle stand that you'd marry him. Would you?" the friend repeated.

"Yeah," I told him. "If he can stand up in front of my family and follow Cambodian tradition, I will." I couldn't believe what I had just said to an absolute stranger. I wondered what my father would say if he knew how I had changed.

The first time Bounchoeurn talked to me was in September during the Buddhist celebration at the little temple inside the camp. The monks had been invited to pray in the temple, so I was carrying food and on my way to offer it to the monks for their prayers. Bounchoeurn was standing outside the little camp store and called out to me. "I want to talk to you!"

"*Poo*, why do you want to talk to me?" I called him Uncle.

"Come in," he told me. "Come inside the store." After I went inside the little store, Bounchoeurn said, "I'm not married right now. If I have the matchmakers go to your barrack and talk to your brothers, telling them I want to marry you, what will you say?"

This was the first time Bounchoeurn had ever talked to me, so when he called me into the little store, I thought he was going to ask me about my friends. Then I remembered the stranger who had talked to me about Bounchoeurn. Still surprised, I answered, "Well, I don't have anybody, only my brothers. You need to go to my brothers. If you follow tradition and have the old people talk to my brothers, asking if I can marry you, and they agree, then I will accept that."

"Really?" he asked.

"Yeah," I answered. "But *Poo*, I don't know you. You need to stand up in front of my brothers, and if they approve, I'll marry you." I could tell that he was pleased with my response.

Many men were interested in me, and I had many suitors, but the rest of them went to talk to my eldest brother instead of talking to me. They would take *Lok Bong* Phong alcohol and drink together to make him happy. Bounchoeurn never talked to *Lok Bong* Phong or my three other brothers; he talked directly to me. We occasionally talked together, but no one was aware of our relationship. I didn't like the other suitors who talked and drank with my eldest brother Phong. Because my father was an alcoholic and had verbally abused my mother, I didn't want to marry a man who drank. At that time Bounchoeurn drank once in a while, but mostly he just smoked cigarettes.

One young man in particular, named Hor, wanted to marry me, but I didn't know it. His uncle was *Lok Bong* Phong's friend, and Hor and I were friends, too. I thought of Hor as another brother. He took a bottle of alcohol to give as a gift to my eldest brother Phong. After drinking together, Hor asked if he could marry me. *Lok Bong* Phong agreed, even though I knew nothing about this visit and request. I found out later what happened.

"Don't worry," my brother told Hor, "I can tell her what to do."

Several days after my conversation with Bounchoeurn, he asked the matchmakers to go to my barrack and talk to my three youngest brothers. I was there when the matchmakers arrived. My brothers didn't know what to expect, but they had an idea that it had to do with me. After the matchmakers formally asked them if I could marry Bounchoeurn, *Bong* Phan, the eldest of the three, turned to me. "*Mii Own*, do you agree to marry this guy, or what?"

My three brothers stood there looking at me, so I said, "Well, it's difficult to live in this camp. You can't protect me twenty-four hours a day. If it's good enough for you to have me marry him, then I'm OK with it." Bounchoeurn was not there for this discussion, just my three brothers, the elderly matchmakers, and me.

Then my brother Phan asked, "*Mii Own*, did you talk to him before?"

"Well," I answered, "Only once or twice I talked to him, but I thought it was about my friends; I don't think he mentioned me. So I don't have strong feelings that I love him. I just want to make sure that he's serious about this."

"OK, if you think that this is good for you, we cannot say no. This is your life. We want to make sure that you feel comfortable to live with him or not," *Bong* Phan told me.

"You know, we never know what's going to happen," I said to my brothers. "But it's really not safe here for me now in the camp with so many men trying to hang around me."

"OK," *Bong* Phan replied. "That's good enough. Probably you're going to have to learn about each other after you're married."

So Bounchoeurn and I planned a wedding party, and all the old people helped with the planning. The elders told us, "OK, wait until the end of the month. We're going to have a big party for the wedding."

We decided what food we were going to have, how many tables we would use, and how many people we were going to invite. We also decided what music we were going to have and what band we would ask to play. All of this was possible because Bounchoeurn was making money, and we could buy the special foods and hire musicians from outside the camp. Bounchoeurn and

I were pleased with all our wedding plans, but then the plans were turned upside down.

Even though my three younger brothers had agreed to my marriage, we had not involved *Lok Bong* Phong. He had been away from the barrack when the matchmakers visited our cubicle. When my eldest brother found out about the engagement, he was very upset. "No! When did you decide this? I am your eldest brother; you can't decide this yourself," *Lok Bong* Phong told me.

"Yes," I said. "You are my eldest brother, but the future is mine, not yours."

Then *Lok Bong* Phong became angry. "My friend's nephew has loved you for a long time. Why don't you marry him?" he shouted.

"Did he ask me? All those men who came to your cubicle — did they ask me?" I asked.

"Did Bounchoeurn ask you?" *Lok Bong* Phong questioned me.

"Yes, Bounchoeurn asked me. We have been interested in each other for almost two months," I answered.

With that, my eldest brother stormed out of our cubicle and didn't say another word.

Two nights after Bounchoeurn and I had made all our wedding plans, *Lok Bong* Phong sent a message to Hor, the one who still wanted to marry me. My eldest brother Phong was on guard duty that night for our barrack, so when Hor came, they drank a lot of whisky, and then *Lok Bong* Phong gave Hor a long-handled knife. At about midnight after everyone was asleep, Hor sneaked into our cubicle and lay down beside me, outside my mosquito net. I was sleeping inside the net next to the cloth partition, with my three brothers on the other side. When I turned over in my sleep, I became aware of someone next to me on the side opposite my brothers. "Who's sleeping next to me?!" I screamed. I opened my mosquito net to look, shouting, "That's a man!"

Hor didn't do anything; he just lay there sleeping. I jumped up, shouting loudly, "Get up! Everybody get up!"

When I shined my flashlight to see who it was, I discovered it was Hor. He lay there drunk, snoring and sleeping without a blanket. I couldn't believe it. I thought of him like a brother, and we always talked. He had never told me he wanted to marry me. I couldn't believe that he would behave this way. In Cambodian culture a young man can't go and sleep next to a girl when he isn't married to her. When I saw him, it made me angry. He had been drinking with *Lok Bong* Phong, who told him where I would be sleeping and let him into our barrack. Although he hadn't done anything to me, he wanted to make me feel guilty because he was there, so I wouldn't marry Bounchoeurn.

I tried to wake Hor up, kicking him and shouting at him, "*Bong*, what are you doing?" All three of my brothers were awake now; the whole barrack was awake. They were all waiting to hear what Hor had to say.

"I love you," Hor said to me. "I don't want you to marry someone else."

"Well," I said to him, "Why didn't you say something to me before I became engaged? Now I'm engaged. What you did was not good to me. If you love me, you have to support me and follow tradition, too. And why did you do this?!"

Hor started crying, and I was furious. I called him every name I could think of, in a polite Cambodian girl's vocabulary, of course.

About that time *Lok Bong* Phong came in to see what was happening, bottle in hand. "Why don't you agree with him? He's been asleep there all night with you?" he asked me.

"Oh, you're the one who let him in!" I shouted at my eldest brother. "If you weren't my brother, I'd report you to the authorities and have you arrested." I turned to Hor and said, "I'm not going to accept you as my husband; you are a bad man and not good enough for me. It doesn't matter if you grab me and take me away; I'm still not going to accept you."

Hor just sat there and cried, saying, "I don't want you to marry someone else. Even if you don't accept me, I want you to stay here. I want it to be like it was before you met this man, when we were friends."

"You're not my mother; you're not my father," I told him. "Don't tell me what to do, and don't ask me after something has happened. You've ruined my life already."

Hor didn't say anything; he just cried. *Lok Bong* Phong didn't say anything; he just continued to drink.

"As soon as it's seven o'clock," I warned, "I'm taking you to the camp authorities, Hor, and I'm going to tell them what you did. I'm not yet eighteen; I'm still only seventeen. What you did was wrong."

The next morning I went to the camp authority and told the person in charge what had happened. "Did he hurt you? Did he touch you? Did he rape you?" the authority asked.

"No," I answered, "I know this man. He didn't do anything to me except come into my room and sleep next to me outside my mosquito net. But I am engaged, and this man knew it."

"OK," the authority said, "What do you want to happen to him?"

"I want him to stay out of my life and pay a fine for humiliating and shaming me," I told him.

The camp authority fined Hor two thousand Thai baht, a lot of money. "How can I pay all this money?" Hor asked.

"I don't care; I don't want to hear that. You're the one who ruined my life," I told him.

Lok Bong Phong was still supporting Hor; he told Hor to take me away from the camp — away from Bounchoeurn and his friends, away from my three other brothers.

"Leave me alone," I said to my brother Phong.

But my eldest brother was determined to force me to do what he said. "I'll take her away from this camp, and then you can take her and marry her," *Lok Bong* Phong said to Hor.

Of course, the people in the barrack could hear what he was saying. They told my other three brothers, "If you don't do anything for your sister now, she isn't going to be safe in this camp."

I was afraid to tell Bounchoeurn what had happened during the night, so I asked an elderly woman, who lived in the same barrack, to tell him. When the elderly woman told Bounchoeurn what happened, she asked him if he still wanted to marry me. "If you no longer want to marry Bounriem," she told him, "she will go to live with her aunt, who is outside the camp in the Thai village of Ta Phraya."

"Tell Bounriem not to worry," Bounchoeurn answered. "I still want to marry her."

"If you still want to marry her, then you must do it tonight," the old woman said.

"How can I do it tonight? I don't have anything ready," Bounchoeurn protested.

"It doesn't matter; just do the best you can today and marry her tonight," she explained.

In three or four hours, Bounchoeurn put together the best that he could. He asked his friends to help prepare some food and gave them money to buy chickens and alcohol. Traditionally, a monk performs the marriage ceremony, but because we didn't have enough time to ask a monk to come to the camp, we had the elderly people as witnesses, and the camp teacher pronounced us husband and wife.

So Bounchoeurn and I didn't get to have the wedding we planned. My brothers — Phan, Phin, and Pheav — were ready to protect me from the possibility of *Lok Bong* Phong creating a scene. But my eldest brother didn't come to the wedding. Instead he got very drunk and took the eight hundred Thai baht that Bounchoeurn paid to my family as the traditional Cambodian bride price. The ceremony was short, and only a few people were invited to it — my three brothers, the matchmakers, and friends from both of our barracks. No party, no music, and no good time. Two chickens, soup, and some fruit on a tray — that was our wedding dinner.

My husband didn't tell me until after we were married that he had a wife and family in Cambodia. When he told me that he had been married, he said that probably his wife had died. I believed him. This was the reality for too many people who lived under the Khmer Rouge; if they weren't killed by Angka, they died of starvation, overwork, or lack of medical care. I didn't say anything. My husband then told me he loved me and wanted to be married to me. I said, "OK; I love you, too."

CHAPTER 19

Bounriem: What Will You Do If She Walks in the Camp Tomorrow?

After our marriage I moved into my husband's barrack. Suddenly having to adjust to being a wife and no longer being surrounded by my family and friends, I felt alone. I felt different from the people who lived there. I spoke a northwestern dialect, and they all spoke an eastern or southern dialect. They came from the cities and were educated; I was a country girl with little schooling. I felt like they were judging me, my ideas, and the way I talked. I could hear the wives talking about me through the bamboo walls.

"Why did he marry a girl like that — low class and uneducated? Why did he marry this girl when his wife is still alive?"

They also made me feel bad by telling me that my husband was married and had children. I first learned that my husband already had a wife and children after we were married. But before he told me, a woman whose husband had been a soldier with my husband told me. Most of the people living in that barrack knew my husband when he was in the army, mostly in Preah Vihear. They and their wives knew my husband's first wife Kim.

"It's not my fault," I told the woman. "I didn't know for sure that my husband was already married, and if he was, his wife was probably dead. If you don't feel happy that Bounchoeurn married me, tell him. I don't care. I can divorce him and go back to my family. It's no problem."

"Oh," one wife replied, "We just want to know what you'll do if Kim walks in the camp today or tomorrow?"

"What do you want me to do?" I responded. "I'm not going to live with her. I'm not the kind of person who's going to stay in a situation of one husband with two wives. Forget it. I will leave if she is alive and returns."

The wives thought if Kim came back, my husband would keep me because I was younger and kick Kim out. If Kim showed up, I didn't want my husband to kick her out. I was young and knew I could find another husband. I didn't know if my husband knew that his friends were treating me

152

this way, but he never said anything about it, and I wasn't going to tell him what was happening. I felt that if this woman didn't tell my husband her concerns about Kim, another one would. If any of them said something to my husband, he kept it to himself.

I found life as a married woman very different from the life of the spoiled, youngest child who had been given everything I wanted and needed. In Cambodia my parents had always given me money, even when I didn't ask for it. When living in my aunt's compound in Ta Phraya, I was making money, but my brothers also gave some to me. Then after moving to Lum Pok Camp, my brothers Phan, Phin, and Pheav continued to give me money to be used as I saw fit. I was free to buy food to cook for the family, or I could buy a treat or lunch for myself.

Now my situation had changed. Besides being gone much of the time, my husband never gave me money to spend on whatever I wanted or needed. But I also didn't ask for it. He would leave money on the little table by our bed, but he wouldn't say anything about it, so I didn't touch it. I didn't ask my husband for money to buy food. When he wanted me to buy noodles or whatever he wanted to eat, he would give me money then, but I never asked him for money.

Another source of irritation had to do with cooking. Before our marriage, Bounchoeurn used to pay a woman, who lived in his barrack, to buy food and cook for him. After I arrived, there was trouble in the kitchen. The woman complained to my husband about me. "Your wife did this, she didn't do that; she said this about me; she didn't cook that dish right."

I called her Auntie because she was older. "*Ming*, if I do something wrong, tell me, not my husband." That was a very difficult time for me.

I didn't complain often to my brothers about my marriage. The one time I did, my brother Phan said, "Well, you know ... that's your life. You're the one who chose him. You're the one who wanted to marry him. It's up to you to make it work."

"I know it was my decision to marry him," I replied. "I need to deal with it."

"But if it's too much," *Bong* Phan told me, "you can come back. I'm here."

I felt that only one person connected with my husband was kind to me in the camp. An old family friend, whom he called *Ming*, lived in a different barrack. Her name was Sophal, but we both just called her *Ming*. She took a look at me and decided that I didn't know how to cook well or talk properly like city people did, so she tried to explain to me and teach me how to do things differently. She wanted to help me learn the correct and proper ways of doing things, to be careful and watch other people. When

Ming Sophal went to another area of the camp to help cook for a wedding or birth celebration, she took me with her and asked me to help prep the vegetables and the seasonings, getting all the ingredients together. She was good to me and made me feel valued.

In my brothers' barrack were the people who knew our parents and loved us when we were children. One woman in particular, *Ming* Tun, used to live in Sam Rong village. Her parents were best friends with our parents. When *Ming* Tun escaped from Cambodia to Thailand, she came to Lum Pok Camp and lived in a different barrack, but she saw me there.

"Oh," *Ming* Tun cried, "That's *Ow* Here's daughter!" She recognized the family resemblance between my father San Here and me.

I didn't recognize her because I was small when *Ming* Tun lived in Sam Rong village, but she knew everything about my family. She would often come to visit me, and even though I didn't tell *Ming* Tun, the older woman knew how lonely I was.

Ming Tun talked to me and told me about my family to comfort me. She knew the San family before I was even born, so she told me all the family stories that I didn't know. *Ming* Tun remembered when my oldest brothers were teenagers, and they would all go to the fields to work and play together. It was comforting for me to know that *Ming* Tun had such a close connection to my family.

Ming Tun advised me to be strong and not listen to what the people in the barrack were saying about me. She told me to wait until the time came when I saw them with my own eyes and heard them with my own ears— when they were speaking directly to me — not being heard indirectly through the partition walls.

"Come visit me," *Ming* Tun said. "We can go to the market; we can go to the field and pick up snails; we can catch some lizards to cook and eat; we can pick vegetables from our garden." She advised me to go somewhere away from where I could hear people talk.

I often followed *Ming* Tun's advice and went away from the barrack. When I remained in the barrack, I heard the women talk. The walls were so thin and there were no doors on the rooms. The women would sit around a table and talk, but they didn't invite me to join them. I felt they saw me as coming from a different world. This made me even more unhappy and defensive. When they wanted to know something about me and my family, they would come to my room and ask me.

"Why do you want to know?" I asked them.

"Oh, we just want to know," one woman answered.

"No," I replied, "I don't have anything to tell you."

My husband was mostly gone during the day, coming to me only in the evening. This was not what I thought married life would be. For the first time in my life, I was alone. I was alone during the day when my husband was at work and after dinner when he went out with his friends, a typical behavior of many Cambodian and Thai husbands, I realized, but it was still surprising for me. I was alone at night until my husband returned to our bed. I was miserable.

Changes were also happening to me. Soon I discovered I was pregnant, a frightening realization as a young girl without my mother and feeling very alone. My periods were always very regular, so after I had skipped two periods, I went to one of the midwives. She felt my stomach and asked me some questions and told me she thought I was pregnant. I asked an older lady in my barrack what to do when I was pregnant.

"You can't walk and eat at the same time when you're pregnant," the older woman told me. "Don't sleep too long; you have to get up before your husband. That way you'll never have morning sickness. Don't carry water from the pond because you shouldn't carry heavy things on your shoulders. Don't bend over to walk under the barrack. Don't let your husband wrestle with you and pick you up and throw you on the bed. That might cause a miscarriage."

I listened to what she said because I didn't have my mother to teach me about being pregnant, and I didn't know what to do or expect. I didn't have to tell my husband when I was pregnant because he was able to figure it out. He knew that I hadn't had a period for some time because when I did, I always wore pads and dressed in black so he would know. Since my husband's first wife had already given birth to four children, it wasn't as exciting for him. I didn't tell anyone I was going to have a baby until I was at least three months pregnant. When I finally told my brothers, they were excited and warned me to be careful. They had been around my sisters-in-law when they were pregnant, so they knew what to expect.

Cambodian tradition taught pregnant women to keep warm and rested by lying down and sleeping with a charcoal fire under the bed. The raised beds in the barracks were made of bamboo slats, and a loosely woven mat was placed on top of that, so the heat from the charcoal fire in the bucket under my bed could easily come up and warm me. I wasn't sick, but I stayed in bed for the last three months of my pregnancy. I didn't know about all the medicines and vitamins available to pregnant women in the west. Because my husband had been a medicine man in the army when living in Preah Vihear, he knew I needed vitamins. He went to the pharmacy in Surin and got some vitamins which he gave to me every morning.

I was young and didn't know about having a baby. When my labor pains started, I thought I needed to go to the bathroom. The bathrooms, Asian squat toilets, were located outside the barrack, and I didn't want to go outside because it was quite a walk. Instead I got the shovel to go behind the barrack and dig a hole.

Once I realized that the baby was coming, I called for help. Soon six midwives from within the camp arrived to help me, just as they helped all the women in the camp when it was time to give birth.

"Oh, *Yeay*! I cried. "Oh, *Yeay*, I'm hurting!"

"Give her some rice soup," one of the midwives called to another.

As soon as I was given rice soup, the pains came again. I cried, "I can't eat! I can't eat!"

"Oh, just a little bit; just eat a little bit," the midwife told me. "You need to have strength; you need to eat something."

It was too painful; I couldn't eat. I was vaguely aware that my husband was around, but the midwives wouldn't let him come inside the room.

"You're supposed to stay out," one midwife told him. "You need to prepare the hot water and make sure there is always a charcoal fire for the bucket under the bed."

My brother Phan came to see how I was doing and called to me from the door. "*Neang*! Do you want some fish? I have the fish that you like, *Neang*."

"Oh, yes, please, *Bong* Phan," I begged. "I'm so hungry." But the minute the midwife put the rice and fish in front of me, the pains came again. I couldn't eat.

My labor lasted for three days, and son Piset was born at one o'clock in the morning of the third day. The six midwives stayed the entire time. They took care of me, taught me how to nurse my baby, cooked, cleaned, rested, and took care of each other.

The older people in the barrack told me we had to have a celebration three days after the birth of our baby. It's a tradition that I wasn't familiar with, but we followed that tradition. People brought food, and some people brought little gifts. Most important, though, Piset was blessed by the old people so the evil spirits would not bother him and he would have good luck.

Recovery time in Cambodia is much longer than in the United States. Traditionally, the new mothers rest for a long time to let their bodies heal from the trauma of their bones stretching out of place during birth. They can get up and walk around a bit, take hot showers, eat, and stay warm. I was still lying on my bed over the warm charcoal fire two weeks after Piset's birth.

The women in our barrack took care of Piset and bathed him. The midwives took turns looking after me. I was told by the midwife not to do a lot of work and lift or carry Piset around. While I was lying down, one of the

Cambodian mother and child seated on a woven bamboo bed, similar to the one used by Bounriem Sao and Baby Piset in Lum Pok Refugee Camp, 1981 (photograph by Craig Faustus Buck).

women would bring Piset to me when it was time for him to be fed. Then someone else would take him away again. My brothers took turns cooking for us, so I didn't have to do any work. The people in our barrack were a lot friendlier to me after Piset was born. Many women don't want people to touch their babies after they are born, but not me. I appreciated their help, and they loved Piset. Life was much better for me in our barrack after my baby was born.

CHAPTER 20

Bounchoeurn: You Have to Do It; We Need You

I was still working for the American and Thai intelligence as an interpreter through *Lok* Tep when I met and married Bounriem. Since *Lok* Tep was working for the Americans, the money I earned probably came from the CIA, but I wasn't told that. It was necessary that the work I was doing remain a secret.

Lok Tep had come to visit the camp, parking in front of the administration office in his expensive car, and talked to the administrators about taking care of me, not putting pressure on me, and letting me come and go as I needed. The camp administrators already knew that *Lok* Tep was connected with the CIA, and they knew my background. They assured *Lok* Tep that I would not be harassed.

When refugees who had actually served in the Khmer Rouge organization came to Lum Pok Refugee Camp, my job was to interview them before they were allowed to move into the Khmer Rouge section of the camp. For security reasons and to keep people from settling old grievances, the camp had two sections— the Khmer Rouge section and the non–Khmer Rouge section. The camp administrators kept an eye on them to prevent fights between the two groups. A person was planted in the Khmer Rouge section, the barrack leader, who would take the people one by one to be interviewed by me. The Khmer Rouge refugees didn't know for sure their camp leader was a spy for the camp administrator, but they probably assumed as much.

I interrogated the Khmer Rouge to find out where they had just come from, who their leaders were now, how many of their group were still in Cambodia and where, which Khmer Rouge unit they had served with, what weapons they had in that unit, and who they presently considered to be their real leader in the camp. I didn't formally interview these people, otherwise they would know that I was trying to get information from them. Instead, I talked to them in a relaxed manner about this and that, as I had learned to do in Special Forces, and gradually slipped in the questions I wanted answered. I never took notes because that, too, would alert the newcomers. When I learned important information, I wrote it down after I returned home to my cubicle.

When I learned something of significance, it was important that I report to *Lok* Tep right away, and then *Lok* Tep would report to the Thai and American military and CIA. I assumed it was the CIA because I had worked with *Lok* Tep for a long time, since Preah Vihear, and knew of his relationship with the Americans. The camp authorities, however, didn't want the people in the camp to know about my work.

Sometimes I would go into the city of Surin, meet *Lok* Tep at a hotel, and talk. At other times I would go into Nakhon Ratchasima, commonly known as Khorat, where the United States had one of its seven air bases in Thailand during the Vietnam War. I would check into a specific room in a specific hotel, lock the door, and speak into the tape recorder that was waiting there for me. I would read from my notes everything I knew about the Khmer Rouge — who was still alive, who was leading, their latest locations and weapons — that I had gleaned from my interviews. I'd spend the night and go back to the camp the next morning. When I would check in to the hotel, the receptionist would ask my name. After I said, "Sao Bounchoeurn," I was handed my key. I was never asked any other questions. Possibly the people at the hotel were also working for the CIA.

While I was busy with my job, I continued to visit my friends and play basketball with them. I had grown up as an only child, with parents who were frequently living away at a military post while I attended school. After I joined the army, my life was the life of a soldier, with military friends and little free time to go back to my first wife and children. I had never really been a family man.

Shortly after Bounriem and I were married, an election was held to choose the Cambodian camp leader. All the men in the camp were required to attend the meeting. My name was placed in nomination to be camp leader along with another man's name.

"No, I don't want to be camp leader," I told those assembled. I didn't want to be camp leader because it was a big responsibility; I probably wouldn't be able to continue my job with American and Thai intelligence if I were made camp leader. As it turned out, it worked better for me by refusing this job. They elected the other man to be camp leader, and I breathed a sigh of relief. Then the UN administrator told the group they needed someone to direct the food program. That person needed to be able to speak Thai.

"The only person here who can speak Thai is Bounchoeurn," said one of my colleagues from Preah Vihear.

"No, I don't want to do that," I told the group.

"Well, it doesn't matter if you want to do it or not," the UN administrator said. "You have to do it; we need you."

This was what most of the people wanted. They wanted me to be in charge of food distribution because I had spent a great deal of time working in Thailand and could speak good Thai. Sometimes a Thai business person would get money from the UN but give only bad food to the refugees, like Grade 3 or 4 rice. With my Thai language ability, I could tell the Thai business person, "Unless you give us better rice, I will report you to the UN and not buy food from your company any longer." The Thai trader would agree and bring a better grade of rice to the camp.

As director of the United Nations food program for Lum Pok Refugee Camp, I didn't receive a salary from the UN, but I made an average of one thousand Thai baht a month, making deals on the side, a common practice in Cambodia and Thailand. The United Nations contracted with a rice company in Thailand to provide the equivalent of three kilograms of rice for each person for one week. Every week when the rice was delivered, I made sure it was counted and arranged for its distribution. There were now ten thousand refugees in the camp, each receiving three kilograms of rice, which came in sacks weighing one hundred kilograms each.

I was also overseeing the refugees who went out of the camp to work. When people wanted to leave the camp for work, they would come to me to ask permission to leave and tell me they would be gone for one week, two weeks, or a month. While they were gone, they would not receive their rations of rice. The same amount of rice would be delivered each week to the distribution center, and after I had given out all the rations of rice to the people who were in the camp, I kept and sold the left-over rice. I didn't take it all for myself; I gave some to the camp leader, some to the Thai policemen, and to anyone I needed to pay off to make the system work.

In Surin Province the Thai government would provide funds to build a dam within a certain amount of time, perhaps five months. If the dam wasn't built within that time, the government wouldn't pay for it, so contractors were always looking for cheap, temporary workers. If they couldn't find enough workers on the outside, the contractors would come to the camp administrator to request permission to hire refugee workers. Even though the refugee workers were making only twenty Thai baht a day, the equivalent of a dollar a day at that time, the contractors would also pay for transportation and food. Although this was less than the local Thai laborers made, the refugees inside the camp had nothing to do and no way of making money, so this was a good opportunity for them. They were given food rations inside the camp, but if they wanted to buy clothing, special foods, or cigarettes, they needed to find a job.

Because I was food distribution director, the refugees needed to tell me if they wanted to work on the outside for an extended period of time. The camp administrator told the contractors to contact me when they needed to hire workers. A contractor would tell me he wanted to hire fifty workers a day. I then told the refugees, "Come on; who wants to go to work? Come and register here." The contractor wanted me to be the supervisor of all those refugee workers. He paid me thirty Thai baht a day to provide workers for him.

When Chinese Cambodian refugees came to me, they wanted to go to Bangkok to work in Chinatown. They told me they would pay me one hundred Thai baht to be able to work in Bangkok. Because they needed more time than the regular laborers in Surin, they were willing to pay that much money for the privilege. However, I could let only five go at a time, and they could stay in Bangkok for only two weeks. According to the rules of the UN refugee camps, the refugees were supposed to remain in the camp. They weren't supposed to go outside to work. Periodically, UN officials would come to visit the camp, and they expected to see a certain number of refugees there. If only five Chinese refugees were gone at a time, they wouldn't be missed as easily as a large group. The refugees carried only a refugee camp identification card, so they didn't have the correct papers to go outside to work. The camp administrators knew what was happening, but they closed their eyes and opened their palms to money I paid them. If refugees came and went to work without causing trouble with the Thai authorities, it was not a problem for them. If refugees caused trouble on the outside, the camp administrators would be blamed for not having a secure camp. They depended on me to make the system work. Corruption existed inside the camps as well as outside in Thailand and Cambodia.

When I was given one hundred Thai baht per person from the Chinese refugees, again, I didn't keep all that money. I shared it with those who helped to make a workable system. I saved up the money, using some for myself, but also to help others. If someone had a baby, for example, I would give fifty Thai baht to the family, as a gift from the Food Distribution Program.

As food director I was also the person the road construction contractor would hire to provide workers to build the roads. Each man I sent out received twenty Thai baht a day, and I received five Thai baht a day from the contractor for each worker I sent. When a worker was sick, I still received the money for that worker from the company. In this way I was able to save up money toward the time when I would finally be able to go to America.

I was food distribution director for about seven months until my son Piset was born. During that time I was respected in the camp, and people would do things to help me, like carry water, to ensure that I would remember them if they ever needed help. Even though Bounriem was a country girl with little education, the people in the camp treated her with respect because she was my wife.

With son Piset's birth and the money I had saved, I decided it was time to ask *Lok* Tep again to facilitate our immigration to the United States. Eventually, *Lok* Tep told me that I could apply for immigration and gave me the application to fill out. *Lok* Tep still needed me to work for him, but he agreed that I should be free to leave the camp with my wife and baby. If I had not been married and a father, *Lok* Tep probably wouldn't have helped with my immigration papers and would have had me stay and continue to work for him. By that time I had worked for *Lok* Tep in the Lum Pok Refugee Camp for almost two years, between 1976 and 1978.

It generally took a long time to process the immigration applications because they came from Bangkok and had to be returned to Bangkok. *Lok* Tep went to Bangkok to get the applications to make it easier for the people he was supporting, or who paid him, and he also returned the completed applications to Bangkok. Baby Piset was only two weeks old when the UN and American team came to interview us. I asked Bounriem if she was able to walk to the office to have our pictures taken and answer a few questions. Although Bounriem was frightened about the thought of leaving her brothers and the camp, she assured me she was able to go to the interview. A Cambodian interpreter came along to help with the interview. Many people were waiting to be interviewed; Bounriem and I were the first ones to be called on that day.

Many countries were interviewing refugees. The Australians and Canadians were accepting people who could speak English; the French were accepting people who had worked for the French government and could speak French. The United States didn't care whether the refugee could speak English or not; he must fit into one of the three categories: he had a relative in the United States, he had worked for the United States government, or he had been a soldier in Lon Nol's army.

If a refugee claimed to be a soldier, the interviewers asked many questions about being a soldier: What was your rank? Where did you fight? What kind of weapon was an M-16? How far can it shoot? If a refugee was a parachutist, they asked questions about parachuting: How many times did you jump from an airplane? What did you do after you jumped? How many strings are there on a parachute? The interviewers were making sure the refugee was who he said he was.

If the refugee was unable to answer the questions correctly, the interviewer would say, "I'm sorry; you aren't what we need. You don't fit the right category. Wait until next time."

When it was my turn to be interviewed, they didn't ask me many questions. They had my application paper with my picture on it, and the first question the interviewer asked was, "Is your wife named Kim Heng Sak?"

"Yes, she is," I answered.

"Now your wife is not with you, right?"

"Yes, she is not with me now."

"And you had a total of four children with her?"

"Yes; our first child died when she was just a baby."

"Your mother's name is Bun Kim?"

"Yes, it is."

"And you now have a second family?"

"Yes, I do."

"You know that in the United States, men are not allowed to have two wives. What about your first wife?"

"She died," I said.

"How did that happen?" the interviewer asked.

"She was living in Cambodia. Many people died," I explained. I was surprised at how much they knew about me.

"Were you the team leader for A-5 Special Forces?"

"Yes, I was."

"Are any of those soldiers in this camp?"

"Yes, there are."

"OK, now you can go sit over there," the interpreter said and pointed to a chair.

Next they took a picture of Bounriem and Baby Piset and asked her a few questions.

"What is your name?"

"San Bounriem."

"How many members of your family are alive?"

"I don't know, but I have four brothers living in this camp."

"How many members of your family are dead?"

"I don't know," she responded "but my mother is dead."

Bounriem was allowed to take the baby and go back to the barracks to rest. It was obvious she was still exhausted from recently giving birth. I was asked to remain while my team members were called in for questioning. I was told to say nothing.

"Who was your team leader in A-5 Special Forces?" the interviewer asked.

Each one pointed at me and said, "He was." That response was all that they needed.

Sometime during the interview process, a strange thing happened, possibly due to misunderstandings during translations. After we received our official papers, I discovered that the interviewer had written Bounriem's name as *Bounroeurn*, the name of her oldest brother, and her last name as *Saim* instead of *San*. The year of her birth was also written as 1959, but she was born in 1960. Perhaps this error was because of the difference in the Cambodian and western calendars, where the Cambodian year runs from April through March, but the western calendar goes from January through December. Bounriem knows she was born in The Year of the Rat, which is 1960 on the Cambodian calendar. But the official translator in the camp wrote that her name was *Bounroeurn Saim* and she was born in January of 1959. That was what was then written on her official passport.

Also during the interview, I had been asked if I knew anyone in the United States. I told them my friend Kin Vann, who was with me in the army and also in Special Forces in Preah Vihear, was in Olympia, Washington. He had written a letter to me, telling where he was. Kin Vann was working as a custodian for the Olympia School District at the time. He had been accepted by the United States because he had been a soldier and had been sponsored by Fern Powers of the Lacey Baptist Church, through Church World Services.

That was it. We were accepted for immigration into the United States. I was so happy, but Bounriem was sad because she would leave her brothers behind. I was happy because I knew Piset would have freedom and be able to go to school, but at the same time, I was worried. I could speak some English, but Bounriem had none. We were also worried that we didn't have any relatives in the United States in case something happened. We were happy and worried at the same time.

After we were accepted for immigration, I wrote back to Kin Vann to tell him we were going to the United States, but I didn't know which place. I asked him if he thought Fern Powers would sponsor us, too. Kin Vann took our names to his sponsor; she wrote a letter to the United Nations High Commissioner for Refugees (UNHCR) at the camp, gave them our names, and said she would sponsor me and my family.

We were finally on our way to Olympia, Washington, U.S.A.!

CHAPTER 21

Bounriem: Everything Will Be Fine

Before we could leave Lum Pok Refugee Camp, Piset needed to be old enough to safely travel. He had to be at least four months old. By that time I was stronger, and Piset was growing and healthy, too. He was crawling like a cricket when we finally left the camp to go to the United States.

I didn't want to leave the camp. When the bus came to get us, I felt like I died again. First, I lost my mother when she died, then I lost my father and oldest brothers and sister when my three youngest brothers and I left Cambodia for Thailand. Then I lost my grandmother, aunt and cousins when we went to the refugee camp. Now I had to say good bye to *Bong* Phan, *Bong* Phin, and *Bong* Pheav. My third oldest brother *Lok Bong* Phong never came to say goodbye to me. He didn't come near me. That hurt, but it hurt more when I had to leave my other brothers—they were the only family I knew I had left.

When we left the refugee camp, five of my husband's friends were also on the bus. The men helped take care of Piset for me. I didn't know where my baby was on the bus because I was crying the entire time. As the bus pulled away from Lum Pok, my brothers shouted to me, "We will follow you; we will follow you!" but I didn't believe it. I thought I would be so far away that I would never see them again. I didn't know where I was going; I knew only that it was going to be a different world. I knew nothing about the United States and never dreamed I'd be going there. I had never seen pictures or movies or even a map of the world with the United States, Cambodia and Thailand on it. All I could think of was the spoiled, little girl I used to be, who had been surrounded by my large and loving San family of thirteen, had become, in a matter of months, the wife of a former soldier and mother of a baby in the small Sao family of three.

When the bus finally left the refugee camp in Surin, after an all-day bus ride, we were taken to the Din Daeng Transition Center in Bangkok to wait for our flight. We weren't there long, but we had to have physical exams before we could leave. Those people who didn't pass the physicals were either treated at Din Daeng until they were well enough to go, or they were sent back to Lum Pok Camp to get well. My husband, Piset, and I all passed our physicals.

I met a sweet, old lady who had a cubicle to herself at Din Daeng. Her name was Peo, so I called her *Yeay* Peo. She had been waiting a long time for her name to be announced for departure, so she was lucky to have a little cubicle that was off on the side, but open to the larger room where everyone else slept. We all slept on the floor. There was no platform built up off the floor to sleep on, like we had at Lum Pok Camp. There was no mat; we were given a used blanket and a mosquito net. That's all. If someone had money, that person could buy a pillow and a blanket that looked new. My husband was carrying money, but he didn't want to buy a pillow and a blanket. He knew we would soon leave for the United States, so he didn't want to have to deal with bedding and wanted to save money for our new life in America.

When we first arrived, *Yeay* Peo talked to my husband and told him about the cubicle. He told her we didn't have one yet, and he needed to go find one for his wife and baby. *Yeay* Peo told him not to worry; Piset and I could sleep with her because she was by herself. I slept with her inside her mosquito net with Piset between us, where *Yeay* Peo wanted him. The cubicle was large enough for only the three of us, so my husband went upstairs to sleep with the single men.

I was feeling exhausted and miserable. Piset was crying all the time because he was hungry, but I didn't have enough milk to satisfy him. I was homesick and missed my family. I told one of my husband's friends, "You know, I want to go back. *Poo,* can you help me? I want to go back to Lum Pok."

This kind man very gently told me, "*Neang,* you have to go. That is your life. You have to go with your husband and baby."

All the people in Din Daeng were good and kind to me, especially *Yeay* Peo. She helped me take care of Piset the most. My husband's friends were also kind and helpful. They took turns helping take care of Piset, watching him crawl everywhere. One of the places where Piset liked to crawl was the bathroom where the people took showers. In the bathroom was a sewer pipe big enough that Piset could crawl into it, so someone always had to keep an eye on the baby. We were like one big family, helping to make me feel a little less homesick for my brothers.

The food in Din Daeng wasn't good — cafeteria food. The kitchen had to serve all the refugees — Cambodian, Lao, and Vietnamese — but the only food that tasted good was the rice. The men would all go get rice together, and we ate lunch and dinner as a big family, including *Yeay* Peo. But the food was so bad, I said to one of our friends, "*Poo,* what are we going to eat? This food is so bad."

The soup would have whole stalks of lemon grass in it — like my family gave animals to eat — not cut up in small pieces. And the vegetables looked like they hadn't been washed — just thrown in the pot and cooked too long. After only a couple of meals, I said, "I can't eat this."

My husband saw that I wasn't eating, so he asked what was wrong. I told him, "I don't ask you for money to buy things, but I want you to buy me something to eat."

"What do you want?" he asked me.

"I don't care — as long as it isn't this," I replied.

Since my husband had wisely saved money to go to the United States, he was able to buy food from the Thai vendors who set up food stalls outside. Our friends didn't have money, though, so my husband shared the better food with them as well. He and our friends went outside and bought from the vendors — barbecued chicken, fried fish, curry, and soup. From seven o'clock in the morning until five o'clock in the afternoon, refugees were allowed to go outside the gate to buy whatever we wanted to go with the rice we were given from Din Daeng. It was much better than the cafeteria food and made all of us feel better.

One day my husband hired a taxi to take us on a tour into Bangkok's center to visit Wat Phra Kaew, the Temple of the Emerald Buddha, and the Royal Palace. Our friend *Yeay* Peo accompanied us. It was exciting to be able to see those famous places, but I wasn't happy. Piset was hungry all the time, and I couldn't nurse him in public. I nursed him every time we got in a taxi, but it wasn't enough. Piset cried. We walked a lot, Piset was heavy, and it was hot and humid. We were used to the heat and humidity, but we weren't used to carrying Piset around when it was so hot.

Yeay Peo treated me like a daughter and helped me day and night. Sometimes one or two of our friends couldn't sleep, so they would come down to the first floor to help me take care of Piset. But with my husband sleeping upstairs, I was still lonely. It seemed like the only time I saw him was at meal times. It made me sad. I didn't want to go to America. I wanted to go back with my baby to my brothers.

Once again, I told our friend, "*Poo*, if I can go back, I will give all my jewelry." I still had the gold necklace, bracelets and earrings that my parents had given me. I was willing to give it all away if I could go back and be with my brothers. Again he told me I couldn't go back. "You and your baby need to go on to America with your husband."

We stayed at Din Daeng only about three weeks. Each morning all the refugees would look at the blackboard to see if their names had been written down with the date of their departure. One morning "Sao Family leaves tomorrow morning" was written on the board. The next morning our name was erased. This happened twice. There were many cancellations. When my husband asked about it, he had to pay a bribe to the man in charge of the board to get our name back on the board. Some people had to stay in Din Daeng for over a year. This was a corrupt system.

When one lady heard that we were finally going to leave for the United States, she said, "Oh, *Neang*, you're so lucky. My family has been waiting for two years."

"What's wrong?" I asked.

"Oh, we were told our sponsor didn't respond yet, so we are still waiting to get out of here," she answered.

Another woman told me, "Our son didn't pass the physical, so we're waiting for him to get healthy. We can't go back to Lum Pok, and we can't go to the United States. We're stuck here in Din Daeng."

Finally, our family was allowed to go to the airport to fly to the United States. My husband had flown many times, but I had never flown, so I was frightened. During the war American planes used to fly over my family's rice fields. We watched them. When I saw the planes at the airport, I thought maybe I would fly on the same airplane that flew over my family home in Cambodia. Even though the international airplanes were much bigger than the military planes I had watched fly over Cambodia, I couldn't believe one plane could hold all the people in our group and fly over the ocean. "Oh, that's too small. How can it fly? How long am I going to be in this airplane?" I cried.

"Don't worry; everything will be fine," my husband assured me.

Yeay Peo departed Din Daeng on the same day we did and flew on the same airplanes to Los Angeles, but she flew on to Portland, Oregon, to be with her son. Much later *Yeay* Peo came to visit me in Olympia. We were happy to see each other again, and she was delighted to see how Piset had grown.

We didn't know where our friends were going. We left Bangkok first, and our friends left later on different airplanes, so we didn't know where they went. We had hoped to find them again, but we never did.

CHAPTER 22

Bounchoeurn:
Going to America

When we boarded the airplane, we saw many refugees, but when we talked to some of them, they couldn't speak our language. There were Vietnamese, Lao, Hmong, as well as Cambodians, going to America.

On the airplanes we were still served rice, since we were flying from Asian countries, but none of us knew how to eat the western food they gave us. We just wanted to drink the liquids. Because we were hungry, though, we ate what was given to us. After tasting a new dish, if we couldn't eat it, we left it. We didn't know what some of the dishes were, and we didn't understand the little packets of salt and pepper. Bounriem and I could eat the bread, but we couldn't eat the mashed potatoes and gravy.

Besides western food, the refugees were introduced to western bathrooms in the airports and on the airplanes. I had seen a western toilet in Hua Hin when I was being trained by the Thai soldiers in Morse code, but I was the only one. Since the majority of toilets in Asian countries were squat toilets, when the refugee men went into the airport restrooms, they perched up on top of the toilet seats. One man accidentally hit the lever that flushes the toilet with his elbow. He was frightened and came running out of the stall. I was able to explain to him how the toilet worked.

Bounriem had a difficult time using the restroom on the airplane. She didn't know how to push the handle to open the door, and I was back in my seat with Piset, so she had to ask the flight attendant for help. The attendant showed her how, so she could help others who asked her how to use the bathroom. She would walk to the back and show the woman, or when a flight attendant came by, Bounriem would motion that a refugee needed help, and the attendant would take that person to the bathroom. There were so many things that were new to all of us.

When we landed in Hong Kong, the airline took all the refugees into the city and put us up in a hotel. We had to ride a bus through the tunnel that goes under the harbor. That was the most frightening experience for everyone. We had never done or seen anything like that before. No one said a word; we were too frightened to speak.

When we finally reached the hotel, we were taken to an elevator. Again, no one had ever seen or used an elevator, and we didn't know how it worked. Fortunately, the airline attendant came, pushed the right buttons, and took us where we needed to go. We had already experienced the western toilets in the airport and on the airplane, but now we were faced with the showers and sinks in our hotel bathrooms. None of the refugees knew how to turn the water on and off or change it from hot to cold to warm. Once I figured it out, I showed Bounriem what to do, and then we helped the other refugees use the faucets. No one from the hotel showed us what to do.

Next door to our hotel room was an elderly Hmong woman all by herself, from one of the Lao hill tribes. I learned by looking at her immigration papers that she was going to live with her children who were already in America. She could speak only Hmong and couldn't communicate with anyone. We heard her crying and crying; she was so lonely and frightened. When we went next door to try to help her, she followed us back into our room and lay down on the floor and cried. There she stayed. Bounriem put a pillow under her head and I covered her with a blanket. In the morning I went downstairs to get food to bring upstairs for Bounriem and the Hmong woman. Bounriem showed her how to use the toilet, sink and shower.

Along the way we all encountered many strange and confusing experiences. In Cambodia and Thailand, and probably also in Laos and Vietnam, babies didn't wear diapers, so Piset and the other refugee babies weren't wearing them. On the flight out of Tokyo, the flight attendants brought disposable diapers for the refugee babies. Because Bounriem was sleeping, the flight attendant took Piset away to diaper him.

At the same time, other refugee families were given diapers for their babies. None of them knew what to do with the diapers, and the flight attendants spoke only English and Japanese, so the refugees couldn't ask for help. One Lao father thought the diaper was supposed to be a hat, so he put it on his baby's head. A Vietnamese parent saw that and decided the diaper should be a hat, too.

When the flight attendant came back with Piset, she saw what had happened. Soon all the flight attendants were helping the parents to diaper the babies correctly. The poor Lao baby cried and cried when the stewardess took the diaper off his head; the tape stuck to his hair and pulled. I was glad the flight attendant had taken Piset to put the diaper on him, or I would have made the same mistake. We didn't know; we didn't understand.

Because our group of refugees, as well as earlier groups, had so many problems encountering western ways, food and technology, the Din Daeng Transition Camp was closed down. From then on all the refugees were first sent to a camp in the Philippines for six months to learn English and western ways.

When we landed in Los Angeles, I didn't think about finally being in the United States. I was worried because I didn't know anyone and couldn't speak very much English. We had to wait in the airport for four hours before flying to Seattle. A United Nations representative took us to an area to sit and wait, but we didn't know where the restrooms were and we didn't know how to ask. Another representative came to ask me if I wanted to go to the restaurant to eat. I had never heard the English word for restaurant and I didn't understand, so I said, "No," and went to lie down on a bench and sleep.

Another United Nations agent came to ask in English if this group of people were the refugees; some of the Vietnamese refugees could speak English and understood that she was going to take them to eat lunch. One of the Vietnamese women could also speak Thai, and, as it turned out, Bounriem could speak some Thai, so the Vietnamese woman told her what the UN woman had said, and asked if Bounriem had any other family members. Bounriem told her she had her husband and son. The Vietnamese woman told her to go get me.

Bounriem come over to me and woke me up. We now called each other Mother of Piset and Father of Piset. "*Pa* Piset," she said to me, "the Vietnamese woman told me they were going to feed us, and we're supposed to go have lunch now."

"I don't believe you, *Mae* Piset," I told her. "Nobody's going to buy us lunch. I'm not going to go."

"If you're not going to go, you take Piset," Bounriem said. "I'm going to go eat lunch with the other refugees."

After they had eaten, the UN agent asked if there were any other refugees that hadn't eaten. The Vietnamese woman who could speak Thai told the agent that Bounriem's husband was over on the bench taking care of their baby. The agent told Bounriem, with the help of the Vietnamese woman, to get a tray of food and take it to me. When Bounriem brought me a tray of food, I was surprised and wanted to know what happened. As she explained to me, I was confused.

"You don't understand Thai, so how did you know?" I asked my wife.

"*Pa* Piset, I lived in Thailand. I didn't tell you that I understand, but I know how to survive in Thailand," Bounriem replied.

We were both lucky my wife could speak some Thai and the United Nations was looking after the refugees.

While we were sitting and waiting in the Los Angeles airport, all the refugees were given I-94 immigration forms. Our family was the last group of refugees to leave Los Angeles that day. All the other refugees had already made their connecting flights to other parts of the country, like Portland, Oregon, and Chicago, Illinois. Later, after we flew to Seattle, while we were waiting in Sea-Tac Airport, I was sitting next to a single Vietnamese man; he saw that my I-94 form said Olympia, Washington. He showed me that his form also said Olympia, Washington, and that we had the same sponsor, Fern Powers. The Vietnamese man's flight to Olympia left earlier than ours, so when he met Mrs. Powers, he told her that he had met a Cambodian family in the Seattle airport who were also sponsored by her. Mrs. Powers hadn't known when our family would be arriving, but she was happy to wait for us.

When we finally arrived at the Olympia airport, Fern Powers was waiting. Bounriem was so happy to stop flying, and so was I, but I was worried about what we were going to do. Mrs. Powers took us to her home, where we spent our first week in America. After that we went to stay with my friend Kin Vann until the federal assistance money arrived. Once it arrived, we were able to rent an apartment at the 1717 Cooper Point Road apartment complex, furnished by items given to us by the Lacey Baptist Church, where Mrs. Powers was a member. This apartment complex had many Vietnamese refugees already living there.

Bounchoeurn Sao standing in front of the Space Needle in Seattle, Washington, 1979 (photograph from the personal collection of Bounchoeurn and Diyana Sao).

After all the church people had gone and I shut the door of our new apartment, Bounriem and I breathed a sigh of relief. Even though we still had many challenges ahead of us, like learning English and finding a job, we were safely in America. Our son Piset would have an education and freedom.

CHAPTER 23

Bounchoeurn:
We Didn't Understand

When Bounriem, Piset, and I first arrived in Olympia, the government helped us for one year. The government gave us $250 a month for three people. They also gave us $75 a month worth of food stamps, and we paid only $90 a month for our apartment. We had enough because many people helped us when we first came, especially the Lacey Baptist Church, through Church World Services, by donating clothing, furniture, pots and pans.

After the first week in Olympia at the Powers' home, we moved to my friend Kin Vann's apartment in the complex across the street from Jefferson Middle School on Conger Street. At that time only one family was allowed to live in a single apartment. We needed to move, but it took over a month before an apartment was available.

While I was waiting for the government to process papers for us, I couldn't communicate well enough, so I needed someone to translate for me. I had been treated rudely by a Cambodian translator at the Department of Social and Health Services (DSHS) when I asked the man for help filling out my papers for the government. The DSHS employee was having his lunch hour at the time, so he refused to help me. That made me angry; I vowed to learn English as quickly and as well as I could, so I could take care of myself and family and help others who were in need.

Finally, Fern Powers found a two-bedroom apartment available at 1717 Cooper Point Road, but she didn't want us to stay there because the complex was isolated and not close to stores, up on the hill in the forest by itself. At that time Capital Mall was just starting to be built, and there was no bus service. Since there was nothing else available, we moved into 1717 along with several other Cambodian families.

When we needed groceries, we had to walk down to Black Lake Boulevard, and then down Division Street to Mark-It Foods, now called Bayview Thriftway, a distance of at least three miles. At Mark-It Foods, shoppers had

173

to mark the price with a black crayon on the items before taking them to the checkout counter. I didn't understand this, didn't know what to do, and was scared, but Olympia was such a peaceful, friendly town that many people tried to help me and my family, including a stranger at Mark-It Foods who showed me what to do.

I had my young wife and baby to protect, and I worried about the long walks up and down the hills, one of us carrying Piset, and one of us carrying the bag of groceries. Often someone would stop the car and ask us where we were going. The first time it happened, I was nervous, but when I said, "1717 Cooper Point Road," the person answered, "OK, get in; I'll take you there." Until I had a car, we were often given a ride.

The Bon Marche department store was the first one to open at Capital Mall, so I walked there to buy a small, black and white TV and carried it back up the hill to our apartment. We were lonely and there was nothing to do, so we wanted to be able to watch TV and to work on understanding the English we heard on the television.

When I started going to school, I first went to Olympia Technical Community College (OTCC), which is now South Puget Sound Community College. I tried very hard to learn, coming home from class to study, asking and answering the questions to myself. When Bounriem asked me why I was talking to myself, I told her I was trying to learn English quickly. I made the spare bedroom my study; I went in there, closed the door, and asked and answered myself in English. Most of the refugees were shy, but I decided not to be shy. When I went to class, I spoke up and asked questions about words and phrases I didn't understand. When I heard a phrase on TV that I didn't understand, I asked someone what it meant. Teachers were kind to me and wanted to help me learn English.

Other refugees studied in the OTCC classes with me, but they didn't learn English as quickly. Bounriem and I lived in an apartment at the back of the 1717 complex, facing the forest, while the others lived in a central location. When the refugee men came home from class, the others would stop and buy beer and get together, but we were isolated, so I wasn't distracted and could study more.

In order to go to class at OTCC, I had to apply for a basic grant. I was told by my advisor that I could apply for a student loan. I didn't know what that meant, but I signed the paper where I was told to sign. Then the financial aid person gave me $700; I didn't understand about this money. I was told to go ahead and use it to buy books, so I did. When a new session started, I was given money again. I didn't understand what was happening.

When I finished my classes, the college sent me a bill, saying I owed money. "No," I said. "I did not ask for this money. You told me to sign the paper, but I didn't understand what I was signing. No one explained it to me. I thought the government or the school was giving me this money."

The college waived the payment and I didn't have to pay back the student loan because I complained and fought it. But my friends had to pay the money back on their student loans. If they had complained and fought back, probably they would have had their student loans waived, too.

After studying at OTCC for a while, I heard there were also extra English classes at St. John's Episcopal Church in the afternoon, so I went to those classes, too. The St. John's classes were free, but the refugees had to have a certain level of English to go there. There weren't any beginning classes. After six months at the community college, I was good enough to go to the free classes at St. John's.

After I had been at St. John's for about four months, Mr. Rick Bird, the ESL director for the Olympia School District, came to find someone who could work as an educational assistant (EA) to help with the refugee students in the Olympia schools. He came while the students were all outside having a smoke break. When Rick stood up on the rear bumper of his car and asked for anyone who could speak English, Thai, Lao, and Cambodian, the refugee men turned and looked at me because they knew I could do it. Nervously, I raised my hand.

My first job was with the Olympia School District as an educational assistant for the refugee students at Garfield Elementary, Jefferson Middle, and Capital High Schools. I eventually worked full time during the school year and earned much more than minimum wage, plus medical benefits. I also did work study as a custodian at the community college, where I was paid $2.50 an hour, minimum wage at the time. After we had been in Olympia a year, many more Cambodians had been sponsored by the churches, and someone was needed to translate for them. The new refugees asked me to help and I became their translator.

Eventually, the larger Olympia community found out that I was a translator, so they called the school district to ask for my help. They didn't call me directly. When the hospital or police station needed a translator for a Cambodian or Lao refugee, they called the school district and one of my principals would call me. Often it was during the school day, so the principal would release me from my classes. At other times I was called in the middle of the night when the police had arrested a non–English-speaking Cambodian or Lao refugee. All of this translation was done for free. No one ever paid me for translating. The school district paid me for my EA job and for translating at parent teacher conferences, and OTCC paid me for my work study job, but translating for the community was all volunteer work. Sometimes the police would say they would pay me for my time, but they never did. Occasionally,

I would say I couldn't come in the middle of the night because I was too tired, but the person would say, "Oh, please come; we have no one else to help us." And so I did.

Twice I was honored for my volunteer service with invitations for dinner and a tour of the governor's mansion. Both Governor Booth Gardner and Governor Mike Lowery invited me to the mansion. Once when I took my refugee students on a tour of the State Capitol building, we were visiting the office of then Secretary of State Ralph Munro. Secretary Munro told the students his ancestors had not been born in the United States, but had come over from Scotland. They helped to build the capitol building where the students were standing. The Scottish immigrants never dreamed that one day their descendant would be sitting and working in the very building they constructed. My students and I heard Secretary Munro's advice that through hard work and determination, we, too, could achieve our goals. I never forgot that advice.

One day I was at Garfield Elementary talking to ESL Director Rick Bird. Rick asked me what was in my shirt pocket because it was a very big packet.

"It's my money," I replied.

"How much do you have in there?" asked Rick.

"Eight thousand dollars," I told him.

"Eight thousand dollars! Bounchoeurn, you can't carry that much money around!" Rick gasped.

"I don't have anywhere to put it," I answered.

"You need to put your money in the bank," Rick explained.

I didn't trust the bank, but I went with Rick to the bank downtown and opened an account where I could keep my money. Later I took Bounriem down to the bank to sign her name on the joint account. I told her I wasn't sure if this was a good idea, but Rick told me I needed to do it. Now I feel comfortable having my money in the bank, but at the time, I didn't.

Not too long after that, I was assisting my students, including Sareth Oung, a new Cambodian girl at Jefferson Middle School. During break time the refugee students were talking, and I was half listening as I sat preparing the next lesson. Sareth told the other students that her cousin had married a widow whose son had the most unusual name. This boy was about eight years old, so the Khmer Rouge thought he was old enough to go with the other children to work, collecting cow dung in the fields. His name was Bdei, which means *husband* in Cambodian, so while the children were out in the fields, all the girls teased him and called him all the time, "*Bdei, Bdei!* Husband, Husband!"

I couldn't believe my ears. "My son's nickname is Bdei!" I exclaimed.

"Oh, really?" Sareth asked.

I took a picture out of my wallet and showed it to her. "This is my son Cheally. His nickname is Bdei," I explained.

"Yes, that's Bdei!" Sareth exclaimed.

Then I took out the picture of my first wife and showed Sareth. "This is my wife Kim Heng."

"Oh, yes! I know her! She married my cousin," answered Sareth. "May I borrow this picture and take it to show my family?"

"Yes, go ahead and take it," I told her. Sareth had come to America with a group of orphans and a minister from the Alliance Church, who happened to be her uncle, Un Oung. Sareth knew only my son Bdei and my first wife Kim. She didn't know my other two children — daughter Amarin and son Ketesak. I couldn't believe the coincidence — I found out that Kim and Bdei were still alive from my student at Jefferson Middle School in Olympia, Washington. I was so relieved and happy — my son and first wife had survived — but what about my other two children? And I had mixed emotions — Bdei and Kim were alive, but now I had a new life and a new family. I would have to tell Bounriem.

I found out much later that when the Khmer Rouge took power, they evacuated the city of Pailin, where Kim and the children had been visiting her uncle. They were sent to work in the countryside in Battambang, to the village where Sareth was living. My youngest child Ketesak was only about five months old when the Khmer Rouge took power. He died of malnutrition because the people didn't have enough to eat. My daughter Amarin, who was about three at the time, was also suffering from malnutrition. When the Khmer Rouge sent Kim out to the fields to work, Amarin cried and cried. When she wouldn't stop crying, one of the Khmer Rouge soldiers began whipping her with a wire whip; the ends of the whip cut into her stomach. Amarin complained that her stomach was hurting; a week later she died. It broke my heart to hear this terrible news about my babies.

CHAPTER 24

Bounriem: Reunited with Family

When we first arrived in Olympia, I went to English classes at Lacey Baptist Church, three days a week for two hours a day. I took Piset with me. The pastor's wife, Grace Hannah, picked us up at our apartment and took us to the classes at the church. I studied English in that class until I was pregnant with my second child.

I nursed Piset, as Cambodian mothers always do, but only until we arrived in America. Then I tried to make him drink from a bottle, but he cried and cried for three weeks. I decided to stop nursing because I was so thin, and there was plenty of milk available to buy for Piset, so he could have as much as he wanted. Because I had not yet begun having periods after Piset's birth, I did not think I would be able to get pregnant, but about three months after Piset stopped nursing, I became pregnant. I didn't know I was pregnant until I started having morning sickness. I was so sick I went to the doctor, who did some tests.

"Do you want a boy or a girl?" the doctor asked.

I didn't understand what he said, so the translator said to me, "*Ming*, do you want a boy or a girl?"

"What?" I asked. "What boy? What girl?"

"*Ming*," the translator explained, "You are three weeks along already."

"What three weeks?" I demanded, shocked at what I was hearing. I didn't want another baby right then. I told the translator to ask the doctor, "What should I do? I don't want to be pregnant now. My life isn't easy."

"Have you had a miscarriage since the birth of your son?" the doctor asked me.

"No, I haven't," I answered.

"Would you love to have a girl?" the doctor continued.

"Yes, I'd love to have a girl," I agreed.

Then the doctor told me, "You can listen to me or not. Since you've never had an abortion or miscarriage, if you keep this baby, you will have a girl. Go ahead and keep this one; you will have a girl like you wish." I believed him.

Bounriem Sao with son Piset and daughter Annmarie in Olympia, Washington, circa 1982 (photograph from the personal collection of Bounchoeurn and Diyana Sao).

During my pregnancy, the doctor wanted me to have a checkup once a month, but I told him I didn't want to do that — he didn't give me anything, so why go? I just wanted to stay relaxed. I told the translator to tell the doctor that if anything went wrong, then I would call him. Otherwise, I would stay home. The doctor's pronouncement came true; he delivered our daughter Annmarie. Our children are one year apart — Piset was born in February of 1978, and Annmarie was born in May of 1979.

In the middle of my pregnancy with Annmarie, I started working at the daycare at St. John's church. This daycare was run for the refugees who were taking the four-hour English classes. The children there were refugee children. The DSHS paid me to care for those children. I took care of children for four hours, and then I studied English for four hours, while someone else took care of the children, including my own. After Annmarie's birth, the daycare moved to a new location over by the Olympia Brewery, called Dee's Day Care, no longer run by the church. The owner, named Dee, paid me minimum wage to work there. I could no longer take English classes at St. John's because there was no one to take care of my children. If I left my children at Dee's Day Care, I would have to pay. I was working only four hours a day, the maximum allowed me by DSHS, and I couldn't afford to pay for my children to stay there.

During this time, the International Refugee Commission (IRC) started closing down the refugee camps in Surin, Thailand, in 1980, after the Vietnamese army had liberated Cambodia from the Khmer Rouge rule in 1979. The IRC began interviewing all the families in Lum Pok Refugee Camp to be sent, hopefully, to western countries.

When the interview team talked to my brother *Lok Bong* Phong, the translator asked him, "Do you want to become a Thai citizen or go to another country? Do you have a brother or sister who is living in a third country, like the United States or France?"

Lok Bong Phong answered, "Oh, I have a sister that's living in the United States."

"What's her name? What's her husband's name?" the translator asked.

Lok Bong Phong gave them our names, and the interviewer looked them up in their records to see that we had already immigrated to America. *Lok Bong* Phong had no idea that the IRC in Surin, Thailand, would send him to the IRC in Seattle, Washington, because we were living in Olympia.

The Seattle IRC called me and asked, "Do you have a brother named San Phong?"

"Oh, yes!" I answered. "That's my brother." I couldn't believe a stranger was asking me about *Lok Bong* Phong.

"He's here in Seattle," the agent replied.

This was the brother who did not come to tell me goodbye when we left Lum Pok; we had not been speaking to each other then, but I was overjoyed to hear that someone from my family was now in the United States.

I called my husband and excitedly told him, "My brother's here! I haven't heard about him since we left! I'm so happy! I want my brother to come here!"

So my husband borrowed a car to drive up to Seattle to bring *Lok Bong* Phong and his family to Olympia. When they arrived, they stayed with us until the applications for welfare, money, medical coverage, and an apartment were filled out and processed.

When I first saw *Lok Bong* Phong, I felt like my life had been given back to me. It was so good to have my family with me again. Even though it was a lot of work to have my brother, sister-in-law *Jae*, and children staying with us, having my family here was worth it.

An apartment was found for *Lok Bong* Phong over on the Yelm Highway. It was quiet over there with all the evergreen trees around. When they moved, I continued to visit my brother and his family. We were talking to each other now; I had missed them so much. *Lok Bong* Phong's children were still young, and I enjoyed being around my niece and nephew. My brother still drank and smoked, but I decided that was his life and who he was. It was good for me to have them in the community; I felt supported and was much happier than before their arrival.

I never imagined that my brother Phan would come to Olympia, too. Even though the four brothers were in the same refugee camp, the authorities treated each one as a separate case. *Lok Bong* Phong and his family had moved to a different barrack, and they were treated as one family. *Bong* Phan was treated as a separate case because he was single. *Bong* Pheav was no longer living in the camp when the IRC came to interview people. He had been living for some time with a Thai family, married a Thai teacher, and become a Thai citizen. *Bong* Phin decided to go back to Cambodia and join the resistance army, fighting against the Khmer Rouge. *Lok Bong* Phong told me about my brothers—one marrying a Thai girl and the other becoming a Cambodian soldier. But he couldn't tell me much about Phan. *Lok Bong* Phong knew that *Bong* Phan had an interview with the IRC, but he didn't know where *Bong* Phan had gone after that.

Shortly after *Lok Bong* Phong's arrival, I received another phone call from the Seattle IRC, asking, "Do you have a brother named San Phan?"

"Yes! Yes, I do! That's my brother!" I screamed.

My brother Phan had arrived in Seattle with a family of Lao refugees that were now his friends, so they came along with him to our house in Olympia. I was even happier to see *Bong* Phan, but I had to scold him a bit first. "If you wanted to come to America, why didn't you come with me when I first came, instead of making me feel so miserable, missing my family?"

Bong Phan teased me back, saying, "Oh, it was good for you and made you stronger. You had been spoiled too much."

"Oh, thank you so much, *Bong*," I replied. "Thanks; I wanted my life to be like before — not the life I've been living since I left Lum Pok. It's been so hard for me."

"See, *Mii Own*," he told me, "Now you've learned more than I have."

"I don't want to learn more than you do," I told him. "It's been difficult, and I've felt dead for a long time — since I left you in the camp, until the day I see you now. First I saw our older brother, and now I see you. And how many years have I been dying here by myself, missing my father and my brothers? I sit down with my baby in front of the little black and white TV, but my mind is not with it. My soul is gone. Why am I here? Nobody is around us. My husband has been like a fish in the water, going here and going there, working two jobs and helping refugees. I am born again with my brothers in Olympia."

"*Mii Own*, you've been living quite well. I'm looking at your big apartment full of possessions and at your two healthy, happy children; I'm thinking of the important work Bounchoeurn is doing in Olympia; and I'm remembering our family's lives back in Lum Pok Refugee Camp, in Ta Phraya, Thailand, and in Sam Rong, Cambodia." *Bong* Phan just looked at me and smiled.

My brother Phan lived with us for a while when he first came to the United States, but then he married Ham, the Lao girl from the family who came to Olympia with him. They went to school together to learn English and fell in love. After they married, *Bong* Phan, Ham, and her three sons from a previous marriage moved to California with her family, and I lost my brother for a time. He stayed married to Ham until her sons had grown up to become young men and have families of their own. Then my brother separated from her. It was probably because of his drinking problem. Just like *Lok Bong* Phong, my brother Phan was an alcoholic.

Lok Bong Phong had a close friend who lived in Aberdeen, Washington. Wanting to live near his friend, *Lok Bong* Phong decided to move to Aberdeen in 1981. The Aberdeen friend helped him move there, find a place to live, and sign up with the welfare department in that town. My brother Phong and his family moved to Aberdeen, where they are living still.

Around that time I began working at Godfather's Pizza, which had just opened up on the west side, taking care of the children during the day while my husband was at work, then leaving for work in the evening after he came home. By then we had moved from Cooper Point Road to a larger apartment over on Lily Road near St. Peter's Hospital in Lacey. When I started working at Godfather's, I had to take the bus across town. The older lady in the apartment upstairs, I called her *Yeay*, took care of the children until my husband came home from work.

While working at Godfather's Pizza, I received my green card and decided to legally change my name. The Americans who worked with me had trouble saying *Bounroeurn* and started calling me *Sam*, since my green card had my name as *Bounroeurn Saim*. I didn't want to be *Sam*, and my brother back in Cambodia was *Bounroeurn*, so I wanted an American name. My name is now Diyana D. Sao.

In 1983 while I was still working at Godfather's Pizza in the evening, I worked full-time during the day at Kentucky Fried Chicken. Because my husband was also working at the same time, *Yeay* took care of Piset and Annmarie in her upstairs apartment. It was difficult to be away from my children when I was working two jobs, but it was what I needed to do. I wanted to be independent and able to provide for my family. If I wanted to buy something for my children or for me, I wanted to have my own money and the freedom to do whatever I wanted. I was saving for my children's education and also to buy a house. We didn't want to have to borrow a lot of money from the bank.

Because I was still making only minimum wage at both restaurants, I applied for work at an oyster company out on the bay in Lacey when Piset started school. Of all the jobs I've done, shucking oysters was the most difficult and the job I liked the least. We wore big, thick rubber gloves to protect our hands and shucked as fast and as safely as we could in order not to cut ourselves with the oyster knife. We were paid $3.50 a gallon, and our boss didn't want us to shuck more than ten gallons in one day. I worked there part-time for several months until I was hired by Ostrom Mushroom Farms, also in Lacey, where I worked in the lab preparing mushroom spawn.

I wouldn't say I liked any of the jobs I had, but I liked working at Godfather's Pizza better than the rest. The people I worked with were friendly and I enjoyed talking to them. They saw how hard I worked and liked me. All the jobs were difficult because of the language barrier. It was hard to speak English with all those people and have interviews in order to get the jobs. The progression of jobs helped give me the experience and confidence I needed, though. I took care of children at day care; I washed dishes and then made pizza at Godfather's Pizza; I prepared mashed potatoes and gravy and three kinds of salads at Kentucky Fried Chicken; I shucked oysters at the oyster farm; and I worked in the laboratory at Ostrom Mushroom Farms.

By 1988 a Cambodian acquaintance named Sarat Ken asked me if I'd like to clean houses with her. At that time Ostrom was cutting back on the hours and days we could work, so I had free time to help clean houses. Sarat liked my work and asked if I'd like to go into partnership with her. She asked if I could afford to go 50/50 with her on the business, and I assured her I could do that. We opened Sao and Ken Janitorial Services and worked well together, getting contracts for several buildings. Unfortunately, some of her friends questioned why she was partner with someone who was uneducated. Even though we worked well together, and Sarat could see that I was a competent business woman, after two years she pulled out and decided to start her own business and run competition with me. I hired a lawyer to take care of the legal dissolving of our partnership to protect myself and then had him set up my business as Sao Janitorial Services. I hired a bookkeeper to take care of the books, but I do my own paper work and fill out my own contracts.

When we had Sao and Ken Janitorial Services, we hired my husband to work with Sarat. I was paid as owner, my husband was paid as a worker, and Sarat was paid as owner and worker. I was working for Morningside Cleaning at the time, after I quit Ostrom Mushroom Farms. Now with my business, I have eighteen people hired, and have had people from many different nationalities working for me. Right now my husband; my brother Phath, who immigrated to the United States with the help of my husband; and several Cambodians, Russians, and Mexicans work for me. I have contracts with several buildings in the city, including state office buildings.

After I hadn't heard from my brother for years, *Bong* Phan called me in

1991. He was suffering from severe alcoholism and wanted to come back to Olympia. He was able to stop drinking and work for me until three months before he died in 1994, when he started drinking again. I was happy to have my brother back in my life. It broke my heart when he died.

I set up the funeral ceremony and cremated *Bong* Phan with the money from his life insurance, which I bought for him when he worked for my janitorial business. The cremation ceremony took place in Olympia, and the Buddhist One Hundred Days ceremony was performed in Aberdeen at *Lok Bong* Phong's house. My brother's ashes are interred in the Tacoma Buddhist Temple. In Cambodian tradition a person's ashes can't be sprinkled in many places. Eventually, I will take my brother's ashes to Cambodia and place them in the San Family *stupa*, which I built in Svay Chek at the temple grounds near our family village of Sam Rong. In order to move *Bong* Phan's ashes, I must first get the official paper that gives permission to transport the ashes from the Tacoma, Washington, temple to the Svay Chek, Cambodia, temple. Then I will take his ashes home.

CHAPTER 25

Bounchoeurn:
Everyone Died Except Me

In 1982 I learned that a number of Cambodian refugees were sponsored by a church in Winlock, Washington, close to Olympia. At the same time, I met a Cambodian woman now living close to my apartment in Lacey. One day I asked her where she lived in Cambodia. She told me she came from Don Noy, close to Svay Chek town in Banteay Meanchey Province.

"Oh," I said, "My wife comes from Sam Rong village, also close to Svay Chek."

"Who was her father?" the woman asked me.

"His name is Here, San Here," I told her.

"Oh, he's my father's friend!" she said excitedly. Then she talked about the people in her extended family who now live in Winlock. She cried because she had lost her husband and had no family living near her now in Olympia.

I decided to find out where Winlock was and visit the Cambodians who lived there. When I went to visit them in Winlock, I met one boy who had stayed with his aunt in Sok San Resistance Camp on the mountain in southwestern Cambodia. He didn't know how to read and write Cambodian, so he asked me to write a letter to his aunt for him. At that time in 1982, Church World Services was working in the camp, as well as the United Nations, so letters were able to get through. When I wrote the letter for this boy, I decided to add a message, asking if anyone at Sok San Camp knew if any of San Here's children were still alive. I wrote that if anyone had any information about San Here's family, would they please contact me. I also added that my wife was the youngest daughter of San Here and was living in the United States now.

When the boy's aunt received the letter, she didn't know how to read, so she gave it to someone who could read it for her. When she heard the request for information about any of San Here's children, she ran to San Phath. When San Phath read the letter, he couldn't believe it, but he wrote back. When I received his letter, I asked Bounriem if San Phath was her brother.

"Yes! That's my brother *Lok Bong* Phath!" she screamed. "He's the brother whose ordination as a monk I saw when I was a young girl."

When I knew that San Phath was my wife's brother, I started to fill out papers for him. I wrote to our United States congressmen at the time, Representative Don Bonker, Senator Dan Evans, and Senator Slade Gorton; I also wrote to Senator Ted Kennedy, asking for help. Then I wrote to the United Nations office in Thailand and to the U.S. ambassador to Thailand. The ESL teacher at Garfield Elementary, Zenaida Rivera, helped me with the letters. These people helped me get through the red tape. Their offices contacted the Sok San Camp and found out that San Phath was there, but we were told he couldn't come to the United States unless he got out of that camp. Phath's papers were approved for immigration to the United States, but first he had to leave the resistance camp.

We found out later that Phath had been fighting for the Khmer Srei resistance army along with the Khmer Rouge against the Vietnamese. He had just gotten back to Sok San Camp when he got my letter. He had been helping several people who had been wounded by mines to come back to camp for treatment. His leaders told him he was needed to go back out and fight again, but he refused, saying, "I just got back to camp from fighting; why do you want me to go fight again? I want to stay here; I need to rest before I go back.

Phath had had first aid training, so he usually wore an identification badge from the United Nations and the International Red Cross. He had been able to cross the border into Thailand because of the work he was doing. This time he took three other people with him because he wasn't wearing his Red Cross badge, and he was afraid to go by himself. When he came to the checkpoint at the border, the guards saw the men didn't have badges, so they were searched. The guards took the money they found and allowed Phath and his friends to go through after Phath told them they were going to Khao-I-Dang. When they got to the town of Trat, the four men took the bus to Khao-I-Dang Refugee Camp in Sa Kaew Province. Because they didn't have the right papers, they were not allowed into Khao-I-Dang, so they had to sneak into the camp at night.

I had written to Phath that his immigration to the United States had been approved; he just needed to get out of Sok San. Unfortunately, Phath stayed in Khao-I-Dang for two years, until the camp authorities found out he didn't have official papers to be there. They sent him to Site Two Camp, the camp for refugees who aren't going anywhere. Even though Phath's immigration had already been approved, I lost contact with him once he arrived in Khao-I-Dang. When I wrote to the United Nations, they wrote back that they didn't know where San Phath was. He was no longer in Sok San Camp. I wrote back, asking them to continue tracking my brother-in-law.

For two years Phath didn't contact me because he had lost my address, and there was no official record of him living in Khao-I-Dang. When he was transferred to Site Two Camp, the UN had his name on a list of refugees whose families were searching for them. One day when Phath was returning to Site Two Camp after working for the day on the outside, he saw a number of people looking at the bulletin board. One of his friends saw him and called out, "Hey, your name is on the board!"

When Phath looked at the board, sure enough, there was his name. He was supposed to contact the United Nations, so he went back to his cubicle, took out all the letters I had sent him and the official papers he had been given, and took them to the UN office at the camp. When the UN officials saw all his papers, they told him he was lucky he kept them. They told Phath not to go anywhere because he would have his interview in a couple of days.

The interview was held back in Wat Kok, where he had stayed years earlier; all the refugees who were going to be interviewed were taken by bus from Site Two Camp to Wat Kok. Each person's interview lasted for about an hour, all except Phath's. When it was his turn to be interviewed, the administrator asked him only a few questions.

"What is your relationship to Piset Sao?"

"He's my nephew," Phath answered.

"What is your relationship to Annmarie Sao?"

"She's my niece."

"What is your relationship to Bounroeurn Sao?"

"She's my sister," Phath explained. I had already written to Phath, telling him that my wife's name had been changed on her official papers from her real name Bounriem to her oldest brother's name Bounroeurn, so he knew to say that Bounroeurn was his sister.

"OK," the administrator said, "Now you have to thank the INS because they are going to accept you." Even though his interview was finished, he had to wait along with everyone else until all the interviews were finished. At the end of the day, the bus took them back to Site Two Camp.

Shortly after that, I received a letter from the UN. "We've found your brother-in-law," the letter said. "San Phath is free to come to the United States, but you have to pay his airplane ticket."

I sent $700 to Church World Services for the airplane ticket to give to Phath. Two weeks after his interview, Phath was able to fly to the United States to be reunited with us. He lived in Sok San Resistance Camp six years, Khao-I-Dang Camp two years, and Site Two Camp two years. He arrived in

Olympia, Washington, in 1989, ten years after he escaped from Sam Rong village in Cambodia.

Bounriem was overjoyed to see her brother again, but she was heartbroken when she heard his story.

Phath San's Story

In 1975, shortly after my sister and brothers had escaped to Thailand, the Khmer Rouge entered Sam Rong. They seized everything of any value that they could find — livestock, personal possessions from inside our homes, and our land. We were told to continue to raise rice for Angka and were divided into groups, with a leader for each group. Rather than working in our own fields, we now worked all together under the direction of our group leaders; the Khmer Rouge in Sam Rong were soldiers, so they just watched us with their guns. All the Khmer Rouge were from the outside; none of the people of Sam Rong became Khmer Rouge. No refugees from Phnom Penh or the eastern provinces came to live in our village. Sam Rong was a village of "old people."

We were forced to build a common kitchen, so the entire village had meals together. During the rice harvest, we had plenty of rice to eat, but as soon as we put the rice into storage, Khmer Rouge trucks came to take all the rice away. Then we were back to eating a small amount of watery rice porridge. During the first year, none of the villagers died from starvation or overwork. The only people who died were killed by the Khmer Rouge, like my father *Ow* Here.

One day I couldn't find my father; I searched for him for two days. When I asked my friend if he had seen my father, he told me he had seen the Khmer Rouge take my father in a horse cart past his house and out of town. I knew then that *Ow* Here had been taken to the killing fields. They would have killed me, too, if I asked about him or tried to recover his body. Two days later the Khmer Rouge also took my friend in a horse cart out of town. I never saw him again either. Even though the people of Sam Rong did not become Khmer Rouge, there was obviously a *chhlop*. *Ow* Here had talked of joining his younger children in Thailand. Someone had informed the Khmer Rouge and my father was accused of being a traitor.

In 1976, after *Ow* Here was killed, the Khmer Rouge abandoned Sam Rong and other small villages, moving all the people to Svay Chek. The small villages were isolated and too difficult for the Khmer Rouge to control. We continued our lives as "old people," growing rice for Angka and, depending on the season, alternating between a full rice bowl or watery rice porridge at mealtimes.

In December of 1979, the Vietnamese and Khmer Rouge were fighting each other for domination; they were in our area of northwestern Cambodia. When the Vietnamese army withdrew from our region, the Khmer Rouge gathered all the people from four villages, including Svay Chek, together in Sam Rong village. More than two thousand people were staying in Sam Rong. When the Vietnamese army returned, the Khmer Rouge withdrew, leaving all those people in our village. At that point the Vietnamese army evacuated all of us from Sam Rong to Svay Chek, the district town, while the Vietnamese army went on to the city of Sisophon. Then the Khmer Rouge army returned and moved us back from Svay Chek to Sam Rong. By this time we were tired of being moved around and feared for our lives, so the more than two thousand people from the five villages crossed the border into Thailand by ourselves.

If we had crossed the border in small groups, the Khmer Rouge would have shot at us, but since we were a group of more than two thousand people, and the Khmer Rouge were only a small group, they didn't fire. Instead, the Khmer Rouge soldiers ran away. A number of them took off their black clothes and dressed as regular villagers to escape after us. They didn't escape with us, but they escaped into Thailand after we left.

When we escaped from Cambodia into the Ta Phraya District of Sa Kaew Province, Thailand, we stayed there only three nights in an area surrounded by a barbed-wire fence. When we reached the fenced area, we built little shelters of thatch. The total area was not more than two hundred square meters, so when we slept, we were all lying right next to each other. The Thai government didn't provide mosquito nets, but they did give us mosquito spray. We were also given food, water, and blankets, but the amount of rice was equal to prisoner rations. It was no different than the rations we had been receiving under the Khmer Rouge. The conditions were terrible for the three days we were in Ta Phraya. There were no bathrooms, so a gasoline drum was cut in half, and each half was set in a hole in the ground. Then two pieces of wood were placed over each drum half to be used as a squat toilet.

After three days the Thai government took the more than two thousand Cambodian refugees in buses to Aranya Prathet, another district in Sa Kaew Province, where we stayed for two months. We were not staying in a United Nations refugee camp; we were staying at a temple, Wat Kok. While we stayed at Wat Kok, we had enough to eat; Church World Services and the United Nations provided for us there. While at Wat Kok, after putting together our thatch shelters, our only job was to clean up our own area. The head abbot let us watch television, but there really wasn't anything for us to do. We had more living space here, so we had room to stretch out and walk around. The temple ground was fenced by a regular temple fence, not by the barbed wire of Ta Phraya. We were free to come and go, but there was no work to do to make money. While living at Wat Kok, someone told me that we needed to have money if we were going to go to the United States. My wife Khim Yon and I had our gold that we had hidden in our clothes that we brought with us from Sam Rong. I took our gold and exchanged it for Thai baht so we would have money to go to America.

After two months, the Thai government decided to send us back to Cambodia. I believe that the leader of the Cambodian resistance paid the Thai government enough gold to take the Cambodian refugees back across the border so we could fight in the Khmer Srei resistance army against the Vietnamese. I believe the United Nations knew Thailand was planning to return the refugees to Cambodia, but they couldn't do anything about it because Thailand was putting pressure on them to solve the refugee problem.

When it was time to move all of us from Aranya Prathet to Trat Province, the Thai government appointed several elder Cambodian leaders, including our brother Bounroeurn because he was the oldest. The Thai leaders took the chosen Cambodian representatives outside of Wat Kok for a meeting. When they came back, the elders each talked to their villages. *Bong* Bounroeurn, the leader of Sam Rong village, told us we had to go back to Cambodia now because we were needed to fight for our freedom again.

In the morning all the buses came and took us to Trat, to the border between Thailand and Cambodia. When the buses dropped us off, there was noth-

Cambodian child with noticeable malnutrition in Khmer Rouge camp, circa 1991 (photograph by Bruce Sharp).

ing there, only forest. The forest was so thick that we couldn't even see the sun. This was exactly like the Khmer Rouge dropping the city people off in the Cardamom Mountains and telling them to live there. The difference was we were being sent back into Cambodia to fight with the resistance. Where we were dropped was supposed to be a staging area. When the Thai bus driver stopped the bus, she told me, "I can't take you any farther. I was told to drop you off here. If we have the chance, I will see you again, but for now I must go."

After all the refugees got off the bus, we had to walk about five kilometers up to the top of Buntuat Mountain to Sok San Resistance Camp. Before we left Thailand, the Thai leaders provided us with some materials from the Aranya Prathet market to use in building and furnishing our little houses. They gave us small pieces of plastic, mosquito nets, blankets, and mats. Unfortunately, there was no room on the bus for all the materials, so we had to leave them behind in Aranya Prathet. Anything we took with us we had to carry the five kilometers up the mountain. Even the resistance fighters had to build the camp. There was nothing there when we arrived. There were eleven members of our family on top of the mountain together: my oldest brother Bounroeurn, his wife Prom Soeung, and their two children; my older brother Bounrien, his wife Theuk Chhouy, and their three children; and Yon and I.

It was very difficult to clear land on the top of the mountain. For the first two years, no one did any work for the resistance because we were building the villages. It took two years to clear the trees and build houses. Some of us built sod houses down in the ground. We also used the branches from the trees to weave into thatch for roofs. Each group was made up of ten families, and each group built a village. We were given two hoes and one machete per group to use for tools.

Life under the resistance leaders was more difficult than life under the Khmer Rouge in Sam Rong. Here we had to build our villages, but in Sam Rong, at least we had our fields and houses already there. The first year was most difficult because we didn't have enough food. We were given only two kilograms of rice per week per family, the same as under the Khmer Rouge. We were not free. If someone wanted to join the resistance fighters, they were welcomed, but you would be shot if you tried to escape. There was no difference in living with the Khmer Rouge or the resistance fighters.

The Thai government brought rice and dropped it off at the Thai border at the foot of Buntuat Mountain. I don't know if the Thai government paid for the rice or if the Khmer Srei paid for it. We didn't have to pay for it and we didn't know where the food came from — United Nations, Thai government, or Khmer Srei. It didn't matter. On the day of the food drop, one person from each family would have to walk down the mountain and bring the rice back up. When all the rice had been carried up the mountain, the people from the ten families would pour all the rice together, and it would be distributed from there.

Because we were on the mountain, there was water all around — in streams and waterfalls, so it was not a problem to get water. The water flowed all the time. Some people hunted for small animals and birds in the forest, but not everyone was able to do that.

In just ten days, people started dying. Nothing was there for them and it was too difficult to live. The first Thai food drop was rice, but also cans of condensed milk. When the refugees saw the cans of milk, they started drinking it. It wasn't what they needed. People became sick. There was a nurse in the camp, but there wasn't enough medicine for all the sick people. My wife Yon became sick and died after being in the camp less than a month. She was the first one of our family to go. We were all devastated by her death, but soon more and more of our family sickened and died.

Bong Bounrien asked me for money on the day it was his turn to go down and get rice. I still had all the money I had saved from exchanging our gold into Thai baht at Wat Kok. My brother had planned to buy something from the Thai people who were waiting at the bottom of the mountain with things to sell. He was sick and weak at the time, but it was his turn to go get rice for his family, so he went anyway. *Bong* Bounrien left the camp and went down the mountain, but he never came back. I don't know what happened to him or how or where he died. I looked, but I never found his body.

It's hard to tell why some people died and others did not. Our family members weren't sick long. It happened very quickly. We were sitting and talking as a family soon after we lost *Bong* Bounrien. "I'm not feeling well," *Bong* Bounroeurn said to us. "I'm going to take some medicine and go to sleep." He never got up again, dying in his sleep. Not even a month had passed since our arrival at Sok San before my brothers Bounrien and Bounroeurn sickened and died. The children, aged four, five, and six, all died shortly after their fathers died. Soon after that, I went to the stream to take a bath in the evening. I felt dizzy and fell in the stream. I stayed there all night in the water. The next morning, Theuk Chhouy, *Bong* Bounrien's wife, went to the stream to collect water and found me there. She carried me back to their house and placed me on the bed. She put a charcoal fire under the bed to warm me, and I survived. Eventually, everyone in the family died from starvation and disease, except me. Not until the middle of 1982 did the United Nations finally start providing relief to the Cambodian people living in Sok San Resistance Camp — too late for our family.

CHAPTER 26

Bounriem: Killed for Wanting to Join His Children

I found out about my father's death after I had arrived in Olympia, around 1982, but I didn't really believe it until my brother Phath arrived to confirm it. One of my brother Bounrien's friends escaped to Thailand and eventually came to Olympia. He became acquainted with my husband and told him, "Your wife's second brother is my best friend." He had never seen me before. When he told us what had happened to my father, I didn't want to believe him. Because I didn't know him from Cambodia, I didn't know if I could trust him.

He said to me, "Oh, *Neang*! You haven't heard about your father? The Khmer Rouge killed him because a *chhlop* reported that he was going to go to Thailand to be with his children."

"I know my father," I told him. "If he wanted to go to Thailand, there was nobody who could catch him. He knew the way."

Bong Bounrien's friend tried to explain: "No, a spy reported him to the Khmer Rouge leader, so they accused him of being a traitor and took him away. They put him in a cart and took him out of the village. Nobody knows where they killed him."

After I heard this horrible news, I felt so sad and lonely. My father was killed by the Khmer Rouge in 1976, just a year after my brothers and I left Cambodia. He had been dead for years, and I just found out. Now both of my parents were dead.

Later when *Lok Bong* Phath came to Olympia to live with us, I asked him about our father's death. "*Neang*," he said, "I don't know what happened. Early in the morning I went to look for him, and everyone I met told me a different direction. I couldn't find him. I also had to be careful myself when trying to find out what happened to our father."

I learned that the Khmer Rouge didn't talk about the people they killed. They didn't tell the families what happened to their loved ones. The people were not allowed to show emotion of any kind — no sadness or happiness. In Olympia I can cry over my father's death; in Cambodia *Lok Bong* Phath could not.

My sister Rieng is still in Cambodia, but she and her husband have been separated since the Khmer Rouge takeover, a physical separation caused by the Khmer Rouge that developed into an emotional and, eventually, a permanent one. At the time that my brothers and I left Cambodia for Thailand, *Bong* Rieng and her husband didn't have any children yet. Later they had one son together, so now my nephew goes back and forth from his mother's house to his father's house. My sister Rieng moved back to Sam Rong village after separating from her husband, living in her own home with her son. She built a small house in the same location of the first house my father built when the family first moved back to Cambodia from Thailand.

After our father was murdered by the Khmer Rouge, they tore down his house, so the family home isn't there anymore. I don't have a house in Sam Rong; when I go back to visit, I stay with my brother *Lok Bong* Phong's friend Plong Chin, whom I call *Bong* Chin, and his wife Liem Nee, whom I call *Bong Srei*. We stay in their house in Svay Chek that my husband and I helped to build. We helped *Bong* Chin build his house to look just like the last house my father built. When I saw his house for the first time, not yet finished, only framed, I sat down and cried — I missed my parents' house. I asked *Bong* Chin to build a fence around it, and now he has many dogs to guard the place. I wanted him to have everything that our family had and I supported him to be able to afford it. People in rural Cambodia are very poor and can't afford to have big houses. I was happy to help *Bong* Chin and *Bong Srei*. They seem more like family to me than just friends. They treat me like my sister and brothers do, I feel comfortable around them, and we trust and respect each other.

The land I now own in Sam Rong is the original land that belonged to my father. I didn't have to buy it. Even though the Khmer Rouge took everything from everyone, they never worked our land, and they never lived on it. They used land on either side of our property, but never our land. When the Khmer Rouge were no longer in power in 1979, other people wanted our land, but people in the village would say, "You can't take that land. That's San Here's land, and some of the children are still alive. At least one son lives in Cambodia, another in Thailand, and one daughter lives in another country. It's not a good idea to take their land."

I didn't know that our family land was still available. It wasn't until 1991 that I learned the family land was still safe. I was very lucky. I believe that the spirits of my parents protected our land. My mother died on our land, and my father died because of our land. That's why I want to work hard on the land and help people as much as I can. Four years ago I received the official papers for my land — three hundred hectares of rice land, plus land used for the tapioca fields.

In 1991 my husband, children and I visited Cambodia for the first time since I left there in 1975. My successful business and our savings allowed us to return. At the time it was still too dangerous to travel to Banteay Meanchey Province, so I was unable to visit my old village of Sam Rong. While we were visiting my husband's mother in Phnom Penh, she asked if we would build a *stupa* for her and her family before she died. We assured her that we would build one in Takeo Province at the temple near Tang Russey the next time we were able to visit Cambodia.

We decided to make a Sao San *stupa* to honor both of our families, since I had yet to be able to travel to Sisophon. My sister-in-law found a stone carver in Phnom Penh to do the work. The carving was done in the city, and then the plaques were attached to the outside of the *stupa* with screws. When a new stupa is opened, the monks are invited to perform the ceremony, the ribbon is cut, and the monks bless the new *stupa* for the first time. At the opening of the Takeo *stupa*, at Wat Chambak Bethmeas, all of my husband's relatives who were still alive came for the ceremony. On my side only four members of my immediate family came from Svay Chek. They had to hire a pick-up truck with side benches in the back to take them from Svay Chek to Takeo and back again.

On the Sao side of the *stupa*, only the name of my husband's "papa," his step-father, is written there. On the San side, my mother's, father's, first and second brothers', their wives' and children's, *Bong* Phath's wife's, and my sister-in-law's parents' names are all written on the outside of the *stupa*. After my husband's mother dies, her ashes will be placed inside the *stupa*. Right now there is nothing inside the *stupa*. No one has died since we had it built.

When we present gifts in honor of the family members who have passed away, the gifts are given to the monks to honor those individuals. The monks keep the gifts for themselves or give them to the people who are in need. Each year on *P'Chum Ben* in September, those of the family who are in Cambodia at the time will go to the family *stupa* and ask the monks to come to pray for all the family members who have passed away. Cambodian tradition demands that each year this must be done, even if your gift is very small. Young and old alike must perform this ceremony as long as they are alive. During the seven days of *P'Chum Ben*, Cambodians believe that the spirits of the dead are free, so the living must find and honor them. By giving gifts and remembering the dead, you are making merit for them as well as for yourself.

After my brother Phan died in Olympia in 1994, the next time I went to Cambodia (in 2004), I arranged to have a family *stupa* built in Svay Chek. Since

Bounchoeurn Sao at the opening of the San Family *stupa* in Svay Chek, Cambodia, circa 2005 (photograph from the personal collection of Bounchoeurn and Diyana Sao).

there is no stone carver in Svay Chek, I had to find one in Sisophon. In Svay Chek it's different. I placed my brother Phan's name inside the *stupa*. Nothing is carved on the outside because someone would steal it. Everything has to be placed inside the *stupa* in Svay Chek. Not many people there can afford to build a *stupa*, and because of the extreme poverty, many people steal things like carved names or funeral urns for ashes because they know they can get money by selling them. In Takeo people don't do that. They have more respect for the dead and for other people's property.

When I was finally able to visit Sisophon in 2004, I went to my old village of Sam Rong to visit my mother's grave, but the cemetery had already been turned into a tapioca field. I could not find where she was buried. During the Khmer Rouge rule, they destroyed the cemetery, and after they left, someone else turned the empty land into a tapioca field.

Because I cannot find my mother's bones, each time I visit Cambodia, I perform a ceremony to remember her and all the members of my family who have passed away. I ask someone to write down all the names on a piece of paper of the people in my family who have died. Then I ask the monks to pray for all the people whose names are on the paper. Sometimes I do this at the temple or at *Bong* Chin's house, but most of the time I have the ceremony performed at the San *stupa* I've had built in Svay Chek. I invite all my nieces and nephews, sister and brothers, any of my family still living in Cambodia to join me and help prepare the ceremony.

We invite the monks to come in the late afternoon to the *stupa* to bless all the names. The next day we take gifts to the temple for the people who have died. These gifts are what we think our family members who have passed away would need or like to have to be comfortable, wherever they are. It

Diyana Sao and her brother San Pha on a return trip to Cambodia in 2004 (photograph from the personal collection of Bounchoeurn and Diyana Sao).

might be shoes, a shirt, silverware, dishes, food, or anything they might want. My children bought the game they used to play with their uncle for me to give in my brother Phan's memory. We believe that if we buy gifts and offer them to the monks in the name of *Bong* Phan, in his next life he will have everything he needs and wants—a big house, a big family, a healthy life, good luck, everything.

Right now in the San *stupa* in Svay Chek are the ashes of my brother Pha, who passed away in April of 2010. Cambodians prefer to be cremated, so when *Bong* Pha died, his body was cremated. The family kept the ashes in a funeral urn in the house for one hundred days. Then at the One Hundred Days ceremony, his ashes were taken to the San *stupa* and placed inside where they will remain forever. Because we did not have the bones or ashes of our parents and the brothers and their families who died at the Sok San Resistance Camp, their names are carved on plaques and placed in our *stupa* in Svay Chek and on the *stupa* in Takeo.

This is the way that I can serve my parents in a way that I could not do when I was young. It's sad because this is the only way I can serve *Mae* Yan and *Ow* Here. They passed on before I could help them, but now the spirits of my parents know that I am trying to help the best that I can.

Thank you, America, for bringing me here. Because I am living in Olympia, Washington, and succeeding financially, I am free and have the resources to go back to Cambodia to help my family and the people. I am happy now.

CHAPTER 27

Bounchoeurn: He Was Murdered Because I Was a Soldier

I finally learned about my mother and *Ow* Chham in 1990. After the Vietnamese invaded Cambodia, we were allowed to send letters back and forth to Cambodia. I didn't know who was alive and who was dead, so I wrote a letter from Olympia to my uncle, *Thom* Yim, in Tang Russey. I asked if my mother was still alive, if she had come back to Tang Russey. About two months later, I got a letter back from a brother-in-law I had never met. He was married to my half-sister Naren, Papa's daughter. Naren's husband told me that my mother had come home to Tang Russey. I was so happy to hear she was still alive. I also learned that *Poo* Yoeun survived, but his Vietnamese wife *Ming* Youn died of overwork and malnutrition in the Khmer Rouge work camp in Battambang.

Soon after receiving the letter, Naren moved, but she gave my address to my half-sister Satom, *Ow* Chham's daughter. Satom wrote to me and told me what happened to our father, although she couldn't give me many details. *Ow* Chham, his wife *Ming* Chek, my half-brother Dorn, and his three younger sisters were killed by the Khmer Rouge at Wat Chambak Bethmeas, the same temple where I had been taken near Tang Russey. *Ow* Chham may have been tortured because he was related to me and talked about me. Actually, Dorn wanted to come with me when I left Tang Russey, but he was too young, and *Ow* Chham had told me that *Ming* Chek didn't want him to go because he was her only son. Even though *Ow* Chham lived in Thnol Dach, only five kilometers from Tang Russey, his daughters and wife couldn't go to visit him, and he couldn't go to visit them.

Ow Chham was a good man and everyone liked him. I was told that he used to talk about me and say how much he missed me. Probably a *chhlop* working for the Khmer Rouge overheard my father talking about me and reported it. That could have been enough to get him and his family killed because his son was a military man. Before the Khmer Rouge killed *Ow*

Chham, they tortured him on the temple grounds in the monks' school building. A person who lived close to Wat Chambak Bethmeas heard my father's voice screaming at night, but he didn't know why *Ow* Chham was tortured and killed. I can't forget that my father, *Ming* Chek, Dorn, and his younger sisters may have been killed because of me.

Satom also told me what had happened to her after the Khmer Rouge took over the country. She escaped death because she was already married at the time and living with her Chinese husband Long Heng in his birthplace in Kandal Province. Later the Khmer Rouge separated Long Heng from her and their two children. They put him in a detention center, formerly a school building built by American aid. He was detained because he was Chinese, but he survived because he was a tailor. Long Heng taught the Khmer Rouge to sew. Once they knew how to sew, however, Long Heng was no longer useful to them. Fortunately for him, the Vietnamese invaded Cambodia in 1979, so he was released. Long Heng, Satom, and their children moved to Phnom Penh after the Vietnamese liberation, where they still live.

Our sister Hoeung and her husband had left Tang Russey for Battambang at the same time I did. Hoeung had been sent to work where I was working just when I was ready to escape. She had wanted to remain behind to take care of her sick husband, but the Khmer Rouge wouldn't allow that because she wasn't a doctor or nurse. She was forced to work in the fields like everyone else. I had asked her if she wanted to escape with me, but she wouldn't because of her sick husband. Probably she would have escaped with me if her husband had been well and could come, too. It was a difficult decision for her. As it was, her husband died in the Khmer Rouge work camp of overwork, malnutrition and disease. After the Vietnamese invasion, Hoeung went back to Tang Russey. She has since remarried and lives in Phnom Penh with her family.

Satom and I wrote letters to each other for a year, and then in 1991, I was able to go back to Cambodia for my first visit. I've returned many times since then, but the first time sticks out in my memory. I was happy to be back, but also worried because there was still fighting. I wasn't afraid, just excited. I took my whole family with me — Bounriem, son Piset, and daughter Annmarie. I was able to see my mother, and she was able to meet her American grandchildren. We stayed in a hotel; in 1991 we weren't allowed to stay in homes, only the hotels for tourists. Even though my mother was living in Phnom Penh with my sister, I was not allowed to stay with her. Instead, she could come to the hotel to visit me. *Mae* Kim is still alive, living in a suburb of Phnom Penh with Naren.

Bounriem wasn't able to visit her village of Sam Rong in Banteay Meanchey until 2004. She traveled to Cambodia three times, but was not able to go to Banteay Meanchey until the fourth trip. Her family had to travel to

Phnom Penh to see her. The same happened with my son Bdei who lived in Battambang; he had to travel to Phnom Penh to see me. It was difficult for our families to come to see us in Phnom Penh, too. They encountered soldiers with rifles along the way, who often times treated travelers cruelly. Today, however, it is easy to send money to Cambodia and to visit our families.

Now, both my son Bdei and my first wife Kim have died. Bdei died of liver or heart failure several years ago. No one knew for sure how he died. Kim died in 2009. Again, no one knew why she died. Their deaths saddened me. I had tried to help them, but it was difficult to send money to Cambodia when I first learned that they had survived living under the Khmer Rouge. When I did send money, the family never received it, so it was hard to help them when they were sick. The only way I could give them money was to take it to them, and at that time, the Khmer Rouge controlled the road between Phnom Penh and Battambang, so it was too dangerous to take the risk.

When I first returned to Cambodia in 1991, a surprising thing happened. A policeman came to see me in the hotel, saying, "My commander wants to invite you to a party this evening."

I accepted, but I was worried. I told my mother and sister, "If something happens to me, take my children to Thailand and fly them back to the United States." We had return tickets, so they would be able to use them. That evening, Bounriem and I were picked up in a Soviet-made jeep and taken to a villa in the suburbs. Besides my wife and me, many government people were at this dinner, including the foreign minister and the attorney general. I still didn't know why I had been invited.

One diplomat asked me how I felt coming back to Cambodia. I answered, "Oh, I feel good. So much has improved." I had learned in Special Forces that if we want

Diyana and Bounchoeurn Sao in Olympia, Washington (**photograph from the personal collection of Bounchoeurn and Diyana Sao**).

to learn something from someone, we don't speak against them. They were happy with my response. They wanted me to work with them.

"I know you're an educated person. We want you to come and work with us to help build our country," another diplomat said.

"I like it here," I responded, "but as you know, my wife and children are with me now, and my children are Americans." Everyone was very polite, but I still didn't know why they chose me. All the people on the airplane were staying at the same hotel, but I was the only one talked to by the people from the Cambodian government. They gave me a letter that said I could go anywhere in Phnom Penh. If anyone stopped me, all I had to do was show the letter. At that time Phnom Penh had a curfew at 9:00 pm. Sometimes I came back at 11:00 pm. I just showed the letter and had no problems.

I found out later that the Cambodian government wanted me to help them because I could speak English. At one point early in my visit, I had helped an American couple who wanted to adopt a Cambodian orphan; I went with them to the foreign minister's office to translate. I also went with the couple to the doctor to translate when they had the Cambodian child checked. Because of this, the Cambodian government knew I understood Americans, could speak English, and was a translator.

I was proud that Cambodia wanted me to return, but Olympia is my home now and feels like my birthplace. I'm comfortable here. Of course, I would like to live part of the year here and part of the year in Cambodia with the rest of my family, but when I have grandchildren, that would be too difficult to do. When I'm lucky enough to have grandchildren, I want to be here in Olympia close to them.

Bibliography

Affonco, Denise. *To the End of Hell: One Woman's Struggle to Survive Cambodia's Khmer Rouge*. London: Reportage Press, 2007.

Chandler, David. *A History of Cambodia*. 2d ed., updated. Chiang Mai: Silkworm Books, 1998.

Crew, Linda. *Children of the River*. New York: Dell, 1989.

Criddle, Joan D., and Teeda Butt Mam. *To Destroy You Is No Loss: The Odyssey of a Cambodian Family*. New York: The Atlantic Monthly Press, 1987.

Cummings, Joe, Sandra Bao, Steven Martin, and China Williams. *Thailand*. 10th ed. Malaysia: Lonely Planet, 2003.

Drabble, Margaret. *The Gates of Ivory*. New York: Viking, 1991.

Fifield, Adam. *A Blessing Over Ashes: The Remarkable Odyssey of My Unlikely Brother*. New York: HarperCollins, 2000.

Him, Chanrithy. *When Broken Glass Floats: Growing Up Under the Khmer Rouge*. New York and London: W.W. Norton, 2000.

Ho, Minfong. *The Clay Marble*. New York: Farrar, Straus and Giroux, 1991.

Keat, Nawuth, with Martha E. Kendall. *Alive in the Killing Fields: Surviving the Khmer Rouge Genocide*. Washington, D.C.: National Geographic, 2009.

Kiernan, Ben. *The Pol Pot Regime: Race, Power, and Genocide in Cambodia under the Khmer Rouge, 1975–79*. 2nd ed. New Haven: Yale University Press, 2002.

Lafreniere, Bree. *Music through the Dark: A Tale of Survival in Cambodia*. Honolulu: University of Hawaii Press, 2000.

Lord, Michelle. *A Song for Cambodia*. Illustrated by Shino Arihara. New York: Lee & Low Books, 2008.

Neveu, Roland. *Cambodia: The Years of Turmoil*. Edited by Ben Davies. Bangkok: Asia Horizons Books, 2009.

Ngor, Haing, with Roger Warner. *Haing Ngor: A Cambodian Odyssey*. New York: Macmillan, 1987.

Pa, Chileng, with Carol A. Mortland. *Escaping the Khmer Rouge: A Cambodian Memoir*. Jefferson, NC: McFarland, 2008.

Pran, Dith, comp. *Children of Cambodia's Killing Fields: Memoirs by Survivors*. Edited by Kim DePaul. Chiang Mai: Silkworm Books, 1997.

Ray, Nick, and Daniel Robinson. *Cambodia*. 6th ed. Singapore: Lonely Planet Publications, 2008.

Seng, Theary C. *Daughter of the Killing Fields: Asrei's Story*. London: Fusion Press, 2005.

Siv, Sichan. *Golden Bones: An Extraordinary Journey from Hell in Cambodia to a New Life in America*. New York: HarperCollins, 2008.

Smith, Icy. *Half Spoon of Rice: A Survival Story of the Cambodian Genocide*. Illustrated by Sopaul Nhem. Manhattan Beach, CA: East West Discovery Press, 2010.

Standen, Mark. *Passage Through Angkor*. Bangkok: Mark Standen, 2000.

Streed, Sarah. *Leaving the House of Ghosts: Cambodian Refugees in the American Midwest*. Jefferson, NC: McFarland, 2002.

U Sam Oeur, with Ken McCullough. *Crossing Three Wildernesses: A Memoir*. Minneapolis: Coffee House Press, 2005.

Yathay, Pin, with John Man. *Stay Alive, My Son*. Chiang Mai: Silkworm Books, 2000.

Index

Numbers in **bold italics** indicate pages with photographs.